MW01616778

MAN OF GOD

St. John of

San Francisco

MAN *of* GOD

SAINT JOHN
of Shanghai *&* San Francisco

Translated from the Russian
Compiled by Archpriest Peter Perekrestov

**A Publication of the Western Diocese of the
Russian Orthodox Church Abroad**

 NIKODEMOS ORTHODOX PUBLICATION SOCIETY
RICHFIELD SPRINGS, NEW YORK

English edition translated and revised from the Russian
Arkhiepiskop Ioann (Maksimovitch): arkhipastyr, molitvennik, podvizhnik
published 1991 by the Diocese of Western America & San Francisco
Russian Orthodox Church Outside Russia, San Francisco

English translation copyright
© 1994 by Nikodemos Orthodox Publication Society
All rights reserved

Second printing 1995
Third printing 1997
Fourth printing 2002
Fifth printing 2005
Sixth printing 2009
Seventh printing 2012
Eighth printing 2015

Published by
NIKODEMOS ORTHODOX
PUBLICATION SOCIETY
P.O. Box 383
Richfield Springs, NY 13439-0383 USA

Printed in the United States of America

Publishers in Publication Data
Man of God—Saint John of Shanghai and San Francisco
Translated from the Russian.
1. John Maximovitch, Archbishop, 1896-1966.   2. Saints—Biography.   3.
Russian Orthodox Church—History—Hagiography.   I. Title.
Library of Congress Catalog Card Number 94-67129

ISBN: 978-1-879066-06-9

CONTENTS

ILLUSTRATIONS

cover: Bishop of Shanghai, 1938; *page 10:* Shanghai cathedral, Surety of Sinners; *page 18:* a popular photo of Vladika John; *page 76:* in France, 1950s; *between pages 96 and 97:* see captions; *page 126:* giving a sermon in the Synodal Cathedral of the Mother of God "Of the Sign" in New York; *between pages 160 and 161:* see captions; *page 228:* Vladika John; *page 242:* "With the saints give rest . . ."; *page 251:* Cathedral of the Mother of God "Joy of All Who Sorrow" in San Francisco.

PUBLISHER'S PREFACE

The original Russian edition of this book, *Archbishop John: Archpastor, Man of Prayer and Ascetic,* was published in 1991, to coincide with the twenty-fifth anniversary of the hierarch's blessed repose. Since that time the Council of Bishops of the Russian Orthodox Church Abroad decreed that Archbishop John be glorified as a saint. It seemed fitting to reflect this official recognition of his sanctity in giving a new title to this English-language edition, which goes to press on the eve of this eagerly-awaited event, scheduled to take place June 19/July 2, 1994.

In preparation for the glorification, a special Commission was appointed to examine the remains of the holy hierarch, which were laid to rest in a small crypt-chapel beneath the Cathedral of the Mother of God, "Joy of All Who Sorrow," in San Francisco. The report of the Commission's findings, made in October 1993, has been added to this edition as an appendix.

The fact that Archbishop John's relics were found to be incorrupt, the fact that he is soon to be glorified only confirms the opinion of thousands of people who already venerate him as a saint. (The act of glorification, as Archbishop John himself wrote, does not make a saint; it merely confirms his sanctity: "The righteous [become] saints not through any decree of the earthly ecclesiastical authority, but by the mercy and grace of God.") A majority of these people—who are not only Russians but Americans, Serbs, Greeks, French, and others—became acquainted with Archbishop John only after his lifetime, many through personal experience of his power of prayer. It is only natural that with such veneration should come the desire to know as much as possible about this extraordinary God-pleaser.

While numerous articles have appeared in the years since his repose, a comprehensive biography has yet to be written. The late Bishop Savva of Edmonton collected materials for a Life, and these were adapted in 1979 under the title *Blessed John*, but this was still, in the words of the editors, simply "a preliminary sketch." Additional materials in a second, considerably expanded edition (1987) emphasize Archbishop John as a wonderworker, a fool-for-Christ, something of a maverick, who was often misunderstood and slandered. In compiling materials for this present volume, an effort was made not only to avoid duplicating what has already been published, but to present a balanced, truthful portrait. Here is a similar composite of reminiscences and miracles—materials *about* Archbishop John—to which have been added sermons and decrees written *by* him, showing him as a theologian and hierarch of the Church, "rightly dividing the word of truth"; one who was guided by the law of love while holding firmly to the traditions and discipline of the Church. As a framework for the reminiscences, which touch on all but the earliest period of the Saint's life, a brief chronology has been added. For those unfamiliar with Orthodox terminology, a glossary is also included.

Although scheduled to have been published soon after the Russian edition, the delayed appearance of this English translation appropriately coincides with the Bicentennial commemoration of the Russian Orthodox Mission to America. Archbishop John was not a missionary in the classic sense; his activity was concentrated in shepherding his Russian flock. But wherever he went—Serbia, China, Europe, America—his personal holiness attracted thirsty souls like a spiritual magnet. In introducing its readers to a new or deeper acquaintance with this luminous archpastor, ascetic, and man of prayer, may this volume also serve as a missionary tool, inspiring a desire for those spiritual treasures of Orthodox Christianity, which Saint John so amply possessed and so generously manifests even now, years after his repose.

The Shanghai cathedral, "Surety of Sinners," today a stock exchange.

CHRONOLOGY

1896   Born June 4 in Kharkov, southern Russia, to parents Boris and Glafira. Baptized Michael.

1907-1914   Student at the Poltava Cadet Corps.

1914   Attends Kharkov Law School.

1921-1925   Belgrade Theological Seminary.

1924   Ordained reader by Metropolitan Anthony (Khrapovitsky).

1925-1927   Instructor of religion at Serbian State High School.

1926   Tonsured a monk at Milkovo Monastery, with the name John. In November, ordained hieromonk.

1929-1934   Teacher in Bitol Theological Seminary

1934   Consecrated Bishop by Metropolitan Anthony (May 28); arrives in Shanghai (November 21), where he remains until the end of World War II.

1946   Raised to the rank of Archbishop.

1949   Comes to America to arrange for the immigration of his flock, which finds temporary refuge on the Philippine island of Tubabao.

1950   Becomes head of the Western European Diocese with his see first in Paris, then in Brussels.

1962   Appointed Archbishop of Western America and San Francisco; arrives November 21.

1966   Reposed in Seattle (June 19/July 2).

INTRODUCTION TO
THE RUSSIAN EDITION

THE TIME HAS come to especially invoke the prayerful aid of Archbishop John, that these days dedicated to his memory might be spent in a worthy manner.

This book is being published on the occasion of the silver, i.e., the twenty-fifth anniversary of the repose of our ever-memorable Vladika John. The Lord granted the compiler of this book the joy of gathering revealing materials, which have been arranged into four sections. The book does not pretend to exhaust its subject. An effort was made to avoid duplicating what was printed soon after Vladika's repose, although the section of reminiscences concludes with Metropolitan Philaret's well-known eulogy which he gave at Vladika's funeral. This section tells about Vladika's faith as witnessed by his deeds, about his ready accessibility, his lack of self-interest, his unremitting spiritual struggles.

The section of testimonies concerning his prayerful intercession vividly explains why it is that people's hearts are so drawn to Vladika John, and why he and his power of prayer have become so widely known—everywhere help is needed!

The third section contains some of his sermons. Although not long, it wonderfully conveys the inspiration of an Orthodox hierarch, especially in the sermon about the repentant thief, who, as Vladika explains, manifested such a depth of repentance and humility, the likes of which not one of Christ's disciples was then yet capable of, and because of which he was first to experience *the power of Christ's co-suffering love*. Not without reason did Metropolitan Anthony write concerning Vladika John that he was "a piece of his own heart."

The fourth section is comprised primarily of a number of brief decrees issued by Vladika John, reflecting his strictness, particularly regarding the clergy. With such laborers in Christ's vineyard as Vladika John, being strict and exacting in no wise contradicts their pastoral love. He who is always strict with himself is justified in being strict at times with others.

My first encounters with Archbishop John date back to the time when he was still a hieromonk, at Milkovo Monastery [in Serbia], where, in 1926, he was tonsured by Blessed Metropolitan Anthony [Khrapovitsky]; he was the first Russian to become a monk in Milkovo.

While continuing to be in obedience to Metropolitan Anthony, Father John gave classes on the Law of God in a Serbian high school. Before long (probably still before he became a teacher at the Bitol seminary) his inspired apologetical brochure, *The Orthodox Veneration of the Mother of God*, was printed in Vladimirovo in Carpatho-Russia. The work first appeared in the St. Vladimir Calendar, where it was signed, "Hieromonk John Maximovitch, monk of Milkovo Monastery, Feast of the Entry of the Most Holy Theotokos into the Temple, Yugoslavia, 1928."

I read this work in Milkovo Monastery, which I entered in 1930. Father John would come there on short visits. Abbot Ambrose loved him very much, and later spoke admiringly of his humility and readiness to fulfill any obedience.

I remember how, in 1930, our Bishop Tikhon of San Francisco, after his consecration, was at Milkovo Monastery together with Metropolitan Anthony. In those days Hieromonk John served Liturgy there, assisted by Deacon Savva Struve (later Archimandrite). It was during this same period of time that Metropolitan Anthony tonsured the present Archbishop Antony of Los Angeles, Monk Theophan (who reposed in Mahopac, NY,

13

in the rank of archimandrite), and another monk. That year Father John was making the trip to Milkovo from the Bitol seminary, whose students had come to love their Russian instructor, moved by his asceticism and that fatherly concern which he showed in covering them with blankets and blessing them as they slept.

At that time, Vladika John served in the diocese of the renowned Serbian hierarch, Nikolai of Ochrid, the "Serbian Chrysostom." This archpastor, known to the whole Orthodox world, had the greatest regard for Vladika. He wrote that even then Father John, in visiting the sick with an icon of Saint Naum of Ochrid, healed many. . .

The relationship between Bishop Nikolai and Father John was very close, sincere, and simple. Later, Bishop Nikolai published a small booklet in the series, *Little Missionary,* under the title, "Vender of Belgrade Newspapers—a Chinese Bishop." To a Serbian girl who asked in a letter: Why are there no saints nowadays? Bishop Nikolai replied in the press: "There are, my dear!" and he pointed out the example of Vladika John's ascetic struggle.

And just now, as we are preparing for the twenty-fifth anniversary of Vladika's repose, the coffin with the remains of Bishop Nikolai has been recently translated from America to Serbia, where it was solemnly met by the Serbian hierarchy, clergy and people.

After the death of Schema-archimandrite Ambrose of Milkovo, at the request of the monastery's new superior, Vladika John began collecting material for a Life of this Elder. When I, too, came to him to relate what I knew and rememered about the deceased, Vladika was worn out and sat bent over with his head to the table. "Vladika, you are tired. Bless me to come later," I said. "No! You were saying ..." Vladika raised his head and repeated precisely what I had told him. He was like that also at meetings of the Synod of Bishops; he would be very tired and appeared to doze off. But no! He heard and was fully aware of what went on. Vladika had not yet finished gathering these materials when he had to leave for Shanghai.

Where did Vladika John find strength, such that he never slept in a bed, such that he was ready at any time of day or night to visit the sick, to always console, to instruct, and—not always, but often—to make the impossible *possible*? There are many with personal memories of the wonder-working power of his intercession, and of how he would respond to unspoken thoughts.

Like Saint John of Kronstadt, whose example Vladika John followed, his grace-filled power came first of all from his daily partaking of the Holy Mysteries. Later, he would unhurriedly consume the Holy Gifts, remaining a long time in the altar, particularly on weekdays when he himself served the Divine Liturgy. His prayer and what he experienced at these times are a great mystery about which we dare not, and cannot speak.

Besides this, he was always almost simultaneously with people—listening to them, helping them—*and* in spiritual communion with the saints. Saint John of Kronstadt wrote of himself that he always tried to read the canons to the saints whose service was appointed for the day. So, too, Vladika John, when he travelled, took with him a full set of service books. From the Greek he often translated hymns to those saints for whom, in the Slavonic *menaia*, there existed only general troparia. Those Greek *menaia*, which were Vladika John's constant reading, are now in the library of Holy Trinity Monastery in Jordanville, NY.

Vladika John avidly and persistently tried to ascertain the dates of commemoration of those Orthodox saints of the West, whom the Orthodox East had either completely or all but forgotten. We have a list he compiled with the names of nineteen Godpleasers, chiefly French and Irish.

He never refused anyone his prayers, as is evident from numerous testimonies. I know a bishop who was very anxious that Vladika John take part in his consecration, but Vladika was clear across the continent and could not be present. On the day of the consecration, however, he wrote that at the moment when the Mystery of Consecration was to have taken place, he, too, had offered up the appointed prayers for the new bishop.

Another bishop confided to us that he knew of only two hierarchs who could be said to possess a truly "œcumenical spirit," i.e., who participated in the life of all Orthodox peoples and their local Churches: these were Metropolitan Anthony (Khrapovitsky) and our Archbishop John!

And this is obviously so. The heads of all the Orthodox Churches had the highest regard for Metropolitan Anthony. French and Dutch people thoroughly relied upon Archbishop John as one who would lead them onto the path of salvation. Slavic peoples recall the heartfelt concern which these two archpastors had for them in particular. And American converts, as also French converts, especially love Vladika John.

As the reader can see, for me, recollections of Vladika John are tied to the memory of Metropolitan Anthony and to Milkovo Monastery and its soul—Elder Ambrose. And not only for me!

I have before me the 1935 volume of the magazine, *The Holy Land*. In issues Nos. 6, 7, and 8 there is serialized an article by the well-known church laborer, P.S. Lopukhin, who was close to Metropolitan Anthony and who left us a summary of his sermons. The article is titled: "A Christian Ascetic of Modern Times." In it the author writes that he received almost simultaneously three letters, which he proceeds to quote:

"From Jerusalem I received a photo of Elder Ambrose [of Milkovo], with a heartfelt request to write something about him."

From Poland came a letter: ". . . we were in Pochaev. There we found the same spirit of compelling love as in Milkovo. Everyone there cherished the memory of our Vladika Metropolitan Anthony. And we noticed that people spoke not so much about his erudition and his mind as they did about his sincerity and simplicity."

From Harbin: "Bishop John of Shanghai came to see us. He was here five days, and I followed him everywhere. He bears the same spirit that so impressed me in Yugoslavia; it is the spirit of Metropolitan Anthony and Milkovo Monastery. The same sincerity and simplicity."

In the same article the author relates his last conversation with Elder Ambrose, which took place in the infirmary where Father Ambrose was taken not long before he died. The conversation began on some other topic, but further on I quote:

"He [Father Ambrose] bowed his head in exhaustion. After a moment's rest he smiled and asked:

"'Did you see Grandpa?' [This is how Metropolitan Anthony was affectionately called sometimes—A.A.]

"'Yes, I did.'

"'What did you talk about?'

"'I asked who was closest of all to him in spirit.'

"'Well, now, that's interesting.'

"'He said you and Father John.'

"Father Ambrose raised his head, opened his eyes wide, crossed himself, wanted to say something, and suddenly fell back into his pillow and sobbed. My God, how he wept!

"The next day he was taken to Milkovo to die. I never saw Father Ambrose again, and I treasure the image of this man lying on his death bed and weeping with happiness at this spiritual oneness in God."

With this Lopukhin concludes his article.

The joy of spiritual oneness! May God grant us all to experience the same feeling when we pray at the tomb of our dearly-beloved Vladika John! God grant that, as we pray for him, he would warm us with his prayers before the throne of God and entreat for us strength that we might be renewed. It is for such renewal that God grants us the joy of learning about new saints and in this way to feel their power.

All is possible for God (Mark 10:27)! And the fervent prayer of a righteous man can accomplish much (James 5:16). Amen.

†Archbishop Anthony
Sunday of All Saints Who Shone
Forth in the Russian Land
1991

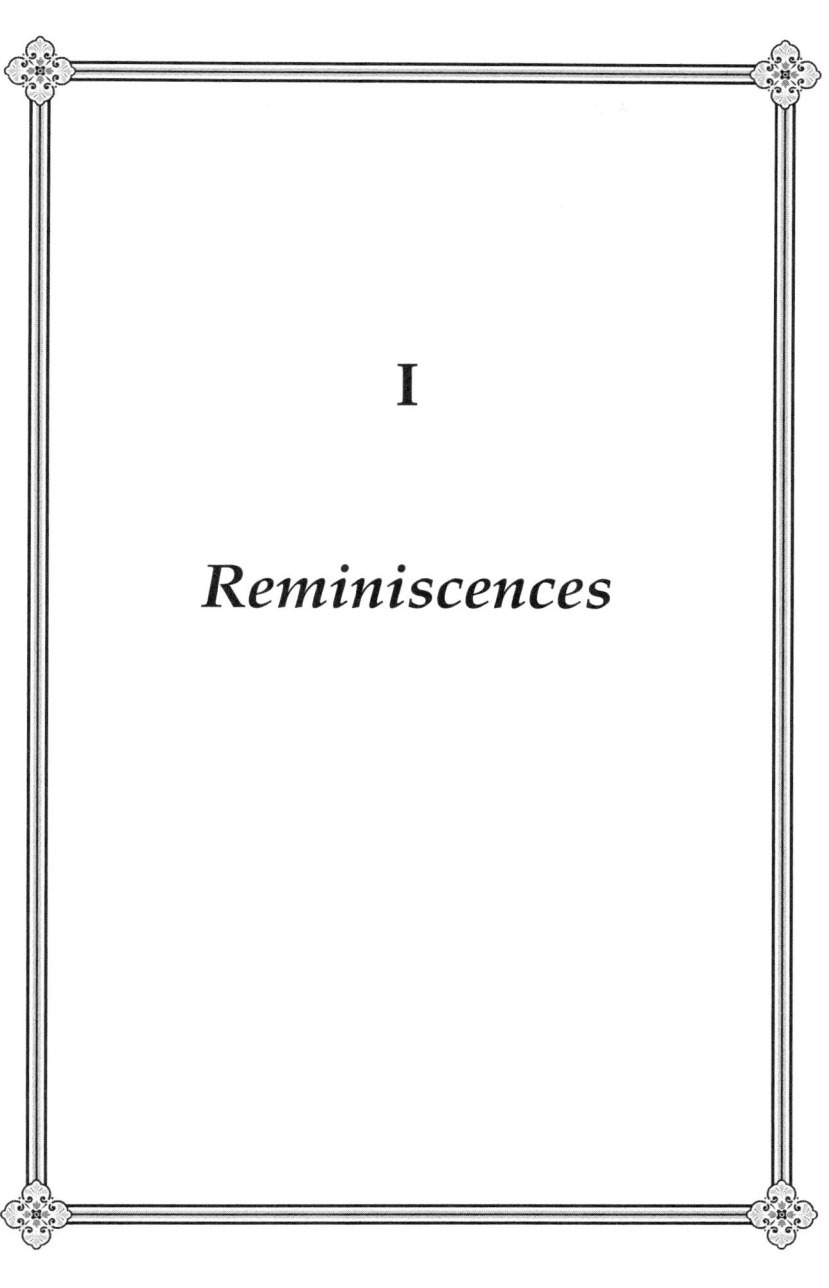

I

Reminiscences

THE CONSECRATION
OF ARCHBISHOP JOHN

THE LAST CONSECRATION performed by Metropolitan Anthony (Khrapovitsky) was that of Hieromonk John (Maximovitch) to the office of Bishop of Shanghai.

Bishop John became bishop at the age of thirty-eight. He came from a noble family in the region of Kharkov, and came to the notice of Vladika Anthony in Kharkov in 1914. After finishing the Cadet Corps, he graduated from law school in Russia and from the theological seminary in Belgrade. Then, having been tonsured a monk by Vladika Anthony in the Milkovo Monastery, he taught as a hieromonk in the Bitol Theological Seminary. In Bitol, Hieromonk John revealed himself as a fervent man of prayer. The local Macedonian and Greek population, for whom he served in Greek, came to love him.

In entrusting him with the episcopal staff, Vladika Anthony said to him: "From childhood I have witnessed a great many episcopal consecrations. Even then, I paid attention to the words addressed to the new hierarchs. I remember how the elderly Metropolitan Isidor of Petersburg and Novgorod would say, in committing the staff to the new bishops, 'It is very simple; just try to fulfill two commandments: Serve well, and do not give yourself airs.'

"More than anything in the world you love the Divine services, and since you are without any pretense whatsoever, you shall be able to fulfill these testaments to their fullest degree.

"Living as a pure virgin, do not become prideful or say, like the Pharisee: *I thank Thee, that I am not as other men are, extortioners, unjust, adulterers, or even as this publican* (Luke 18:11). May the Lord preserve your heart from such feelings! Pray with humility, and this prayer will constantly enrich your heart. This is my humble wish for you, shared by the other hierarchs present: May you love the Divine services, and preserve this love to the end of your life.

"Many bishops and higher clergy, while they were of lower rank, fervently loved the Divine services but, having increased in years and sometimes in wealth, gradually grew cold; but you will never become like them. It always pained me when I heard it said that a certain bishop was indifferent to the services and was not very prayerful, but 'at least he's a good administrator.' Such administrative skill is not necessary in a hierarch. If he would see prayer as his primary duty, the administration would take care of itself, and everything around him would improve on its own.

"Moreover, always refrain from judging your brother archpastors for their lack of zeal, and do not admit any subtle self-deception into your heart. Then every day and every hour the virtues will increase in your heart. Love theology and try to penetrate its depths. With it enlighten your soul and the souls around you, and with your learning give your mind soul-saving nourishment.

"Your path is clear, and it is adorned with the wisdom that comes from humility and with benevolence toward all. Do not despair if, along the way, you encounter ingratitude. Holy Athos formed a special type of versatility in people who combined in themselves zealous activity with the fullness of humility; this is the way all the virtues grow in your own heart and in the hearts of those around you. Then, if you fulfill all these things, remember the words of the Apostle Paul. To whom do they refer? We answer with trepidation: to our Lord Jesus Christ: *For such a high priest became us, Who is holy, harmless, undefiled. . .* (Heb 7:26)."

The consecration of Bishop John was distinguished by the warmth of heart felt by those present. Besides the Russian hierarchs, there participated a delegate of the Serbian Church, the renowned theologian and preacher, Nikolai [Velimirovich] of Ochrid, and other members of the Serbian clergy.

At the trapeza, one of the speakers characterized the consecration in this way:

"Many luminary archpastors were kindled here, but they were remnants, as it were, of old Russia; they were born and raised by her. The new bishop, however, is a young scion from that life which, with all its storms and tribulations, did not break the Russian spirit. A bearer of this spirit appears in this young bishop, who was greeted in Bitol by the first sons of the Church—the representatives of the Greek population—and also by those who came to him here, exalted representatives of the now powerful Serbian Church. May the future path of Russia continue in this vein."

Bishop John remained at the see of Shanghai until the end of World War II, after which, with the establishment of the Communist regime in China, he assisted the exodus of a significant part of his flock from Shanghai and, afterwards, the emigration to the United States of those who had found refuge on the island of Tubabao in the Philippines. Toward this end, Bishop John conducted ardent appeals in Washington. Later, when his flock had been accepted into the United States, he was appointed Archbishop of Western Europe.

Archbishop Nikon
in *The Life of Metropolitan Anthony*, Vol. 5

MY MEETINGS WITH
VLADIKA JOHN

I FIRST MET the young Hieromonk John Maximovitch at the beginning of his ecclesiastical career. We maintained contact from 1928 through 1934, that is, until he left for the Far East to be Bishop of Shanghai. I saw him again during the final, brief period of his service as Archbishop of Western America and San Francisco (1963-66). Thus, I was a witness, as it were, of both the first and last phases of Vladika's pastoral life.

I met Vladika John in the summer of 1928, during the school holidays. Not quite twelve years old, I was studying at the Russian secondary school in Belgrade, and had entered the third form. I served in the altar of Holy Trinity Church, which at that time was the main cathedral of the Russian Church Abroad. In this church there often served the head of the Church Abroad, Metropolitan Anthony, and other archpastors of the Diaspora. One Sunday, there were not enough acolytes, and one of the subdeacons (I think it was Ivan Gardner) recruited me. Vladika John, like most young people close to the Church, loved and revered Metropolitan Anthony as a great Church leader; he was for him an inimitable example in his personal life, a living embodiment of meekness, humility and love. He spoke to me of this more than once, knowing that I also loved and respected Metropolitan Anthony. Vladika John followed the reposed Metropolitan's example in many respects, especially in his personal interactions, which were simple, direct, spontaneous, often affectionate, and, it seemed, with a light southern Russian humor.

Our acquaintance began very simply. After one of the services, Vladika asked me my name and where I lived. On learning that I lived not far from him, or to be exact, from the house where his parents lived, he invited me to walk home with him. From 1929 to 1934, Vladika taught at the theological seminary in Bitol, in southern Serbia, and only in summer, during school holidays, did he live with his parents in Belgrade. Later, when I myself became a teacher at a secondary school, I understood why Vladika was so successful as a teacher in the seminary, in spite of a speech impediment. He was not only an excellent pedagogue (he knew how to adapt his methods to the age and maturity of his class), but he also loved his students, who repaid his love. In conversation, Vladika loved to bring up many examples from the lives of the saints, which made his discourse more vivid and familiar. It was easy to turn to him for advice, and one was always sure of receiving a clear and concise answer. From then on, I always walked home with him, grew closer to him, and grew to love him.

I had an opportunity to meet his parents, whom I occasionally saw in church. During the services they seemed strict, especially his mother, but later I discovered that they were kind, warm people. Vladika did not resemble them in appearance; judging by one photograph, however, he bore an amazing resemblance to one of his ancestors (I think it was his great-great-grandfather), who died in 1873, Michael Alexandrovich Maximovitch, and in whose honor, most likely, Vladika was named at his baptism. His ancestor was a great scholar, a kind of Renaissance man; he was not only an educated botanist and zoologist, but also an expert in the history of Russian literature, a philosopher, and a master of Little Russian folklore. He was first a professor of botany, and then of Russian philology. He was also rector of the University of Kiev. In his youth he was acquainted with Pushkin and Gogol. Another well-known ancestor of Vladika John was the Metropolitan of Tobolsk, Saint John (Maximovitch), enlightener of western Siberia, who reposed during the reign of Peter the Great. In the eighteenth and nineteenth centuries, the Maximovitches were well-known nobility, landowners of the Poltava region. Vladika himself graduated from the Poltava Cadet Corps. Vladika's parents later lived in Kharkov. His father was for a short time a Marshal of the Kharkov nobility, and Vladika himself finished law school there. During his student years, Vladika met the distinguished Archbishop Anthony [Khrapovitsky] of Kharkov, later Metropolitan of Kiev, who had a strong influence on him. It should be noted that the most ancient ancestors of Vladika John were Serbian nobility, who left their native land after its conquest by the Turks at the end of the fifteenth century. (One might note here that Tsar Ivan the Terrible's maternal grandmother, Princess Elena Glinskoy, was also one of the Serbian nobility refugees.) Vladika John loved very much the Orthodox Serbian people and Serbia, as did the entire Russian émigré population in Yugoslavia. The latter consisted primarily of former Russian military and their families, and, in general, of the Russian intelligentsia.

Thirty years later, as Archbishop of San Francisco and Western America, Vladika John would visit our parish in Seattle. On the first day of his visit he invariably stopped by to see me, since I lived just opposite the church. He would come into my room, in a half-basement apartment, where there was a separate entrance from the garden. Sometimes he would come by several times, during the day and in the evening. He would sit in an armchair and rest. Sometimes he remained silent; at other times he would begin talking right away. He would recall our Russian Belgrade, his Abba, Metropolitan Anthony. Vladika loved and knew Russian history well, and it was interesting to listen to him. Like Metropolitan Anthony, he was politically conservative and a monarchist. He believed in the rebirth of Russia. He was indulgent towards other people's shortcomings, forgiving; he never judged. When I asked him an awkward question regarding the unpleasantness in San Francisco in connection with the construction of the cathedral,* he immediately "fell asleep"

---

* During the construction of the new cathedral in San Francisco, the Russian community became bitterly divided, one group accusing the other of mishandling funds. The matter was taken to court, where Archbishop John, head of the accused parish council, was exonerated.

for a few minutes; I never brought up the subject again. Sometimes Vladika would abruptly change the course of our conversation and bring up various family matters which might be troubling me, matters I hadn't told him about. One could confide in him; his advice was always simple and straightforward.

On Saturday, July 2, 1966, Vladika came and sat with me for about forty-five minutes. He was supposed to go with the wonder-working Kursk Icon to a certain ill person, and then on to Canada. When I asked him whether he would stcp by again during this trip, he responded briefly: "God only knows what will happen with me today or tomorrow." I accompanied him across the street into the church building, where George Kalfov was waiting for him. George and I stayed downstairs while Vladika went up to his room. A short while later we heard a loud thud from upstairs. We ran up to Vladika's room and saw him lying on the floor. We helped him up and sat him in his armchair. When we asked what had happened, he answered: "I don't know; nothing like this ever happened to me." At that moment, Vladika experienced a slight shudder through his body, and then left us forever. The paramedics whom we called from the neighboring block confirmed his death, which had been quick and easy. The ruling hierarch of Seattle at that time, Bishop Nektary, and the rector, Archpriest Andrei Nakonechny (now both reposed) served a panikhida right there in Vladika's room, and again, after the body was placed in a coffin, inside the church itself. On the following day, Vladika's body was already in San Francisco.

Such was my last meeting with Vladika John, whom I knew and loved for forty years. And now, twenty-five years after his death, I still feel his loss very much. When I visit the sepulchre where Vladika now lies, I always turn to him for help and advice.

Yury K. Khruschoff

"NOW THAT IS A BISHOP!"

ONE COULD say that I was attached to Vladika John from my early childhood, in the church in Belgrade. At that time he was not yet forty, and his hair was still dark; I was just an ordinary little boy, but I loved Vladika John deeply. Vladika John was Bishop of Shanghai, but often visited Belgrade. Whenever he came to Yugoslavia, he came to the church and served. Everyone knew him, loved him, and considered him their own. I remember how I would press my head against him, and he would say: "Don't butt into me." These, then, are my first impressions of Vladika John. Of course, we knew that there were two pillars of our Church, which we could hold onto: the wise and very subtle Vladika Metropolitan Anastassy, and Vladika John, who was remarkable for his holiness and asceticism. Afterwards, everything was turned upside down. As a result of Yugoslavia's submission to the new [Communist] regime, the Russian Church Abroad left Belgrade, and all contact with Vladika John was lost.

I heard a great deal about Vladika John's ascetical struggles; how he never lay down to sleep, but slept sitting up. That he was a man of prayer was obvious. One sensed that Vladika was surrounded by an aura of prayerfulness.

I met Vladika John for the second time in my life in 1950, when he was appointed to the West European diocese. The situation there was very difficult. The Church was struggling financially, as were the clergy, myself included. Economically, Vladika John could not help me: there were no parishes and therefore no place to send me. However, Vladika John received many donations of church articles, cassocks and the like. One day (I was a young, 26-year-old priest at the time) he said to me, "Try on this cassock." I tried it on, and couldn't tell if it fit or not. And Vladika John stood on his knees to see whether the cassock reached all the way to my feet. Such humility!

Later on, Vladika John visited us in London. He usually visited us every year on the Feast of the Dormition of the Mother of God, the patronal feast of our church. Vladika John was an outstanding personality. Everyone loved and revered him, but not in an idolatrous way. It was, rather, a profound deference to his ascetical struggles, and to himself, as one who voluntarily carried on this spiritual struggle.

Vladika John routinely visited churches of other faiths, where the grace of Orthodoxy might still manifest itself, especially in the form of holy relics of saints whom we revere in common, who were glorified before the Schism of the Christian Churches. Following this practice, Vladika John expressed the intention of visiting Westminster Abbey. At one time it may have been a holy place. In spite of the devastation wreaked by Henry VIII, the Abbey was miraculously preserved as a functioning church. Now, however, it no longer possesses the holiness it once had as an ancient church. Now we simply come to see it as one of London's tourist attractions. Vladika also went to see it, but after spending only a short time there, he left, saying, "There is no grace here." It is true, one could find there the remains of renowned figures of England, of the country's political founders, writers, and scholars, but not of saints.

Here is yet another impression I had of Vladika John. He was coming by train to London, from France as I recall. A group of clergy—the late Vladika Nikodim, Archpriest George Sheremetieff, and I—met Vladika at the train station. At that moment, there came out of the train station a hunched-over old man, wearing sandals on bare feet, carrying a heavy icon on his chest, and with a klobuk that was slightly askew. Although he was not an elder (*starets*), he had the appearance of one, as if worn down by life's concerns. Vladika came out of the train station and an Englishman, a simple man, said: "Now *that* is a bishop!" He felt a tremendous spiritual strength in Vladika. It must be added that the same impression applied to Vladika John as to all bishops, that is, when they are in church, you feel that it is a day of celebration. Although you think, "This isn't a feast day; it's an ordinary day: three stichera from the Octoechos, three from the Menaion on the tone 'Lord I have cried'; there is no doxology or polyeleos"; nevertheless, you feel that it is a feast day, a great holiday, because Vladika John is there. This should apply to all bishops, but that is far from true. It applies, apparently, to bearers of holiness, such as Vladika John. Wherever he was, there was something special, an invisible light, that which we call grace, although we don't really understand this word.

Vladika John served with great flair (this is too secular a term), with great feeling and deep involvement in the church service. While his sermons were virtually unintelligible to the ear, when they were read they made a great impression. Only two or three people standing at the front of the church were able to hear him; the rest was lost. Vladika John considered it his duty to preach, but he had difficulty pronouncing words clearly, and it was hard to understand him.

Vladika John could be very strict and very forbearing at the same time. If he knew that someone could do better, he was strict with him, but if he could see that the person could not manage, he was very understanding and forgiving. I noticed two things about Vladika John: on the one hand he was pedantically strict about the order of the services. For example, he would expect you to sing the sessional hymn or the exapostilarion; it wasn't important in which tone, but it had to be sung. On the other hand, he could be exceptionally understanding. For instance, I know of two cases where Protestant ministers converted to Orthodoxy. Vladika baptized them and, although they had been married twice, he ordained them. Thus, in him was a strictness as well as an incredible kindness. If anyone took offense at Vladika, Vladika himself would ask forgiveness of that person, even though the other could sense that he himself was at fault. Vladika saw his flock as truly his flock: he was closely bound to it. He constantly visited the sick and went to parishioners' homes.

On theological issues Vladika and I discussed very little. He was greatly pressed for time, and I was shy about bothering him. However, I know that every translation that I sent to him, even the most insignificant, Vladika John received with great enthusiasm, praise and gratitude. And this gave me noticeable energy to continue this work, knowing that there was someone who would find the time, even if it tore him away from sleep or rest, to read it.

Vladika John's services were extremely long. Perhaps this was necessary as an ascetical practice, but there were few who could endure it. However, now that Vladika is gone. I remember how wonderful it was to live with him and pray with him. You had someone to whom to open your soul, someone to support you, someone who, if you fell, would pick you up again, who would give you courage, show you compassion, give you spiritual strength. This was a saint. Without him, you have the feeling that your whole life is passing between pieces of ice, and that warm heart is not there.

I know that Vladika read thoughts. Once I had a very bad thought, and Vladika turned around and looked at me very sternly. Vladika's clairvoyance was hidden; in order to avoid sinning by false humility, he preferred never to admit this gift.

During the last months of Vladika's life, I was in San Francisco. Vladika received me with such warmth, that I simply cannot express the joy I felt in my heart during those two months. He had reached such an unattainable level of holiness that during that last period it was almost frightening for me to be with him. Imagine if you were to actually see an angel before you; you would feel awestruck in his presence. As he approached the time of his death, Vladika was already in the realm of God's grace.

Did Vladika John foresee his own death? It is difficult to say. If he did, as some say, then, out of his own modesty, he concealed it. In any case, knowing that he wanted to reimburse me right away for my travelling expenses to San Francisco, I said to him: "It's all right, Vladika; it can be done another time." "No, no, it must be done right now." "Why?" "Because it must be so." Then he directed me to supervise courses in theology, which I did gladly. Then Vladika said to me: "All right, now that you have rested for a month and a half, it's time you get to work—serve and work." And then suddenly came the unexpected news, the dreadful news, that Vladika had died.

Bishop Nektary was in Seattle, and it was my duty to preside at the first panikhida for Vladika John in the cathedral in San Francisco. It was unforgettable. We started with a resounding: "Blessed is our God" [*Blagosloven Bog Nash*], and then you start to cry, and the concelebrating priest follows suit and also starts to cry. The deacon's voice breaks and he cannot get through the litany. . . The entire city was crying, including the clergy. Vladika John departed this life, bearing the aura of holiness and boundless love for people.

Archimandrite Ambrose Pogodin

EXAMPLES OF HOLINESS AND GRACE

OVER THE LAST fifty years, the Russian Church Outside of Russia not only accomplished great cultural and spiritual works, but also provided many examples of holiness and grace. Space limits us to only six examples, although there were many spiritual strugglers.

. . . The third of these was Archbishop John Maximovitch, who, during his life, was considered by many to be a fool; only after his death was he valued for his high Christian standards. He saved thousands of his flock from China, and was an amazing ascetic and man of prayer.

Pierre Kovalevsky
from the book *Russia Abroad*

A REMARKABLE STUDENT

Russian STUDENTS, like Russian professors, differed from Serbs. The majority of the latter graduated from seminary and prepared to become priests. They regarded the study of theology as a step facilitating their ability to move up the hierarchical ladder. Their relationship to the Church was more casual, although many of them were also sincere believers. We Russians, however, were preparing to serve the persecuted Church; no secure career, but total uncertainty awaited us.

Among us were a significant number of rare and gifted people, who left their mark on the life of the Russian emigration. Undoubtedly the most remarkable of them was Mikhail Borisovitch Maximovitch (1896–1966), later Archbishop John. Of slight stature, with massive, broad shoulders, puffy cheeks, and red lips protruding from a reddish, Little Russian-style moustache, he made a great impression of concentrated inner strength. As he did not associate much with other students, it was only toward the end of the course of study that I got to know him a bit better, and we had a few friendly conversations. He was very poor and earned a living selling newspapers. Belgrade in those years would be covered with impenetrable mud during its rainy season. Maximovitch wore a heavy fur coat and old Russian boots. He would tumble into the classroom rather late, thickly covered with street mud, take out a soiled notebook and chewed-up pencil, and start taking lecture notes with his large handwriting. Soon after that, he would fall asleep, but as soon as he woke up, he would immediately resume his writing. Many of us were curious to find out what sort of notes Maximovitch managed to come up with, but no one had the gumption to ask if they could read his notes. This unusual student became the most remarkable bishop of the Russian Church Abroad.

After graduating from the university, he entered monasticism and became a priest. For a time he taught at the seminary in Bitol. In 1934 he was consecrated bishop and was sent to Shanghai. There Bishop John led the life of an austere ascetic: he denied himself food and sleep, wore sandals without socks in winter as well as in summer, and his cassock resembled more the attire of a beggar than that of a bishop. His behavior would provoke a feeling of embarrassment among those around him because of his foolishness. Some considered him to be abnormal, but this did not stop him from carrying the responsibility of seeing to the material and spiritual needs of his flock, or from being untiringly helpful to all those in need. He started an orphanage for homeless children, whom he managed to evacuate, first to the Philippines and then to America. Many Russians are indebted to him for their deliverance from the Communists, when the latter occupied Shanghai. After leaving China, Bishop John settled in France, and in 1962 he received the cathedral post in San Francisco, where he died on July 2, 1966. Many now revere him as a saint.

N. & M. Zernov, from the book Russia Abroad

RECOLLECTIONS OF
AN ARCHPASTOR ASCETIC

Do NOT FORGET that next to the Theological Faculty in Belgrade, where I am sending you for good and soul-profiting studies, there is a 'living academy'—our Abba Metropolitan Anthony [Khrapovitsky], my previous mentor and benefactor, who is today a great teacher and hierarch of Christ's Universal Church. Drop by frequently to see him, because from him you will receive and draw a richness of knowledge and wisdom which are scarcely obtainable from any contemporary theological school." With these words Metropolitan Dionysius sent me to Yugoslavia, in January of 1932, when I was threatened with being kicked out of the Warsaw University (because of a protest provoked by an action of the ministry prohibiting students from using their native tongue at gatherings of the Theological Circle).

Metropolitan Anthony received me as one dear to him. I became a regular recipient of his abundant love, kindness and attention. The Elder would be offended and reprimand me if I did not stop by to see him in the evening or during the course of the day.

It was in the Metropolitan's humble quarters that I also became acquainted with Hieromonk John (Maximovitch). I often observed the paternal kindness which the Elder-Metropolitan showed towards Father John: in the movements of his eyes, in every word directed toward Father John, there shone joy over a spiritual son, complete trust, and gratitude that this son was multiplying his God-given talents.

Several times I had occasion to be in the home of Father John's parents. I was amazed at the number of Serbian students who made a "pilgrimage" to see him. The Serbs are not generally admirers of their own monasticism, but here, as soon as Father John appeared in Belgrade, Serbian students would literally besiege him. The righteous life of the monk-ascetic, his uncommon strictness towards himself, and his love-filled heart—this attracted the attention and the hearts of the Serbian students.

The Lord allowed me to be present at Father John's episcopal consecration and, afterwards, to meet him as a bishop in Metropolitan Anthony's quarters. "Be careful, Vladika, that your hierarchical rank does not spoil you. . . . Don't take a fancy to fine dishes; you know how people like to prepare delicious fare for bishops. . ," the Metropolitan would say jokingly to the young ascetic Bishop, and the Elder's face would radiate with joy for the new hierarch of God.

Our people like pontifical services and attend them eagerly. But, as I observed in Belgrade, the Liturgy celebrated by Vladika John attracted an unusually large turnout. His speech was sluggish and hard to understand, but the church would be packed.

In 1935 I returned to Poland for my pastoral service. In 1936 I received a letter from Vladika John from Shanghai, and shortly thereafter some of his sermons. While in Paris in 1958, I spoke to him personally. Many people there did not understand Vladika. His external appearance, the fact that he wore no shoes, disturbed them. P. S. Lopukhin told me that there were even complaints about Vladika sent to Metropolitan Anastassy. In one of the complaints the petitioners asked that the Chief Hierarch order Vladika John to get some shoes. Metropolitan Anastassy complied and wrote Vladika a letter. The parishioners, overjoyed, rushed to present their Archpastor with new shoes. Vladika accepted the gift, thanked them, and "used" the shoes. . . he carried them under his arm! but did not wear them on his feet. [The Russian verb, носить, "to wear," means also "to carry."] Again complaints to the Metropolitan, again the Metropolitan Abba wrote to Vladika John concerning obedience and received in answer: "Your instructions were carried out— you wrote that I should use shoes, but did not write that I should wear them on my feet, and so I used them, i.e., carried them. But now I shall wear them." And so Vladika began striding around Paris in shoes.

"Your Vladika John leaves a strange impression on people. Many are repelled by his external appearance, but one thing is sure—he is a man of God, an ascetic and man of prayer," D. N. Fedchenko, a parishioner of the Russian Exarchate in Paris, told me. He then proceeded to relate the following incident from Vladika's life in Paris:

There was a sick Russian woman in one of the hospitals there who was unable to move and whose condition was hopeless. The doctors had reconciled themselves to her imminent death and tried to ease her last hours of pain. In the evening hours, on the threshold—as the nurses thought—of this woman's last night, Vladika John entered the sick woman's ward. He came on his own, without being called by anyone, and stood by her bedside. Vladika prayed for a long time, blessed the unconscious woman, and left. The nurses and aides watched how the "strange Russian priest" prayed, standing by her bedside. And who would believe it? —around midnight the woman got up from her bed and demanded her clothes so she could leave the hospital! The astonished nurses called the doctor who, upon checking the woman, found her completely well. In asking her what had transpired, it became evident that "someone in black came to her and told her that she was well and could go home." The sick woman did not name the "visitor in black" who ordered her to get up and go home, but it was not difficult for the doctors to determine that it was Vladika John.

On May 16, 1963, in a discussion concerning the difficulties in San Francisco, Metropolitan Anastassy said to me, "I do not recognize Vladika John. Previously he was quiet, silent and meek, and now he is showing persistence, has livened up and is uncompromising. . . " What happened to the archpastor-ascetic? His whole life was a total surrender to God and the service of the Church, excluding any personal gain or, all the more, the interests of any cliques. The negative (and, within the Church, devastating) phenomenon of cliquishness was completely alien to Vladika John. But it existed and exists. Vladika saw that within the Church a matter of principle was being altered for the sake of cliquish and personal gains and interests, and he became vigorous, firm and unyielding. His attitude to all questions of church life was founded on the principle of the matter, and his evaluation of events and facts did not depend on the author or protagonist of the given question, occurrence or event. Archbishop John did not know how to sacrifice objectivity for the sake of personal friendship, personal preference or, all the more, for personal favors.

Vladika John was unusually strict in canonical questions and in faithfulness to Orthodox-Russian traditions and customs. At the same time, he was a stranger to church provincialism.

This was made evident when, as Archbishop of Western Europe, he reinstated the veneration of the saints of France (Gaul) who lived before the Schism.

Once I was asked by the librarian of the Theological Faculty of the University of Belgrade, "Tell me, what is your attitude towards Metropolitan Anthony and Father John?" Over thirty-five years have passed since then, and the Lord has allowed me to meet with many active Church leaders and members, to hear and see a great deal within the Church confines, but I can still hear the librarian's question. On the basis of the answer, the librarian would measure the spiritual level of the respondent and determine his degree of suitability for service in the Church. This question is still relevant today. Even now it remains a true measure in determining the spiritual quality and suitability of laborers in Christ's vineyard.

Bishop Mitrofan Znosko-Borovsky

SHANGHAI ACOLYTE

I GLADLY SHARE with you my personal reminiscences of then Bishop John of Shanghai, recalling the following words of Saint Nestor the Chronicler and praying his prayer:

"I entreat you, my beloved brothers, do not judge me for my ignorance if, being so filled with love for this saint, I decided to relate absolutely everything I know about him, for I feared lest the words of our Lord concerning the wicked and slothful servant apply to me. . . . But first of all I appeal to the Lord: O Almighty Lord, bestower of grace, Father of our Lord Jesus

Christ, help me, enlighten my heart that I may know Thy commandments, open my lips that I may tell of Thy wonders and the glory of Thy saint." (From the Preface to *The Chronicle of the Veneration of Archbishop John* by Bishop Savva of Edmonton)

I, too, am "filled with love for this saint," but I fear my own ignorance, my inability to convey "the glory of the God-pleaser." I don't know where to begin, how best to arrange the incredible number of the most profound, grace-filled impressions concerning this great Saint, which are engraved forever in my heart.

Not knowing where to begin, I copied out by hand several of Vladika's letters addressed to me between the years 1949 and 1962. I did this in order to relive that compunction evoked by the spirit-bearing instructions of that holy Hierarch, and note that Vladika began each letter with a deliberate eight-bar Cross of the Saviour, the Cross he so loved. He dated these letters according to the Orthodox calendar, ignoring altogether the civil calendar, and wrote exclusively in old orthography. Nameday greetings he wrote always on the very day of the commemoration, for which reason I only received them a few days later. This Saint did not permit even such a trivial "falsity" as sending congratulations before the actual Feast!

Vladika began his episcopal service in Shanghai in 1934, the year I was born in this large, international, commercial port city of China. My family's home was just three blocks from the majestic cathedral dedicated to the Mother of God, "Surety of Sinners." On Sundays and feast days my parents would walk with us children to this cathedral. Next to the cathedral was a Catholic school, the "Collège de Sainte Jeanne d'Arc," which my brother and I attended from 1939 until 1949, when we left Shanghai for the island of Tubabao. I dimly remember the solemn consecration Vladika performed, of the enormous gold crosses, which were then raised onto the five cupolas of the newly-completed cathedral. Next to the cathedral a diocesan house of several storeys was built, surmounted in the center by a bell-tower. I remember behind this house the unfinished foundation for a second church, where Vladika always performed the blessing of the waters on the Feast of Theophany. During the summer, when school was closed, my brother and I frequently came there and played in the spacious church yard.

One hot summer day, when I was eight or nine years old, I walked into the vast, always cool cathedral to get some relief from the heat. It was a weekday, about seven in the evening, still quite light. The evening service was in progress, celebrated by one of the priests; the cathedral was all but empty. At his place near one of the massive columns, between the altar and the right entrance, Bishop John stood behind an analogion spread with service books. Subsequently I learned that Vladika daily attended all nine of the services appointed by the Orthodox Church, and that he communed every day. After the service I approached him for a blessing. He asked my name and invited me to his quarters "for a talk." I'll never forget how, before leaving the cathedral, he made full prostrations in front of each icon—and there were many—as if he were temporarily parting with his close friends, the saints. I followed him, holding his staff. My childish soul was at once drawn to this extraordinary man, unconsciously sensing that deeply-Christian love which Vladika had for people, especially children.

For the first time I stepped into his large study on the second floor of the diocesan house. The entire right corner of the study, from the ceiling to the level of the analogion standing there, was filled with countless icons of all sizes. For some reason it seemed perfectly natural to me when Vladika, on entering his study, began unhurriedly making prostrations before the icons and again prayed at length. Finally he sat down at his desk, which was literally heaped with papers, and talked with me for a long time. As in later conversations, he spoke about the Church, about the life of her righteous ones and saints, about the martyrs, about church feasts. I didn't want to leave this extraordinary man. It was already dark when Vladika blessed me and told me to go home.

I began attending services in the cathedral every day, morning and evening, and serving in the altar. On weekdays Vladika himself often consumed the Holy Gifts, remaining in the altar, deep in prayer, long after the priest had gone. And always, before leaving the cathedral, he would venerate all the icons.

While talking with me in his study, Vladika would occasionally doze off for a few moments. I learned that he never slept in a bed, and only succumbed to brief periods of sleep in a chair or on his knees before his beloved icons, in which position his secretary, Mr. Kantov, would occasionally find him.

One evening, during one of our conversations in Vladika's study, the phone on his desk rang. Vladika answered it. I don't know who it was, but I'll never forget how at one point in the conversation Vladika dropped the receiver and dozed off. The receiver lay in his lap, but Vladika, dozing, continued for a long time to listen and respond to the person at the other end of the line. According to the physical laws of nature this was impossible—either for Vladika to hear the person who called him, or for that person to hear what Vladika replied. Nevertheless, from what was said—and it was a lengthy conversation—it was clear that this is just what miraculously transpired!

Once Vladika was brought dinner in his study. I remember: there was a plate of borscht and some pudding in a mug. He was alone; I was in an adjacent room where I was brought my dinner. Through the open door I watched as Vladika poured the sweet pudding into the plate with the borscht and proceeded to eat this unappetizing concoction. At that time, it seemed to me, a child, these were perfectly natural things for Vladika to do.

All of us boys, acolytes, loved Vladika, in spite of his strictness. (Once, for some mischief, Vladika had the watchman take a belt to the offenders.) For me, Vladika became a hero, and I decided to imitate him in everything. When Great Lent came, I stopped sleeping in my bed and lay on the floor; I stopped eating normally with my family and ate only bread and water, etc. My parents got worried and took me to Vladika. After listening to them, Vladika asked the watchman to go to the store for some sausage. To my tearful remonstrance, "but it's Great Lent," the wise archpastor ordered me to eat the sausage and always to remember that obedience to one's parents was more important than self-willed fasting. "What should I do now, Vladika?" I asked, still desiring some "special" ascetic practice. "Attend the church services as you already do, and at home do as your father and mother tell you." I remember how hurt I was that Vladika didn't prescribe any "special" podvigs.

I remember another extraordinary incident which I personally witnessed. It was a weekday and the Liturgy was celebrated by one of the cathedral priests. Vladika John stood in his usual place. As I recall, I was serving in the altar, although I can't remember for sure. I do remember how this priest, during his sermon, verbally abused Vladika, pointing at him and using such words as "snake," "scorpion," "toad," "hypocrite," and the like. Vladika continued standing in his place, and showed not the slightest reaction to his priest's outlandish attacks; he continued to read from some book there on his analogion. Papa later told me how he and many others, upset by the priest's intolerable behavior towards his hierarch, asked Vladika to punish the offender, but Vladika took no measures, saying that it was his personal affair. What holy meekness! In general, no one ever heard Vladika utter even a single word of judgment—of anyone.

The late Archpriest Seraphim Slobodskoy told me how he once asked Vladika, "Who is responsible for the deplorable strife surrounding the San Francisco cathedral" (then under construction)? Vladika answered very simply: "The devil."

"Care of souls"—this best defines the principal motivation of the whole life and activity of this great man of prayer and holy life, great not only in our lukewarm age, but—I firmly believe—in the whole history of the universal Church of Christ. How otherwise can one explain all that to which I was a living witness? How, for example, his face would literally be transformed during Divine Liturgy on great feasts, emanating an unearthly light; and his eyes, always full of divine love, clearly reflected that ineffable joy—unattainable for us sinners—at the presence of the Holy Spirit. Or how on Pascha night he flew around the vast Shanghai cathedral, as if borne by angels, shouting from an excess of jubilation the victorious proclamation: "Christ is Risen!" "Christ is Risen!" It seemed that his genuine exultation knew no bounds; he was entirely suffused in the joy of Christ, Whom he loved with a consummate, genuine love.

But what was most amazing was his gift of being able to see into the human heart and draw it to Christ. Were it not for this righteous man, I would never have even thought of serving the Church in the priestly rank. It was incredible how precisely he foretold what would happen to us! In October 1949 he wrote to my brother and me—we were only thirteen and fifteen years old and had just arrived in Australia from the Philippines but already were going less frequently to church—warning us: "In departing from the paths of the Lord, we can get only temporary satisfaction from carnal pleasures; later we feel the bitterness of that evil which had seemed so sweet." Today, thirty-five years later, I still cannot read these prophetic words without burning tears of gratitude.

He knew that I would write to him, May 19/June 1, 1960: "How I should like to talk with you personally, Vladika! So much has happened, so much has imprinted itself on my mind after our time in the Philippines that I do not even recognize myself. The spiritual aspirations of my youth have long ago drowned in a sinful, materialist environment." But the righteous one saw that my spiritual aspirations had not "drowned" altogether, and he continued to call me to serve the Church, advising me "to get a theological education and for this purpose to enroll in Holy Trinity Seminary. May the Lord help you and bless you on this path!" (Letter from January 18/31, 1961)

Of course, I have no words to express my gratitude for the love of this unforgettable archpastor. During the earthly life of a hierarch we exclaim: "By the prayers of our holy Vladika, Lord Jesus Christ, Son of God, have mercy on us!", but inasmuch as God is not the God of the dead, but of the living (Matt. 22:32), according to the incontrovertible words of the Saviour Himself, to this day I continue to call upon Vladika John for help with that same prayer.

I constantly thank God that He granted me to be a witness of His great Saint, by whose prayers I did not sink utterly into the vanity of this world. I am certain that the day will come when the Church on earth will glorify Vladika John as one of those "of whom the whole world is not worthy," and we shall render thanks to God, "wondrous in His saints."

Archpriest George Larin

A RIGHTEOUS MAN
OF THE 20TH CENTURY

CHILDHOOD. Tomorrow something special is antici-pated. . . They are going to raise the crosses onto the cupolas of our new Cathedral of the Mother of God, "Surety of Sinners" (Shanghai). I recall a sea of heads around the church—like on Pascha. My father lifts me up, and through the crowd I try to see Vladika as he blesses the prepared crosses. I raise my head. Somewhere far above, the main cupola is etched against the sky, and suddenly. . . I am transfixed with wonder. Reflecting the rays of the sun, a gold cross floats upwards. Lord! How splendid!

Here, next to the cathedral, is the diocesan house. Although we were afraid, we boys liked to climb up to the top floor and look out at the passersby. Sometimes Vladika would find us there. We would guiltily press against the wall, but he would call us affectionately to himself, rumple our hair and, giving his blessing, send us on our way with a kind word.

Behind the church house was a courtyard where we would play. Vladika, who usually went everywhere on foot, in passing by this courtyard always went in to see the children. He blessed us and spoke with us good-naturedly. I can still see his smiling face.

As a high school student I fell seriously ill and was admitted to the Catholic hospital on the outskirts of the city's English quarter, where Vladika lived. My condition was critical. I remember what joy flooded my heart when I saw beside my bed the kind face of dear Vladika, his sparkling eyes full of sympathy. How Vladika prayed! I lay in the hospital for several weeks, and each week on a given day Vladika came; he consoled me and prayed. Truly, this was a good shepherd! Vladika could have assigned one of his priests to visit the sick, but, in spite of the daily services, of being weighed down with diocesan affairs and concerns with the orphanage, and the rather primitive state of the city transportation system, Vladika himself covered long distances, partly by tram, partly by foot, visiting the sick and suffering in hospitals and prisons, thereby fulfilling the injunction of the holy Apostle Paul: *In all things shewing thyself a pattern of good works* (Titus 2:7).

And can anyone forget the service on Pascha night in the cathedral? How Vladika shone; it was absolutely unearthly. Each time he censed he seemed to be propelled around the cathedral. How he exultantly exclaimed, or rather shouted out the victorious paschal greeting! I've never seen anything like it anywhere. And in general, Vladika served with a rare prayerful concentration, so that those concelebrating and the people were penetrated by a spirit of prayer and reverence.

During the war, conditions were very difficult for the Russians in Shanghai: there was the Japanese occupation and pressure from the Soviets. Vladika shared all our misfortunes and deprivations. The war ended. The Soviets were ready to swallow the entire Russian China. But God was merciful. It was likewise difficult for Vladika to orient himself, having no contact with Metropolitan Anastassy, who at that time was restoring the life of the Church Abroad which had been thrown into disarray by the war. Besides which, Vladika had a trusting soul. Although he was accused of political wavering, in his heart he never betrayed his true convictions, which he demonstrated not only in bringing repentance before the Sobor of Bishops but in taking charge, as spiritual leader, of the exodus of Russian refugees from China, first to the Philippines and then to America.

On the island of Tubabao, the Lord granted me again to meet with Vladika and to experience his favorable disposition towards the unworthiness of me, a lonely and lost wanderer. Although Vladika had a visa for the United States, he considered it his first duty to share exile with his spiritual children, whom God's Providence had cast onto islands of palm trees and typhoons. Within no time church life was in full swing. A temporary diocesan office was organized, the convent was settled, three churches were opened, and, in the spacious military barracks adjacent to the convent, there arose a "cathedral," which by Pascha was adorned with a hand-made onion dome.

Vladika left for America. Everyone knows how, by the strength of his spirit, he succeeded in securing from the "powerful of this world" permission for his persecuted flock to enter the States. Experiencing freedom, people reacted to it in different ways, and in different ways expressed their gratitude to the Elder. One thing can be said for certain: Vladika never concealed in his heart malice towards anyone, and towards those ill-disposed towards him he acted as if there was nothing between them. This trait particularly impressed me. Oh, if only we all could conduct ourselves like that in our difficult time!

When later on I was in Washington, I couldn't help but notice the mark which Vladika left behind—both in church life and among those living there in general.

Time passed. In the fifties the Lord directed my steps to Paris; at that time Vladika was living in Versailles. I shall never forget my meeting with that good shepherd.

Vladika lived at the Cadet Corps. I arrived unexpectedly. His secretary met me and directed me to Vladika's study on the top floor. I ascended the wide staircase, trembling with anticipation. Portraits of Russian tsars gazed at me from the walls. I knocked on the door and was answered, "Amen." (At that time I didn't know that one should say the prayer, "By the prayers of our holy fathers. . .") I went in. At a desk piled with letters and papers, Vladika sat writing. The sight of him—without shoes, in a torn cassock, his hair disheveled—was a touching image of meekness and simplicity. I hesitated in the doorway. On seeing me, Vladika exclaimed, his face lit up with a smile; he jumped up from his chair and after blessing me locked me into his embrace. I was unable to restrain my tears of joy. Our conversation was a torrent of recollections, tumbling from one incident to another, one acquaintance to another. In this short time, it seemed as if we relived the past several years.

On learning that I was planning to travel around Europe, Vladika got a copy of the Holy Trinity Calendar and gave it to me, pointing out the parishes located in Europe. "Go with God. As soon as you arrive in a city, go to the local priest. Tell him that I sent you." With God's help, and with Vladika's wise advice, I toured almost the whole of Europe, acquiring both spiritual nourishment and friends and acquaintances who showed me the sights as no tourist agency could possibly have done.

It came time to leave. Vladika suggested that we go downstairs to the church, located next door. There Vladika served Vespers and then saw me on my way. I approached him for a blessing, but he said, "No, no. I'll see you to the tram." It was a fair distance from Vladika's residence. I felt awkward about his accompanying me, but Vladika insisted. When the tram pulled away, I continued for a long time gazing at the bent figure of the elder, blessing me on my journey.

The years passed. University. Marriage. Military service. Work for the Church.

All this time letters arrived from dear Vladika, inspiring and full of concern. And then, quite unexpectedly, Vladika suggested I enter the service of the Church. Just at this time the Synod of Bishops was discussing the canonization of Father John of Kronstadt, something Vladika was actively working towards. And I had a wonderful dream: Father John of Kronstadt blessed me and told me not to be anxious. The same day my wife underwent a difficult operation. But her health did not improve. We were terribly despondent. Unexpectedly there came a phone call from Vladika, who said to my wife, "Agree to the ordination, otherwise you will continue to have problems." Afterwards Vladika came to visit us; we had dinner and a nice conversation. As he was leaving, he suddenly turned to my wife: "Well, my dear, the diaconate or the priesthood?" although not a word had been said on the subject in the course of the evening. There's no need to say what impression Vladika's pointed announcement made on us. We submitted to this decision of our abba. On his next trip to the East Coast, Vladika himself ordained me to the diaconate. And, just as Vladika had said, after I became a deacon my wife's health noticeably improved.

Thus passed several years during which Vladika never forgot us with his letters, and whenever he came to New York he invariably contacted us by phone. Then came a new offer from our abba—to become a priest in his diocese. Again we deliberated, and again my wife fell ill. Here we decided that Vladika evidently was offering us a means of healing. And we made the decision. But Vladika was no longer among those living here on earth. The Lord granted me the calling of a priest, and today I cannot refrain from testifying that a second time my wife's health was restored without any medical intervention. We have no doubt in the intercession and prayers of dear Vladika.

No longer do letters arrive from Vladika, but we sense the unwaning strength of his care for us, and we live with his memory. The bent figure of the elder, distantly reminiscent of St. Seraphim, rises before our eyes. Here he is, a modern saint, a follower of the wonder-working St. John of Kronstadt. A genuine unmercenary who sought no glory in the archpastoral calling, who had no interest in honor or elegant vestments. A good shepherd, the first to give an example of concern for his neighbor. A pastor who lived by the Church, in the Church and for the Church. A Christian who conquered anger within himself, making his face to shine with a joyous smile. A loving father. A hierarch who labored unremittingly. A man who knew no limits in his ascetic exploits. A slave of God, struggling day and night in concentrated prayer of the heart. An intercessor before God for people who received through him healing and the realization of their hopes. . . Truly, brethren, *Such a high priest became us, who is holy, harmless, undefiled, separate from sinners, and made higher than the heavens* (Heb. 7:26). Throughout his difficult life, the ever-blessed Vladika John followed this injunction of the great Apostle, and in large measure succeeded in fulfilling it. And this is all the more remarkable considering that Vladika lived in our time, when humanity has grown impoverished in faith and piety. Here, no doubt, lies the root of that misunderstanding which so often met Vladika even among some apparently churchly people. However, that which the Lord allowed as a way of testing people during Vladika's lifetime is now dissipating like smoke, and with each day this chosen luminary of righteousness shines ever more brightly, strengthening the faithful in bearing the Christian podvig of humility, patience and love.

Archpriest Valery Lukianov

RECOLLECTIONS ABOUT ARCHBISHOP JOHN

MY FIRST meeting with Archbishop John took place at the Lesna Convent, located at that time in the suburbs of Paris. The church was situated within the great hall of the convent. I had heard a lot about our dear Archbishop and very much wanted to see him. The Liturgy had not yet begun when we arrived, but the Archbishop was already standing in the middle of the church, in his white under-vestment, waiting to be vested, while the faithful were standing along the wall. There were already quite a number of people, and I stood to the side. Glancing at Vladika, I noticed that he was of short stature, slightly hunched, and had rather unkempt hair. For some reason I felt sorry for him. I thought: How difficult it must be for him! And I began wholeheartedly to pray for him. He stood motionless, but as soon as I started praying he abruptly turned his head in my direction and looked straight at me, his eyes penetrating my very being. This unexpected gesture sent shivers down my spine—I felt such joy!

At first the Russian Orthodox Church Abroad did not have its own church in Paris, and we rented a Lutheran church. Nor did we have a choir; we gathered singers from various parishes, and I too was part of this conglomerate choir. Once—I cannot remember if it was before the Cherubic Hymn or before Communion—the choir had no piece to sing, and as a result there was a long pause. People in the choir started asking me about Vladika, and I began telling them what I had heard. Suddenly I had a feeling that I must keep quiet. After all, the Divine Liturgy was in progress, and it must be that our conversation was not pleasing to Vladika. I felt awkward, but the singers were so interested in what I had to say that they insisted I continue. I thought the feeling I had could be just a figment of my imagination, and I resumed talking. Again I sensed Vladika ordering me to be quiet—this time rather sharply—and I desisted. Everyone kept asking me to go cn. "I cannot!" "Why not?" they asked, and I answered that Vladika does not want it and does not permit it. Here is a second example of Vladika's gift of clairvoyance. It was impossible for him to have actually heard what we were talking about.

I went to visit Vladika several times. He lived at the Cadet Corps* outside Paris, in Versailles, where he had a small monastic cell on the top floor of a house. In this cell there was a table, his armchair, and several chairs around the table. There may also have been another small table and a dresser. In the corner there were icons and a stand with books. I cannot remember the exact arrangement; at that time I wasn't interested. There was no bed in the cell; Vladika never lay down to sleep. Sometimes, as we were conversing, he would nod off, sitting in his chair. At that point, I would stop, but he would immediately say, "Go on, go on; I'm listening." And indeed, Vladika responded to all my questions. All night long, Vladika would pray, leaning on his staff. Sometimes he prayed on his knees; it is likely that when making prostrations he would doze off a bit in this position, on the floor. This is how he exhausted himself!

When Vladika John was not serving and was at home, he always made a point of going barefoot, for the sake of mortifying the flesh. Even during severe frosts. He used to walk barefoot in the freezing cold from the Cadet Corps residence, which was on a hill inside the park, down a steep path to the church, which was located at the front gate. Once, he hurt his foot; doctors were unable to treat it, and there was danger of blood poisoning. It became necessary to send Vladika to the hospital, but he did not want to lie down in a bed. Since this was against hospital

*A military school for boys, similar to that which Archbishop John had attended as a boy. Founded by Russian emigrés, the Cadet Corps in Versailles was the last Russian institution of its kind.

regulations, Vladika finally conceded. Nevertheless, he put a boot underneath himself, so that it would be uncomfortable for him to lie there. The nurses said, "You brought us a saint!" Every morning a priest would come to him and serve Divine Liturgy, and Vladika would partake of the Holy Mysteries.

In a wing near the entrance gate of the Lesna Convent lived a young man whom Vladika had brought out of China. His body was twisted, and he walked with a severe limp; his hands were deformed and his speech was impaired. Although he looked mentally retarded, he was of sound mind. He smiled a lot, and everyone liked him. Then he became seriously ill (he had been diagnosed with meningitis) and was hospitalized. When Vladika was told that the man's condition was hopeless and that he might not live through till the next day, he immediately went to him and prayed over him for a long time. The following day the man was released from the hospital with a clean bill of health. What happened to him after that I don't know.

When Vladika arrived in Paris, there was a severe housing shortage. In order to start a church, two adjoining garages in a row of garages located in a courtyard were rented. Inside they were fashioned into a little church. After a few years, Vladika managed to find a house and to convert it into a house-church. (It now has an exact copy of the miracle-working Kursk Icon of the Mother of God, with a piece of the original.) I personally liked the garage church: it was small and rude, but it had a very prayerful atmosphere. Our dear Vladika often came to us and served there. It was so easy to pray with him! People found his prayerful disposition to be contagious. I often went to him for Confession. He knew how to confess you in such a way that, without realizing it, you would recall your sins and leave feeling peaceful and joyful, happy to have experienced heartfelt repentance. The Lord allowed me, the unworthy one, to do a lot of work in this church. Glory to God for all things! And although Vladika ate nothing during the entire Passion Week, on Pascha he was more energetic than anyone, joyful, beaming, so that all those praying were involuntarily drawn to celebrate with him.

One lady (she did not belong to the Church Abroad) told her girlfriend that she wanted to go to the church where Vladika John was serving. Her friend did not want to go, because Vladika John was not of her jurisdiction. But then she agreed to go, and even to venerate the Cross; however, she would not kiss Vladika's hand. At the end of the service both ladies came up to the Cross. The one who had resisted coming "melted" under the profound impression of the service and decided to kiss Vladika's hand after all. Vladika let her kiss the Cross, but abruptly withdrew his hand. The lady gasped in astonishment. How could he have known?!

During one of the Passion Week services, before we had a permanent reader, a layman was reading It was a lorg reading, and he thought Vladika would not notice if he turned two pages at once. Vladika, standing in the middle of the church, without any book, "Tsk-tsk'ed" disapprovingly, and from memory recited everything the reader had skipped. This lesson served the man for the rest of his life.

Once a visiting priest came to us (we did not yet have our own at that time) and served the All-night Vigil. The Vigil lasted only forty-five minutes. We were scandalized. So much had been omitted that we decided to report it to Vladika, in hopes that he would chastise the priest into proper observance of the church rubrics. But Vladika only smiled and said, "Well, there's no way to satisfy you! I serve too long (on Holy Saturday, services began at 9 A.M. and by 4 P.M. they hadn't yet reached Communion; after that Vladika shortened the service), and the other serves too short!" We felt so ashamed that we had judged the priest, and even Vladika. To judge anyone is terrible, but especially clergy. And how kindly and humbly Vladika gave us this lesson!

E. G. Chertkov

FOR THE GLORY OF GOD
AND ALL THE SAINTS

A SMALL GROUP of sisters and I spent four years as refugees in Amman, where we had fled from the Gornensky monastery during the 1948 Arab-Israeli war. The Most Blessed Metropolitan Anastassy, predicting that our monastery in the Holy Land would be lost, intended to send us together with Archbishop Nikon to the United States, to the Novo-Diveyevo Convent. At that time Archbishop John was being transferred to Europe, and Metropolitan Anastassy wrote to me in Amman, "Vladika John is going to Europe, and I am placing you in his hands. He will not abandon you." With Vladika John's blessing, while waiting for a visa to the United States, we took refuge for two years in the Lesna Convent in Fourqueux, near Paris.

The first meeting. In order to officially introduce ourselves to Archbishop John, we had to go to Versailles. Mother Flaviana from Lesna accompanied me, together with the elderly nun Agafina. I was warned that Vladika John might be rather stern. To everyone's surprise, Vladika was exceptionally attentive and affectionate. In giving us some refreshment, he poured three spoonfuls of sugar into my cup. He wanted to "sweeten" our fate, as it were, sensing how much poverty, illness and grief we had experienced during our four years as refugees.

In Lesna, the nuns were expecting Vladika John from Versailles. They were making preparations for the service, and Abbess Theodora asked our Sister Catherine, the choir director, to sing "Champion Leader" in Arabic, which she liked very much, at the end of the service. Sister Catherine hesitated, afraid the other sisters would not like it, but she decided to obey the abbess, and our sisters sang this. The service ended, and everyone went in to receive a blessing; the last one in was Sister Catherine. Blessing her, Vladika said, "So, you sang it after all, and you did well!"

On a certain feast day, everyone had prepared for Holy Communion and was waiting for the arrival of Archbishop John. Among the guests from Paris was a thirteen-year-old girl, who refused to prepare for Communion, as she was afraid to go to Confession to the stern-looking abbot Nicander of Valaam. The nuns and visitors went out to meet Vladika. When this girl came up to the Archbishop, he blessed her, put his hand on her head, and said, "You are going to prepare for Communion!" She did, and was glad.

Another instance: Vladika was at the convent. Preparations were being made for the evening service. Someone went to get Vladika but could find no trace of him. When he finally showed up, we learned that the sorrowful Countess Olga Kapnis had been asking for Vladika's holy prayers for her young relative, who was in the hospital with a nervous breakdown. Her situation was so serious that they wouldn't let even her parents in to see her. Without delay Vladika had gone to the hospital, insisted that he be allowed to see the girl, spent time with her and returned for the service. To the great amazement of the doctors and family, the girl recovered and returned to a normal life.

During the reading of the kathisma, Vladika always stood with his elbow propped on an analogion, looking half-awake. At the far end of the church, Sister Xenia whispered, "He doesn't sleep at night; now he's dozing." Vladika immediately turned around and looked at her. She was ready to fall through the floor.

Time passed. All the negotiations regarding our visas to America had failed. Vladika John was then Archbishop of Brussels and Western Europe, and England was under his jurisdiction. On his return from a trip to England, he decided it was there that we should establish ourselves. We received a visa and work permit for England without delay. With his holy prayers and fatherly concern, there was founded the first Russian Orthodox Convent in London, in honor of the Annunciation. At our leave-taking of the Lesna Convent, in sending us off to our new life, Vladika John said, "You will be in a big city, but live as though you were in the wilderness."

After many difficulties, a suitable building was found for the living quarters. Having looked everything over, Vladika said to me, "The sisters are from the Holy Land. They need heat. Make sure they have it right away." Central heating was installed, but we had an unfortunate mishap: the worker broke the faucet of the water heater, and the whole floor of the kitchen and closet was flooded with boiling water. On his next visit Vladika found out about this, and asked for the "Book of Needs" (*Trebnik*) and for some holy water. He read a prayer over the furnace, sprinkled it all with holy water, and prayed at length over the heater and electrical system. He asked that we hang there an icon of the Mother of God, the "Unburnt Bush." Since that time, thanks to Vladika's prayers, everything works fine.

Whenever he visited England, Vladika John always stayed with us at the convent. He never lay down to sleep, but rather rested, seated in an armchair in the office next to the church. At night we heard how he would often go into the church.

Knowing that the sisters had all been pupils at the Bethany school in the Holy Land, Vladika gave us his blessing to work with children—teaching catechism, Russian language, and singing. Once Vladika was at our convent when school lessons were in progress. Among our pupils were some of their English friends. We introduced the children, and they came up for a blessing. Surrounding Vladika, they didn't want to leave. Outwardly Vladika John was not very attractive, but even non-Orthodox felt his spiritual grace, and, in leaving, the English children said, "You're so lucky to have such an Archbishop!" With Vladika's prayers we have been working with children now for thirty-six years.

After visiting the church warden, Count Vladimir Klein-michel, Vladika declined to take a taxi, preferring to return to town via the underground. The warden accompanied Vladika to the station. As he was leaving, the ticket agent asked him whom he was seeing off. "That was our Orthodox archbishop," replied the warden. "I'm a Baptist," said the ticket agent, "but I can see that your archbishop is a saint."

During one of Vladika's visits to our community, there was a phone call from France, notifying us that Archimandrite Serge had died. Vladika ordered that the funeral be postponed, and said that he was returning to France at once. Early in the morning we saw Vladika off to the station by taxi. The young cab driver, an Englishman, asked if it were possible for him to have a blessing. Vladika turned around and blessed him. The driver then said to us: "What a wonderful, extraordinary arch-bishop; he has a rare inner strength."

At one time, there lived in London a Russian family from China. One night the husband called me, frantic with anxiety. "For God's sake, tell Vladika John that my wife Olga is in the hospital critically ill. Her blood pressure has shot up very high, and the doctors fear for her life as well as the life of our unborn child." I called Versailles, hoping to catch Vladika there. He himself answered the phone, found out all the details, and then said not to worry, that all would be well. Afterwards, he thanked me for calling him. By his holy prayers, everything worked out fine, and a healthy girl, Katherine, was born.

A friend of our community, Paraskeva Dimitria, lay ill in a coma. At our request, Vladika John went to see her; he prayed and blessed her. That same day, she got up, healthy, and with tears related how she had felt her illness suddenly leave her. Others told me that whenever Vladika put his hand on a person's head, one felt the power of grace, and one felt light in one's soul. Vladika fulfilled the Lord's commandments with self-sacrificing love, and the Lord answered his holy prayers.

It was the feast day of the Dormition of the Mother of God, the patronal feast of the London cathedral. When Vladika returned to the convent, we fell into a discussion about the conducting of services, and he mentioned, rather sorrowfully, that during the Vigil at the cathedral no one had sung the "eight tones" stichera. The nuns offered to sing them for him right then and there. Vladika listened, beaming. He often served at our place and brought us great consolation. He loved the singing of the nuns and valued a knowledge of the intricacies of the services. For the Feast of the Protection of the Blessed Virgin, Vladika John sent us a greeting, which we hung on our cliros: "On the day of Saint Romanus the Melodist, crowned by the Lord for his enviable singing ability, I ask that you relate my greetings to all the nuns and sisters who work diligently for the Church and participate in the liturgical services with their singing. May the Lord bless them with His mercy for their diligence and hard work for the glory of Christ's Holy Church. I ask the Lord's Blessing on you, on all who glorify the Lord with their singing, and on the entire convent." [signed] Archbishop John.

Abbess Elizabeth

WITH VLADIKA
THROUGH THE YEARS

Shanghai, 1938-48.

In Shanghai, Vladika John unceasingly manifested his concern and attention and spiritually guided us children. Every year he personally administered the catechism exams at all the Russian schools and orphanages throughout the city. He required that all the children know without fail the name of their own saint, the story of their life, and on their saint's day that they receive Communion.

The school's annual patronal feast, the day of Saints Cyril and Methodius, the first teachers of the Slavs, was celebrated by having the children from all the schools participate in the Divine Liturgy on that day at the cathedral. The choir consisted of youth singers from different schools. After Liturgy, food was served in the cathedral courtyard. In the midst of the hundreds of children, Vladika himself was present.

I grew up and lived in the Saint Olga orphanage at the convent with Abbess Ariadna, and studied at the S. E. Dieterix girls' high school. Vladika felt that [at the convent] the girls should participate in serving him and putting on his vestments during the services. From the age of ten to sixteen I was fortunate to be assigned as a server for Vladika.

For a few years I also went to Saint Sophia Catholic school. The nuns there were missionaries, who tried to convert the children to Roman Catholicism, and Vladika struggled against the idea of Russian Orthodox children going there to school. He would come to the school gates at the end of the school day, meet us and bless us. He would sternly tell us that we should not be wearing those uniforms or go to that school, that we had our own, Russian schools.

Christmas was celebrated according to the old Russian tradition. After the solemn Vigil at the convent, we, a group of girls' school teachers, led by one of the nuns, walked through the sleeping city to the cathedral with a lighted Christmas Star to glorify Christ and to congratulate Vladika with the Feast. He received us in his quarters, beaming with joy. After glorifying Christ, we went up to him by turn for his blessing, and each of us received from him a small bag of sweets, which filled up large baskets piled up in his cell. As a Christmas present, we gave him woolen socks which we had knitted ourselves. (To our chagrin, we later saw these same socks worn by street beggars.)

From the windows of the third floor of the convent building where our orphanage was located, we would see Vladika walking the streets in pouring rain and bad weather, winter and summer, in the direction of his children's home, the Saint Tikhon of Zadonsk house. Along the way there was the "House of Mercy" for men, and a refuge with a church for elderly women; further down there was a prison. We knew that Vladika would visit all of those institutions. Sometimes, on his way back, he would visit us as well. At the convent his arrival was announced by a joyful ringing of all the bells. In bad weather, wet through and through, wearing sandals on bare feet, he would go into the convent church, venerate the altar and all the holy miracle-working icons, and then he would go up the back stairs to the third floor, to the children in the orphanage. After singing *Eis pollá eti Déspota*, we would approach Vladika for his blessing. He would ask us our saints' names, what their life stories were about, and from which Evangelist the day's appointed Gospel was read. He also wanted to know if we had enough to eat. During World War II, when times were really tough in terms of getting enough food, the orphanage would get soup from the public cafeteria. Then Vladika would taste the food himself, scooping up a spoonful straight from the pot.

In spite of his strictness towards us, we were drawn to Vladika, and, whenever we saw him walking through the city, we ran toward him to receive his blessing. With Vladika, we children had a good and happy time.

America, 1962-1966.

In 1962 we joyfully greeted Vladika John's arrival in San Francisco. I was married by then, and we had three children.

Vladika's concern for his flock did not cease. He struggled against mixed marriages, against the changing of Russian names to foreign names, against the celebration of Christmas with other faiths. Vladika's authority and personal concern for the upbringing of children in America convinced us parents that he would guide us and correct us. He used to say to us: "Living in a free country, we must especially take advantage of the freedom of religion, and not abandon or change our traditions." His influence was demonstrated, for example, in the children's request that Santa Claus (Grandfather Frost) bring them presents on January 7 [December 25th O.S.], and not on December 25 (as per the civil calendar).

Our work with Vladika during the very difficult years in San Francisco brought our family especially close to him.

In spite of all Vladika's trials, he continued to visit the sick and handicapped Russians and to give them Communion, as he had in Shanghai. I often had to drive Vladika in my car. Vladika continued to give his attention to children, including our own. Our eight-year-old son learned to read the Horologion by staying with Vladika after Liturgy. He conversed with three-year-old little Musenka, let her kiss the Cross and gave her a prosphoron; smiling, he listened to her little chatter, while the warden, lawyers, and other community members waited for him with pressing church business. . .

Vladika's rapport with children was evident when Musya was in the hospital for a gland operation. In unfamiliar surroundings, she couldn't fall asleep, and was always crying. The nurses were afraid to go into the children's ward, because she started wailing even louder. In the morning, the nurse called me from the hospital and asked, "Who was that, dressed all in black and with a black beard, who came to Musya at 11:00 P.M.? We became alarmed when he went into her room, thinking she would go into hysterics and wake the other children. To our surprise," she added, "when Musya saw him, she stopped, broke into a smile, and talked with him. After he left, she peacefully fell asleep."

61

1964-1966. Oregon

We were saddened by my husband's career transfer to the state of Oregon, because of having to leave Vladika. With regret, he blessed us on our way with icons of Saint Nicholas and Saint Seraphim of Sarov, which he took from the walls of his cell.

After we moved, Vladika maintained contact with us: he wrote us letters, sent the children cards on their namedays, thanked us for remembering him when he received little packages from us, always signing his letters, "With love, Archbishop John." Sometimes he stayed at our house en route from Seattle to San Francisco. He was with us in Oregon also with the miracle-working Kursk Icon.

The last time Vladika was at our house was late one evening; he was on his way to San Francisco, and was accompanied by a priest and an acolyte. They were all exhausted from the trip, and my husband tried to convince Vladika to spend the night, but Vladika never missed Divine Liturgy or Communion, and he wanted to travel through the night to San Francisco. Finally, however, he agreed to stay with us and to serve Liturgy in our house in the morning. Our whole family was to take Communion, and Vladika confessed each one of us. He told me to read the Gospel for about ten minutes every day. As part of our preparation for Holy Communion, he gave us spiritual instructions and had us read an Akathist to the Mother of God and the entire order of preparation for Holy Communion.

That was on November 12, 1965. Although it was the last time we saw Vladika alive, we, his spiritual children, feel that Vladika is still with us.

Tatiana Kennedy Urusov

FROM SHANGHAI
TO SAN FRANCISCO

I REMEMBER HOW, in 1934, on the Feast of the Entry of the Mother of God into the Temple, Vladika John arrived in Shanghai from Yugoslavia. We had waited a long time. When, in 1933, our Shanghai hierarch, Archbishop Simon, died, the head of the church mission, Archbishop Victor, had written a request to the Synod to send us a new bishop. A reply came from the Synod that they would send us the same kind of prayerful individual as Vladika Simon had been. We waited a long time for this new hierarch. The day of his arrival was occasion for a great celebration. All the clergy, community organizations and school children gathered at the cathedral to greet Vladika John. After a short moleben there was a reception. At the trapeza I remember how Vladika John smiled on seeing some sugar: "So much sugar?" "Yes," we replied. "In Yugoslavia," he said, "it's unavailable; there isn't any!"

One of the first good works Vladika John did there in Shanghai was to found an orphanage. He gathered children off the city streets. First, he found four children, then more were gathered. One rich man donated a large house for the orphanage. The smallest of the orphans was four years old. Vladika was very affectionate with children.

Vladika John served Liturgy every day, all year round. Different priests would assist him in rotation. The services were very long. With his arrival, Vespers took place in the evening together with Compline. During Compline, at the very beginning of the service, there were always readings from one of the three canons to the saints. At six o'clock in the morning was the Midnight Office, followed by Matins and Liturgy. Vladika John did not have much of a musical ear, but he insisted that all verses appointed to be sung, be sung and not read. At Vespers and

Matins he stood with the clergy on the cliros. He was very strict with the clergy. The polyeleos was always sung in full (i.e., the whole Psalm). Many people didn't like the fact that the services lasted so long.

The children from the orphanage assisted Vladika during the daily Liturgies. The orphanage was located thirty minutes away by foot from the cathedral. When it rained, the children came to church barefoot and served barefoot. Vladika John served in sandals. He never slept lying down. He was very clean: every morning at four o'clock he took a cold bath, even in winter.

Vladika particularly revered the days on which martyrs were commemorated. For some reason it sticks in my mind that he had a special love for Martyr Tryphon.

In 1938 Vladika travelled to Yugoslavia to attend the All-Church Council. Before he left, his flock entrusted him with numerous communications. At this Council, Vladika John was the secretary, and among the communications were some complaints against him, which he read aloud just as calmly as if they did not refer to him at all.

After World War II, many Russian émigrés in Shanghai, including some clergy, took Soviet passports. The head of the mission, Archbishop Victor, was among those who did so, as was the senior rector of our cathedral, Protopresbyter Michael Rogozhin. We, together with Vladika John, did not follow this example. I remember that Vladika John received an announcement from the Soviet consulate that Archbishop Victor was coming to Shanghai. Vladika John gathered together all of the clergy and announced that he would not meet with Vladika Victor. We supported him in this.

When Archbishop Victor arrived in Shanghai from Peking, eight Komsomol youth accompanied him as he walked toward the cathedral, where Father Michael had just finished a moleben. We watched these events from the church house. The next day, it happened I had to meet with Archbishop Victor. He called us "Johnites." "Yes, and do you know why we favor Vladika John?" I asked him. "If you want to know, I will tell you. Who brought Vladika John here? You brought him to us. After Vladika John's arrival you yourself came here many times and said to him: 'Vladika John, I respect you, I recognize your high standards in life, and you are a good leader. Continue in this way. And if the clergy don't listen to you, don't hesitate to chastise them.' Vladika, didn't you say these things?" "Yes, I did," admitted Vladika Victor. "That's why we listen to him. And now you are against Vladika John. You are now a Soviet citizen, and it is impossible to have any interaction with you. I am Chinese; our clergy remained White, but you are Soviet [Red]. Do as you like..."

After the evacuation of Russians from Shanghai, Vladika John travelled through Hong Kong to the Philippines. Then he was transferred to Belgium. In Shanghai, Hieromonk Modest (he died as abbot in the Holy Land) was a close soul-companion of Vladika John's, and in San Francisco, Archimandrite Mitrofan was very devoted to him.

Because Vladika John was very busy from morning till night, he was almost always late to services. He ran about all day long, visiting hospitals and homes. He had no concept of time; he didn't even wear a watch. He himself always delivered a homily during the Liturgy, but it was difficult to understand him. Before the sermon all the acolytes would go out to the center of the church to listen to him.

Vladika John loved services and their order. In Shanghai there were pastoral meetings every Thursday. If someone was absent, he demanded a full explanation. At these meetings, most of the time was spent on questions of how to serve. Vladika would ask the priests about certain unique aspects of some of the upcoming services, testing their knowledge.

Vladika John was altogether uninterested in food. People prepared food for him, but never knew when he would actually eat. He loved tea, he never drank alcohol.

Vladika John never discussed worldly matters with me, only spiritual matters. Even when there was the unpleasantness in San Francisco in connection with the building of the cathedral, Vladika did not share his sufferings with anyone. In San Francisco, the congregation loved him; he had saved all the Shanghai refugees.

Protopresbyter Elias Wen

REMEMBERING VLADIKA JOHN

MANY PEOPLE have heard the story of how, on being informed that he had been chosen to be bishop, Vladika John was convinced there had been some mistake. On his way to the Synod meeting to which he had been summoned, he met up with an acquaintance and told her that an unfortunate mistake had been made, that some priest John had been chosen to be bishop, and they had invited him instead. On his way back, he met with the same acquaintance, and told her that it was even worse than he had supposed, that in fact it *was* he who had been chosen to be bishop. That acquaintance was my mother, the deceased novice Maria (née Dmitrievna Shatilova).

My mother was a childhood friend of the future Archbishop John. She knew him when he was a student in Belgrade and later, when he was a monk. She had corresponded with him when he left for China, but for various reasons, this correspondence was interrupted.

When I was nine or ten years old there was a Sobor of Bishops of the Russian Church Abroad and the archbishops were to serve in Saint Vladimir's Church in the small town of Casse-ville (today Jackson), New Jersey. We lived in Vineland, some seventy miles distance. My mother sent me to this celebration to-gether with our rector, expressly to receive a blessing from Vladi-ka John. Since my mother had not corresponded with him for many years, he did not know about our family.

"How will I know which of the hierarchs is Archbishop John?" I asked. With her unique humor, my mother replied that the one who looked the least like an archbishop would be Vladi-ka John. She also said that he was a bit hunched over, and some-times wore boots without socks.

On arriving at the church, without seeing or speaking to anyone, I went straightway into the altar in order to serve. Sud-denly Vladika John came up to me and led me out of the altar (he never uttered any unnecessary words in the altar). At the cliros, he greeted me with the words: "Hello, Styopa! How is your mother, Marika? How are your brother and sister?" Then, with a smile and sparkling eyes, he looked at me intensely and asked how it was that I had recognized him. I became embar-rassed, remembering mother's description, and shyly muttered something. Only many years later, when I was studying at Holy Trinity Seminary and learned about the gift of clairvoyance, did I understand how amazing it was—not that I had recognized him, but that he had recognized me, knew me by name, knew who I was, and knew about our family.

Here is another interesting episode. My brother Paul, although not in the military, lived for several years in Vietnam during the war, where he searched for wounded or orphaned children, and found them places in orphanages and hospitals. There he met a Vietnamese woman, Kim En, his future wife, who worked with him, helping these unfortunate children. My brother told her about the Orthodox faith, about Saint Seraphim of Sarov and other saints. During difficult times in her life, an old man, like an elder, appeared to her in her dreams, showing her what to do and comforting her through difficult circumstances. Once I sent my brother a cassette of monastic singing, and some religious books and magazines. On receiving the package, my brother showed Kim the literature and was amazed when she pointed to the cover of one of the magazines: "That is the old man who appears in my dreams and comforts me." It was the well-known photograph of Vladika John walking in the cemetery of Novo-Diveyevo Convent in Spring Valley. Later Kim was baptized into the Orthodox Church, taking the name Kira.

A third episode I wish to relate is the following: In connection with preparations for the celebration of 1000 years of the Baptism of Russia, the lecturer Vadim Scheglov came to a conference in our diocese. His wife Zoya is an icon painter. When she was still living in Russia and working as an icon restorer, she noticed one day that a sweet fragrance was emanating from an icon of the Mother of God sitting on the shelf of her workshop. It was a Tikhvin icon. After the Scheglovs moved to America, Zoya had a dream in which a young monk walking through a cemetery directed her to paint three icons of the Mother of God. He gave the names of all three, but Zoya remembered only one: the Tikhvin, and she painted this icon. When her husband Vadim came to our conference, we gave him accommodations in our church in Burlingame. In consultation with his wife, Vadim gave this Tikhvin icon to our church as a gesture of thanks. When Zoya came later to San Francisco to the Millennium celebration, she saw in the sepulchre the photograph in which Vladika John was walking through the cemetery at Novo-Diveyevo. She was stunned. "This is the one who appeared in a dream and told me to paint the icons of the Mother of God! Who is he?" When told that it was Vladika John, she became confused, because in her dream the monk called himself Michael. Then she learned that Vladika's secular name was Michael. The novice to whom she recounted these things told her that the Mother of God icon in his cell was the Tikhvin. . . !

Archpriest Stefan Pavlenko

VLADIKA JOHN KNEW THE
CHARACTER OF THE SERBS

ONE YOUNG SERB was a seminary student in an Orthodox seminary in Paris. He was faced with a dilemma: Should he
get married, or become a monk? He went to Versailles, where
Archbishop John was living at that time, and asked him: "Should
I become a monk?" Vladika John had lived for a long time in
Serbia, and was well acquainted with the mores and character of
young Serbs. He knew they could be stubborn and impulsive,
and he emphatically told the young Serb, "No."

This Serb became a monk anyway. When this Serbian
monk had the good fortune to meet Vladika John once again,
this time in America, Vladika blessed him with the beaming face
of one who knows Serbs through and through. Vladika knew
that if you told a Serb, "Yes, you should become a monk," that
he wouldn't do it. . .

Bishop Daniel of the Serbian Orthodox Church

WITH VLADIKA JOHN
IN FRANCE

I WAS A parishioner at the Russian Orthodox Church in
Meudon, outside Paris, when Vladika John arrived there. He
amazed us by reading people's thoughts. A woman came to our
church, who had recently been widowed. She was thinking
about entering an old people's home and wanted to talk to Vladika about something. The service ended, everyone approached
to kiss the Cross. The woman also kissed the Cross, but disap-

peared to the back of the church, without having said anything to Vladika. Vladika asked her friend: "What is on that lady's mind? She wanted to talk to me."

In the Lesna Convent in Fourqueux, Mother Flaviana told me that they hadn't had rain for a long time, and their vegetable garden was drying up. Then Vladika John came; he served a moleben, went around the garden in procession, and it started to rain.

Mrs. Petukhov, who knew Vladika John from Shanghai, told me that Russian refugees from China lived on the island of Tubabao in tents. One morning, Vladika went around to all the tents and blessed them. That very night a typhoon raged through the island, but left them untouched.

After World War II, our Russian Church Abroad lost its church in Paris. As a result, not a single church of our jurisdiction remained in that city. The closest one was in Meudon. At first Bishop Nathaniel came there and, later, Vladika John. Vladika John established a temporary church in Paris, but he lived in Meudon with Father Alexander Trubnikov, and also in Versailles, and he would go to Paris to celebrate services.

Our church, dedicated to All Saints of Russia, consisted of two garages. Inside, it was cleanly painted and adorned with icons. Here Vladika John served. Also, the Grand Duke Vladimir Kyrillovich attended services here.

Not everyone loved and respected Vladika. Once, in Meudon, Vladika came out of the altar with the chalice, and when he pronounced the exclamation, a woman parishioner said something bad and immediately fainted. They took her out and brought her home. Never again did she say anything bad about Vladika.

Another time, at a sisterhood meeting, I heard a woman criticize Vladika. I protested, but seeing that my words had no effect, I said good-bye and left. Afterwards, I learned that the woman who had been so critical was on her way home from the meeting, when she stepped off the sidewalk into a stationary bus and broke her arm. She was for several days in the hospital. Her arm never did heal properly.

My husband was a taxi driver and often drove Vladika from Paris to Versailles and from Versailles to Paris. On these trips he never set the meter, so he lost time and money. And what happened? The first day he drove Vladika, a passenger left his account book behind, and my husband went to the address indicated in the book. It turned out that the book belonged to a shopkeeper and he was in great need of it. He was overjoyed to have it returned, and told his clerk to give the driver a box of his best oranges. And so it was that Vladika's ride was paid with a grand "tip." On another occasion, my husband received a box of fine chocolates...

Maria Skachkovskaya

WITH VLADIKA
AT CHRISTMASTIME

THIS TOOK PLACE in 1963 or '64 when I was thirteen or fourteen years old. I was the senior acolyte in the Church of All Saints of Russia in Burlingame and, because of my duties there, I was rarely able to attend services in San Francisco. But my parents allowed me to serve Vladika John at the Old Cathedral on Christmas. I remember how regally the church was decorated, with huge fir trees, and with what honor we acolytes attended Vladika John during the service.

The next day, after celebrations in the Saint Tikhon of Zadonsk orphanage, where Vladika lived, I had the opportunity to go with him to visit the sick in five hospitals. There were four of us: Vladika, the driver, Paul Lukianov (now Hieromonk

Peter), and myself. Paul and I loaded the car with several dozen small presents, and we drove off. On the way, Vladika took out of his velvet pouch a tattered Horologion, published before the Revolution, and asked us to read the Psalms, which we did.

Since Vladika often visited the sick, the hospital personnel knew him well. In every hospital Vladika knew precisely where to go to get a list of the Orthodox patients. In one of the hospitals, Vladika walked into the office, went to a desk, opened a drawer and himself took out a list already prepared for him.

Words cannot describe the faces of the sick people when they saw Vladika. In every room we entered, we sang the Troparion and Kontakion of the Feast of the Nativity. Vladika John consoled every patient and gave them each a present. Often, people of other faiths would call Vladika over to them, and Vladika would go bless them, too. Even a Russian Jewish lady kissed Vladika's hand, with tears in her eyes after receiving a present from him. . . And all day long Vladika was beaming with joy.

Reader Vladimir Krassovsky

VLADIKA HAD AN
INCREDIBLE MEMORY

I WISH TO share with you some of my recollections of the Saint—and his incredible memory. It must have been 1952. There was a meeting of the Synod of Bishops in an old building on West Seventy-seventh Street in New York. Vladika John and I met, and wished to become acquainted. In the course of conversation, Vladika asked if I had a little sister who had died in infancy. "Yes," I replied. "How is it you remember?" I knew, of course, that little Natalia was a year older than I: born in 1905 on

March 10, and baptized April 10, she died of meningitis a month later, on May 10, 1905. Vladika even remembered where she was buried: in the sepulchre, next to the cathedral of the Peter and Paul fortress in Saint Petersburg. There, my father and his parents, and others of our relatives, are also buried. The church was built in the shape of a cross. Little Natusia was buried under a window in the left apse (the north apse?). And Vladika knew even this. . .

On another occasion we met at the entrance to the Synod on Ninety-third Street in New York; Vladika was coming out as I was going in. Vladika told me that it was the anniversary of my brother Oleg's repose. I myself had forgotten about it. Such a memory Vladika had.

Her Highness Princess Vera Korstantinovna

EULOGY BEFORE
THE MEMORIAL SERVICE
FOR ARCHBISHOP JOHN

In the name of the Father, and of the Son, and of the Holy Spirit!

AMONG RUSSIANS there has long existed a popular belief that bishops of the Orthodox Church die in "threes" (within, of course, a certain period of time). And just now this belief has involuntarily come to mind. A year and a half ago, soon after the last Bishop's Council of the Church Abroad, the elderly Archbishop Stephan died. Then, just over a year ago, the orphaned Church Abroad prayerfully accompanied into the "way of all the earth," her spiritual father and primate of many years, the never-to-be-forgotten elder, Metropolitan Anastassy. And now, finally, a third name.

Yesterday, during the All-night Vigil, there was an urgent telephone call from Bishop Nektary in California, bringing us the mournful news that one of the senior hierarchs of our Church, the alternate to the Chief Hierarch of our Church, the archpastor-ascetic, Archbishop John, had died suddenly in Seattle, where he had gone with the wonder-working icon of the Mother of God. Shattering news.

Thinking now about Vladika John, I remember what happened more than thirty years ago, when my late father, Bishop Dimitri, knowing what sorrows and troubles awaited Blessed Metropolitan Anthony, Chief Hierarch of the Church Abroad, in Yugoslavia, invited him to the Far East, to Harbin, where church life was beginning to thrive. "You will rest here, Vladika," wrote Bishop Dimitry. Metropolitan Anthony answered as follows:

"My friend, I am already so old and so feeble that I cannot think of making any journey except the one to the cemetery. . . . But instead of myself, I am sending you—as my very own soul, my own heart—Bishop John. This small, frail individual, almost a child in appearance, is some sort of miracle of ascetic steadfastness and strictness in our time of general spiritual paralysis". . . . So did his great Abba characterize the still young and only recently consecrated Vladika John. This is how Vladika John was then, and so he remained. And even in our time, before our eyes, he was the same "miracle of ascetic steadfastness," a supreme example of a spiritual, prayerful disposition.

Vladika John was always praying; Vladika John prayed everywhere. With good reason did the young and similarly spiritually attuned Hieromonk Methody note perceptively, still back in Harbin, "We all 'start' praying, but Vladika John does not need to start; he is always in a state of prayer. . . " No matter what changes occurred in his outward situation, in the external conditions of Vladika John's life and his work, prayer and the Divine services were of primary importance to him; nothing could distract him from this. No single individual can possess all perfections and be the bearer of all gifts. Everyone can err—

no one is free from erring. But those who had contact with Vladika John as a man of prayer, as an archpastor concerned with human souls and always ready to come to their aid, those who experienced the power of his prayer, either personally or with their close ones—these people will never forget Vladika and will always carry in their hearts the grateful memory of that warmth and light which he imparted.

Vladika is gone—and that unceasing prayer with which our great man of prayer was aflame, praying ceaselessly "in behalf of all and for all," has been cut short. But the Church Abroad will not forget him. We trust that Vladika John will find mercy and boldness at the Dread Throne of the Lord of Glory, and there will pray for his close ones and for his flock, just as he prayed while here on earth. . . . And our duty, the duty of grateful love, is to answer his prayers with prayer. Let us pray for his pure soul, that the Lord will give him rest with the saints. Amen.

† Metropolitan Philaret

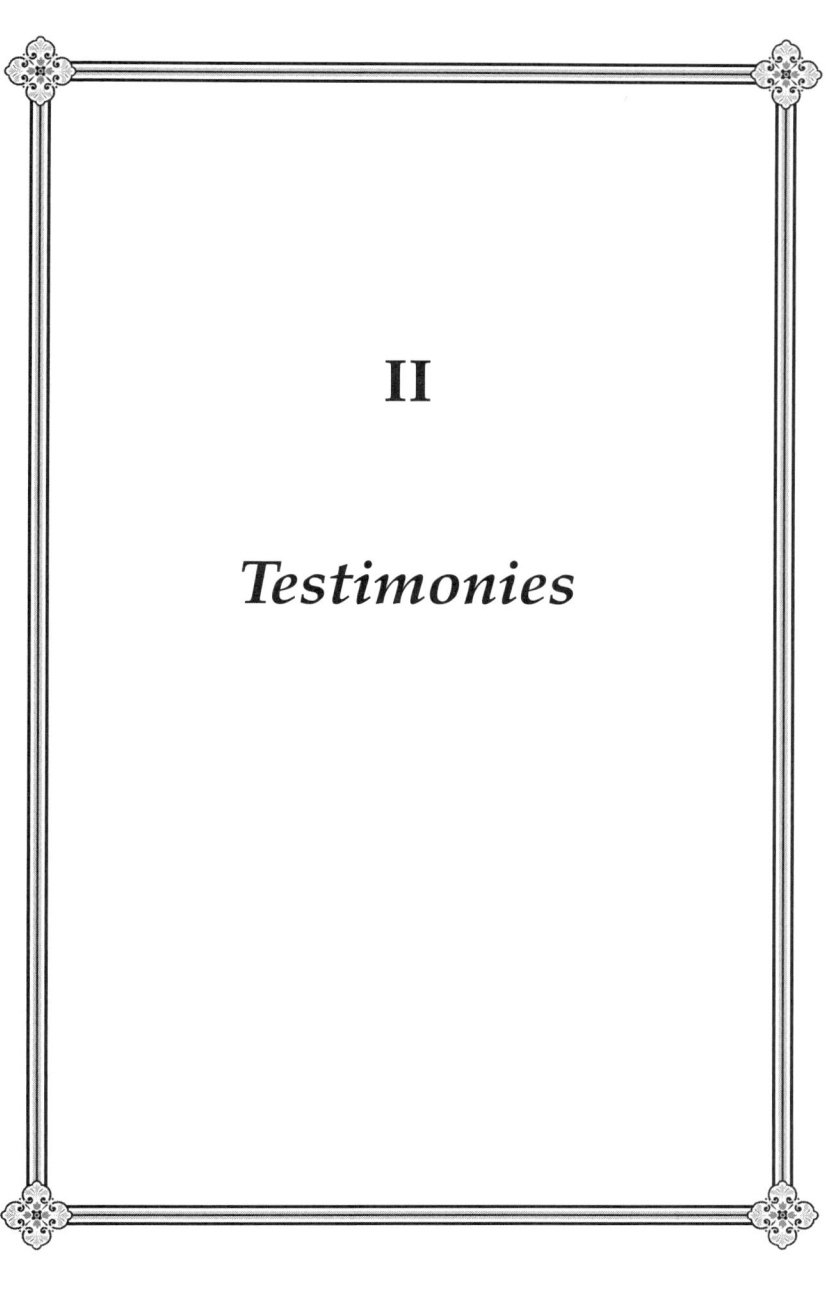

II

Testimonies

Vladika helped many times—
in many ways

In 1953 we were living in Paris. My daughter, Olga, was not yet five years old. In early October she had an operation to remove her appendix. She recovered and all seemed to be well when suddenly she developed a fever. The doctor, a very good man and wonderful physician, came to the house almost daily. All kinds of tests were made to determine what was wrong with Olga. Her temperature remained high through the month of December and finally the doctor insisted she be taken to the hospital, where she would have round-the-clock care.

All our close ones and acquaintances were concerned and prayed with us. Towards evening a friend came and suggested that we go to Vladika John to pray. "He will pray and everything will be resolved." At that time Vladika lived in the Cadet Corps in Versailles, outside Paris. On the way, my friend, Maria Iliodorovna, told us about Vladika's power of prayer, about how he helps people, and that I should listen to what he said at the end of the service of intercession *(moleben).*

A service was already in progress when we arrived. At the candlestand I asked that my request to have a moleben served after Liturgy be conveyed to Vladika. At the end of the service the man in charge of selling candles approached me and said that Vladika had to give Holy Communion to some sick boys in the Corps infirmary and that the moleben would be served by a priest. My heart sank; we decided to wait for Vladika.

We waited in silence. I wanted to pray but my thoughts were too occupied with my daughter; she could die at any time. Soon Vladika came and I told him about Olga's illness. Vladika served a moleben and, when at the end he held the Cross for us to kiss, he placed his hand on my shoulder, looked at me and smiled. "Everything will be all right, Mama; your daughter will recover, all will be well." Having blessed us, he gave us a prosphoron. "Go with God!" My heart felt unbelievably light and I firmly believed that indeed all would be well.

That night Olga had hallucinations. I placed compresses on her head, and prayed. Towards morning her temperature dropped. When I began to get her ready to go to the hospital, she complained that her hands and feet hurt; some round spots had appeared on them which were sore to touch. I phoned the doctor and told him about the spots. He said that now he understood what was the matter and that it was not necessary to take Olga to the hospital. He came at once and diagnosed the problem as subcutaneous tuberculosis, which could be treated at home. All she needed was rest, good food and care. Seven months later my daughter had fully recovered. I believe that she was healed through the pure and holy prayer of Vladika John. Glory to God, all turned out well, just as Vladika said.

For three years we tried to make arrangements to move to the United States. Finally, in 1961, we received permission to immigrate. I was pregnant and was quite worried about how we would manage on our arrival in the US. We had lived in France for thirty-five years and had many friends and acquaintances, but there we had no one. Now we had to leave my mother, brother, sister and friends. After speaking with my spiritual father, Father Mitrofan, I took his advice and went to see Vladika John. I came with my husband and daughter, and Father Mitrofan took us all into Vladika's room. Many candles were burning in front of Vladika's icons. His desk was covered with letters, many had money on top of them, waiting to be sent. Vladika helped everyone in whatever way he could—but primarily through prayer.

Everything about the room was simple, holy, peaceful. Vladika blessed us, and when our daughter came up to him he smiled at her, "Ah, this is Olechka who was so sick; yes, everything will be fine!" I told Vladika about our plans and my anxieties. He listened with closed eyes—it was hard to tell if he was simply concentrating or praying. "Well, go, go; one can live anywhere. Only hold fast to our Church, then all will be well. If you don't, you'll have trouble." Vladika gave his blessing for our move. We came to the States and everything turned out well, as Vladika had foretold.

In 1962 we were living in New York. From Paris my mother sent a letter saying that on New Year's Eve my brother had been attacked by some Algerians who had beaten him unconscious and taken his money. It was payday, and in France people received their wages not by check but in cash in an envelope. My brother was taken to a hospital where an X ray showed that his skull was cracked. His eyes were swollen and filled with blood; he was in a frightful state. The doctor said he must have been hit with a pipe or metal rod. My mother was informed of what had happened only at noon the next day. She rushed immediately to the hospital. My brother told her that that night Vladika John had come to him, had given him Holy Communion, prayed, touched his head, and asked if he were in need of money. My brother was embarrassed to accept money from Vladika and declined the offer. Having related the incident to my mother, my brother asked how Vladika knew that he was in the hospital and that he was without money. After all, my mother herself hadn't yet learned of it!

Many, however, who knew Vladika, knew that it wasn't always necessary to ask Vladika. The Lord Himself sent him, indicating where and to whom to go. Vladika didn't sleep, his nights were occupied in prayer; the Lord would reveal to him who was in need of help, and Vladika would go. In the Paris hospitals everyone knew Vladika, and he was admitted at any time of day or night. He always knew where to go. My brother did not know Vladika personally, but Vladika would go to anyone, either by car or by foot.

When a second X ray was made of my brother's head, no crack was visible and he speedily recovered. The doctor was baffled!

We maintained our ties with Archimandrite Mitrofan even after our move to the States. Whenever he came to New York, we would bring him to our home for a few days. We so enjoyed listening to his stories about his life with Vladika John. He was very attached to Vladika and was a faithful spiritual son. Whenever we had some misfortune in our family I always wrote to Father Mitrofan, who was living at that time in California.

In 1979 my mother, then eighty-one, fell seriously ill with cancer. After a brief stay in the hospital, the doctor informed my sister that my mother would soon die. She was taken home in order that she might at least have the consolation of dying at home. Everyone looked after her. I was called in Connecticut, where we lived, to come quickly before mother died. I came and undertook to care for her completely myself, in order to give the other family members a rest. Her condition steadily deteriorated; she suffered terribly and the doctors or nurses came almost daily to give her injections to alleviate the pain. Medicines didn't seem to help, and it was agonizing to see her suffer so. Praying, I remembered Vladika John and straightway wrote to Father Mitrofan, telling him where I was and what had happened to my mother.

The reply from San Francisco came quickly. Father Mitrofan sent some cotton with oil from the perpetually burning vigil lamp over Vladika John's tomb. He wrote: "Anoint the affected area daily, making the sign of the Cross with the words, 'Lord

Jesus Christ, Son of God, by the prayers of our dear Vladika John, heal and ease the suffering of the sick Elena!'" Every morning after my prayers, I anointed the affected area, praying as I did so, and within a few days I noticed that afterwards my mother would peacefully fall asleep. Within a week she asked that the injections be stopped. "Vladika is helping me; if the pains recur, pray and anoint me with the oil." I continued to anoint her every day and she, without suffering, quietly and peacefully faded away. She died on the eve of the feast of Archangel Michael. I believe that through the prayers of Vladika John, the Lord granted her a painless Christian ending to her life.

We had in our midst a holy man—Vladika John, and did not appreciate him. But to this day Vladika does not abandon us in his prayers.

Valentina Dikova, Kansas

Healing from illness after being anointed with oil from the sepulchre of Vladika John

This happened in late 1977. My husband, Priest Michael Konstantinov, flew overseas to visit his uncle who was very ill, while I stayed home with our small children. In his absence I learned from the doctors that I had a large growth on my thyroid gland which required an operation. I was very upset; I was afraid to have surgery on my throat. My anxiety was made worse by my husband's being away. I used to go quite often to our convent, New Shamordino, and I shared my distress with the late Abbess Helena. She advised me to take holy oil from the vigil lamp from the sepulchre of Vladika John of Shanghai, anoint my neck with the sign of the Cross, and appeal in prayer to Vladika John. I did so. On my third visit to the doctor he determined that the growth was shrinking by itself and no operation was necessary. Lord, how happy I was that I would be home with the children, that I was healed by the prayers of Vladika John of Shanghai.

Ever since then, whenever I fly to San Francisco, I bow down before his holy relics with gratitude for his mercy to me, a sinner.

Matushka Irina Konstantinovna, Sydney, Australia

Improvement in health after a panikhida at the sepulchre

Unfortunately, I don't remember the exact details, but I will try to relate in general terms what happened.

Letters often come addressed to our cathedral, requesting prayers in the sepulchre of the ever-memorable Vladika John. Sometimes these letters get delayed at the candlestand, waiting for a priest. One such letter from Boston was misplaced and only two or three weeks later was discovered and passed on to me. The letter came from the late Sergei Yulevich Conus, requesting prayers for his wife. In the sepulchre I served a panikhida for Vladika John, and then a litia for the health of Sergei Yulevich's wife. I wrote about this to Sergei Yulevich, and enclosed in my letter some postcard photos from the sepulchre. A few days later I received a phone call from an excited Sergei Yulevich, who asked at what time I had served the panikhida. I answered that it was about ten o'clock in the morning. Sergei Yulevich then informed me that about one o'clock EST (between Boston and San Francisco there is a three-hour time difference) that day, after a prolonged and serious illness, his wife became better and for the first time in several months she got out of bed! This couldn't possibly be a mere "coincidence," especially when one considers the number of similar cases.

Archpriest Peter Perekrestov, San Francisco

Saved from drowning

In August 1988 my wife and I went for vacation to Hawaii, to the island of Kuai. We had been there many times, and there where we stayed was a good beach for swimming.

My wife and I are both good swimmers and therefore we don't worry about one another when we go swimming in the ocean. This time, on the night of our arrival, a hurricane had swept the island. Nevertheless, we went for a swim that day as usual.

My wife stayed close to shore while I struck out into deeper waters for a proper swim, Suddenly, out of nowhere, a big wave lashed at me and I was dragged under by the current, away from shore. (I later learned that after a hurricane there is a strong undertow.) Knowing that it is futile to struggle against an undertow, I gradually swam to the surface and made my way towards the shore.

I swam in until, when I stood up, the water was at shoulder level, and I began walking towards shore. Suddenly another great wave caught me and again I was pulled under. Although I had little strength left after the first wave, I managed somehow to swim to the surface. This time I had been carried even farther from shore, and I realized that in spite of all my efforts I would not be able to reach shore against the current. I tried to attract my wife's attention, but she was on the beach standing with her back to the water.

Sensing that I was perishing, I cried, "Vladika John, help me!" Instantly my wife turned around and saw my perilous state. She ran towards a group of Hawaiians there on the beach, asking for help. Grabbing their surfboards and ropes, they paddled out to me, secured me to one of the boards and brought me to shore.

I firmly believe that without the help of Vladika John I would have drowned—and no one would have noticed.

Alexis Cattell, San Francisco

Help after a memorial service for Vladika John

On January 29, 1979, we flew from Los Angeles to San Francisco. On February 4, Archimandrite Mitrofan suggested we go to a memorial service at the tomb of the ever-memorable Archbishop John.

I submitted a commemoration slip for the health of the sick slave of God, Nicholas, whom we had left in the hospital in Los Angeles. When we arrived home in Vermont, I called Los Angeles to inquire about Nicholas' health. His wife answered that he was already home and I could talk to him. When I asked him when he had gotten better, he thought a moment and replied: "It was on Sunday at four o'clock." That was the very day and hour I had given his name for commemoration at the tomb of Vladika John.

Nadezhda Paganuzzi, Florida

Vladika appears to a child and heals him

Hegumen Anastassy from the Old Cathedral advised me to write to you about a blessing which my son Christopher received.

It happened in 1983. Christopher, who was then three years old, went to an ear specialist who found that he had a thirty percent hearing loss, due to an accumulation of liquid behind the ear drum, caused by repeated ear infections. His impaired hearing contributed to a slowness in learning to speak. An operation was scheduled to drain the liquid and implant tubes.

That spring, my two older sons (twelve and ten years old) had gone to visit Hegumen Anastassy in San Francisco. Brother James, Father Anastassy's assistant, showed them Archbishop John's sepulchre and they brought home oil from the vigil lamp burning on his tomb. I anointed Christopher with this oil before his visit to the speech pathologist, and again two days before his operation, with the words, "Lord Jesus Christ, Son of God, by the prayers of the ever-memorable Archbishop John, heal the ears of my son Christopher."

The next day Christopher had a final examination before the operation. The doctors discovered that his ears had healed. There was no hearing loss and all the liquid had disappeared. The operation was cancelled. It was a tremendous relief for us, but we were even more amazed by what Christopher told us: "That man made my ears better." He repeated this several times. Once, after prayers which he finished with the words, "Thank you for making my ears better," I asked, "Who made your ears better?" He pointed to a postcard of Vladika John which stood in the corner with our icons. Again he repeated, "This man made my ears better." He said this so insistently that I know he believes that Blessed Vladika John healed his ears. I don't know how he knows this, but he does; he insists on this, and we believe him. I have no other explanation; I only know that my son is now better, and we are very grateful for the prayers of ever-blessed Archbishop John.

Agape Ketrenos, Portland, OR

Vladika—guardian of family life

I have been helped numerous times by the holy prayers of Vladika John, which continue to this day. I should like to relate at least one incident.

Many years ago I became pregnant with a child neither my husband nor his family wanted; we already had several children. It was very difficult for me both physically and emotionally because I was very sick. I often went to dear Father Mitrofan, who comforted all by his Christian love and warm prayers. We prayed to Vladika John and thanks to his holy prayers everything smoothed out at home. My father-in-law even helped my husband with our other children while I recuperated in the hospital after the birth of the baby. It was a boy, whom we named John in honor of the holy hierarch, Saint John of Tobolsk, Vladika's ancestor.

L.T., California

Healings through the prayers of Vladika John

Thanks to the fervent prayers of Vladika John, my father, Nicholas Michailovich, quickly regained his health after a third heart attack in the summer of 1962. My father had already suffered two heart attacks, in 1954 and 1958, and thereafter he spent a month each year in the Ardennes under the care of a doctor. My sister, Baroness Maria Nikolaevna Apraksina, and I were at the doctor's when he told us that our father's condition was hopeless. Suddenly Vladika John appeared in our father's room and started to pray. Our father soon regained his health completely and returned home to Brussels, where he lived another four years . . .

Valentin Collenga Stadnitsky graduated from the Poltava Cadet Corps. Vladika John also studied there and the two became acquainted. After the Second World War, Valentin Collenga moved from Yugoslavia to Brussels, where he lived with his sister, Mme Dobrovolsky. Washing windows one day in the apartment, he fell from the second floor onto the street. This happened in 1959; he was 65 or 66 years old. So many bones were broken that the doctors held absolutely no hope for his recovery. Vladika John arrived at the hospital together with Father Chedomir Ostoichem and began to pray at the dying man's bedside. Father Chedomir later related that for the first time he heard how Vladika John conversed in prayer with God.

The next morning the doctors couldn't believe the sick man hadn't died; what's more, he began very quickly to recover. Within a month he left the hospital completely healed and lived for a long time afterwards. This was told me in detail today by Vera Alexeevna Stassen, the granddaughter of Archpriest Vassily Vinogradov, first rector of our cathedral parish in Brussels.

Philip Gering was born in Brussels in 1943. Together with his brother Dimitry, he conscientiously served Vladika as an altar boy. Philip was operated on for what was thought to be simply appendicitis, but it was found to be cancer; his condition was hopeless. However, by the fervent prayers of Vladika John, Philip soon recovered completely—something the doctors of course did not expect. He graduated as an engineer from the university in Louvain, worked in Canada, and lives now in Italy.

Reader Vladimir Kotliarevsky, Brussels, Belgium

Vladika helps in giving birth

My wife gave birth to our second son on 12/25 February (Forgiveness Sunday) this year [1990]. We were both very anxious about the birth because our first son, born in 1988, nearly died at birth (thankfully he is all right now) and my wife had been told that for any future children she would have to have a cesarean. A few days before the birth I anointed her with some oil from Blessed John's sepulchre, and his prayers before the throne of God were wonderfully answered for us. My wife gave birth quite normally (no operation was required) and she was in labour for only three hours! It all happened so quickly in the early hours of Forgiveness Sunday that we were all taken by surprise, including the doctors, who were preparing to operate on that day. The baby proved to be larger than our first one, which just added to the confounding of the doctors, who were sure my wife could never deliver a baby normally.

Then, about a month ago, my wife, who is breast-feeding the baby, developed all the symptoms of having a breast abscess. She had a nasty one after the birth of our first son and ended up having two operations and contracting septicemia which made her very ill. Once again I anointed her, and within forty-eight hours all the symptoms had gone! God is truly glorified in His Saints.

Naturally we are very thankful and, although Blessed John has not been officially canonized, we have named our son Iain (Gaelic for John).

unworthy priest Ian Prior, Aberdeenshire, Scotland

Helping children

Some time ago my daughter developed an unsightly planter's wart on the side of her foot. It was in such a place that it hurt and became irritated when she wore shoes. Apparently the only way to be rid of it is either to have it burned off or cut off with a razor blade. We live pretty well in the country and at that time I had no transportation to go to the doctor. We therefore decided to anoint her foot with holy oil from Blessed John's sepulchre and I suggested that she read a canon to him for three days, which she did. After the third day the wart had completely disappeared; all that remained was a faint white circle where it once had been.

Then, one night not long ago, our three-year-old Alexander awoke about eleven o'clock crying bitterly with an earache. I myself had been up the night before with illness as well as being extremely run down from lack of sleep. I thought of anointing his ear with holy oil from Blessed Vladika John, but much to my shame I felt that I had not the faith to ask for his intercession with "nothing wavering," as the Holy Scripture bids us. So we continued most of the night, he crying and I not knowing how to console him. I gave him eardrops, Tylenol, warmth, etc., but nothing would help the poor little boy. Finally, in desperation—it was now about four in the morning—I prayed, "Please, Blessed Vladika John, help Alexander. You help so many others, and I promise I will write to Father Peter." I fetched the holy oil from the main icon corner and anointed his ear. The moment I did so the child gave a sigh of relief and lay down and went to sleep.

Something remarkable has also occurred with his behavior since that night. He used to be so hyperactive and would not listen, but now, still lively as ever, he actually listens and tries to obey. He himself asked me, "Please Mama, ask God to help me," and he prays for this himself.

Glory be to our God who is glorious in His saints. . .

Katherine Doll, British Columbia, Canada

Vladika is praying

Forty-seven years have passed, and I have not forgotten the help we received through the prayers of Vladika John.

My husband began having headaches. We thought they would go away but they only grew worse. Finally he had to quit work—he was thirty-nine—and the family was left without a breadwinner. What were we to do? How were we to live? Some kind people advised us to go to Peking (we lived in Tianzin) which had a large hospital where they took X rays and performed complicated operations. There we learned that my husband had a brain tumor requiring an immediate operation. Again, what were we to do, where were we to get the money? A kind man was found who paid for the entire procedure, two hundred and eighty dollars.

My husband was admitted to the hospital, while I stayed with some acquaintances in the Russian Mission in Bej-Huan. Vladika Victor lived there at that time, and there were daily services in the church. In the morning I went to church, and after Liturgy I asked Vladika Victor to serve a moleben for my sick husband. "We'll serve a moleben," said Vladika, "but you write to Vladika John in Shanghai; he really knows how to pray. I'll give you his address." I did not delay in following Vladika Victor's advice. The operation was performed. For a whole week my husband remained unconscious, but then he gradually began to recover, and after a time he began to work a bit. I never did receive an answer from Vladika John.

Seven years passed, and we émigrés were evacuated from Tianzin to Shanghai where we were settled in the French barracks. Vladika came frequently to visit us and serve Liturgy. One day my husband was walking in the courtyard when he met Vladika walking in the opposite direction. Vladika came up to my husband and said, "Why didn't you send your son to me to school?" Vladika had never seen my husband before and didn't know we had a son. I consider this to be supernatural. I also believe that my husband recovered through the prayers of Vladika John. My husband died in 1987.

For a long time my sister's arm caused her intense pain. She turned to doctors and tried home remedies; nothing helped. Then she decided to appeal to Vladika John and wrote to him in San Francisco (she lived in Los Angeles). After a time the pain in her arm went away, and my sister even began to forget her ordeal. Once she went to San Francisco and attended Liturgy. When at the end of the service she went up to kiss the Cross, Vladika John asked her, "How is your arm?" Vladika had never seen her before! How did he recognize her and know that she had had trouble with her arm?!

Everything written here is the truth. I wrote as God laid it on my heart.

Anna F. Khodireva, Sacramento, CA

Deliverance from a sinful
and shameful habit

From childhood I suffered from a habit, about which it is embarrassing even to speak. It stayed with me even after I grew up. I tried as hard as I could to rid myself of this habit, but couldn't. During Great Lent I would refrain from it, but I would await impatiently the coming of Pascha so that I could. . . (how awful! to desire Pascha in order to. . . !) once again indulge in this habit.

When I realized that this habit was becoming an addiction, I tried sincerely to break it, but without success. Several times after indulging in it I would tell myself, "Enough. This is the last time." But the next day, or even later that same day, it would usually be repeated. In desperation I turned one day in prayer to Vladika John: "Vladika, you see that on my own I'm powerless. Help me!" And the urge for this passion disappeared. This is the extent of the miracle, but what a miracle! I then felt immediately (or realized?) that Vladika had healed me, and in my prayers I always thank him. Many years have passed and Vladika continues to protect me.

A.S.

Vladika eases pain from arthritis

My wife has suffered for some time from arthritis, but when she became pregnant earlier this year the symptoms more or less disappeared, which is what usually happens. If the arthritis comes back during pregnancy, however, this causes great suffering, because a pregnant woman really cannot take any effective medicine without fear of harming her baby.

Two weeks ago we were on vacation in Dallas, staying with Matushka's father. After we drove from her sister's to her father's house that evening, her knee became extremely swollen and it was difficult for her to walk. Because she could not take any medication, and because of the thousand-mile drive still ahead of us, this was, of course, very discouraging. I prayed to Vladika John and firmly promised that if he took care of Matushka's knee, I would send an account of it to you. Within twenty-four hours, her knee was much better, and by the time we had to leave, two days later, it was quite healed, entirely without medication of an earthly kind.

Glory be to God, and blessed be the memory of His righteous servant, Archbishop John!

Priest Steven Allen, Denver, CO

Vladika helps a family

I'd like to share with you a miracle which we received through Vladika John.

Our family—I, my husband and three children—came to America in 1963. We were not greeted very warmly by our new country. They found something wrong with our son's lungs and he had to have an operation. My husband was already ill and couldn't find work. I managed to find work, but it was very difficult to support the family on one income.

We didn't know Vladika John, but here in America we heard about him and about the miracles he worked. We began thinking how we could arrange to invite Vladika John to our home to tell him about our situation. We had no money, and so we postponed doing this.

As it happened, Vladika John himself came to us unexpectedly one night at eleven o'clock. We told him about our son, who was in the hospital. Vladika went up to my husband and for several moments looked him straight in the eyes. He then made the rounds of all the rooms, asking who slept where, and left, without saying anything else.

Soon my husband got a job and worked there for ten years, making it possible for the children to receive a higher education. Vladika visited our son in the hospital; he even brought the Wonderworking [Kursk] Icon. Most often he visited our son late at night. Soon our son recovered and everything was normal.

Two days before his repose, Vladika John visited us and asked after the health of my husband. Foreseeing his repose, Vladika nevertheless continued to be concerned about his flock.

A second miracle occurred with our other son. At work I received a phone call from his school and was told that the right side of his face was paralyzed. A specialist, after examining our son, told us that he had a pinched nerve, and that an operation was necessary. We began discussing when to schedule the operation. Leaving the doctor, we went straight to the cathedral, where we found Vladika John and told him everything. At that time our sons still served as acolytes. When our son who was ill approached Vladika for anointing (it was the eve of Saint Nicholas day), Vladika anointed him with a large sign of the Cross on several places on the afflicted side. Our son's condition improved, and when we returned to the doctor, he examined the boy and said that an operation was not necessary. Pressing my hand, he acknowledged that it was a miracle.

Tamara Bogatskaya, San Francisco

A fortunate outcome

I should like to share with you how Vladika helped me in a difficult period of my life. In 1987, after being happily married for six years, my wife filed for divorce. Her attitude towards me became so aggressive that she not only convinced the judge to evict me from my own home, but she insisted that she be awarded all our possessions, and on top of that she demanded a substantial promissory note, plus money belonging to my relative.

95

The legal proceedings for these groundless demands had been going on already for a year and a half, when this relative, the priest of the Saint Sergius of Radonezh parish at the Tolstoy Foundation in New York, advised me to turn in prayer to Vladika John, pointing out that Vladika himself had suffered from unjust legal prosecution.

I took his advice and on Sunday the priest served a panikhida on behalf of Vladika John. The very next day I was informed that I had to appear in court for a final hearing. For some reason a new judge had been assigned to the case, quite different from the one who for the past year and a half had sided with my wife. To my surprise and immense relief, the judge cut through all this red tape and fairly divided everything in half.

There's absolutely no doubt in my mind that this was the result of a certain "interference" from above. The unexpected turn of events occurred right after the prayerful appeal to Vladika John.

I might add that for another year and a half my former wife tried to have the court ruling changed, but without success.

V.T., New York

"I'm praying"

In 1956 I was working as a hairdresser on Catalina Island. Returning home from work, I always tried to go for a dip in the ocean to refresh myself. This time, as I entered the water, I felt a terrible pain at the back of my neck. I decided to go home immediately.

The next day I went with my husband to see Dr. Rebukhin. My neck had become stone hard. For the next three days the doctor tried everything but nothing helped. Then he analyzed the fluid from the swelling. Three days later we received the results: it was a very malignant carbuncle abscess, seventy-five heads right at the cerebellum. The doctor finally found one

96

Metropolitan Anthony [Khrapovitsky], Bishop Tikhon of San Francisco, Elder Ambrose and the brotherhood of Milkovo Monastery in 1930. In the back row at the far right—Hieromonk John.

Hieromonk John with Serbian students of the theological faculty.

Bishop John in Serbia. On either side of him stand the Bartoshevich brothers—the future Bishop Leonty and Archbishop Antony of Geneva.

Bishop John in the St. Nicholas Church in Shanghai.

Bishop John with Bishop Juvenaly in Shanghai.

Shanghai: blessing the school children in the courtyard of the cathedral.

Shanghai: Bishop John with clergy and members of the Circle
for the Beautification of the Shanghai Cathedral.

Shanghai: Bishop John with his flock at a festive outdoor trapeza.

Bishop John on the island of Tubabao in the Philippines.

1949. Bishop John arrives in San Francisco, where he is met by Archbishop Tikhon.

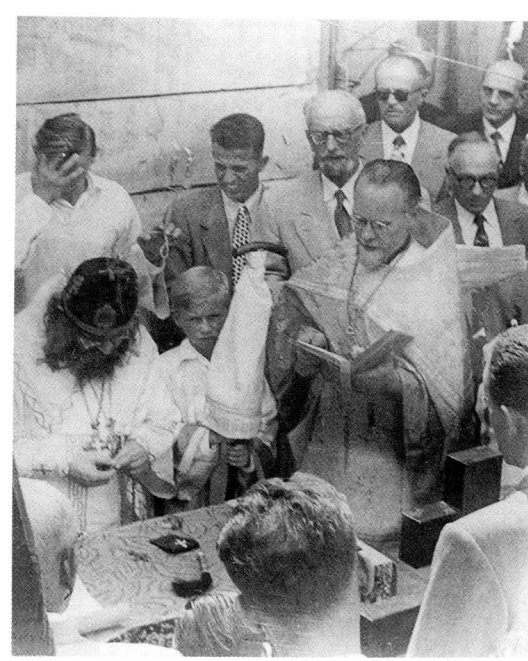

left: Blessing of the cornerstone for a new church in Caracas, 1953.

below: A visit to Venezuela, where his parents lived.

Vladika John, 1950s.

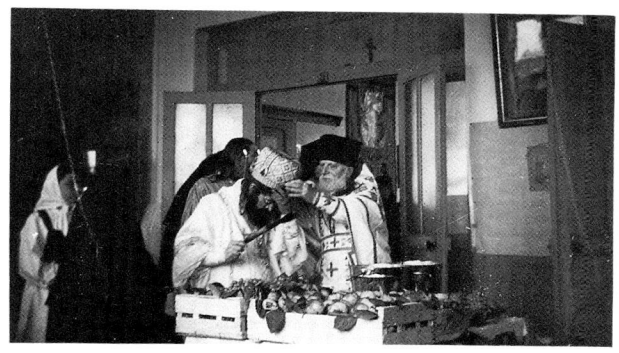

At the Lesna Convent in Fourqueux, 1954 or 1955. *Top:* blessing the fruit harvest; *Middle:* with Abbess Elizabeth and Abbess Theodora. *Below:* with the nuns.

Funeral at the Lesna Convent in Fourqueux.

Above left: with a novice; *above right:* leaving Lesna; *below:* blessing a garden.

Versailles, 1950s. With students of the Cadet Corps.

London 1955. With Abbess Elizabeth at the Convent of the Annunciation.

medicine to heal the abscess. I went to him daily to have the dressings changed, morning and evening.

My head was all swollen. When the pus began draining, the swelling in the center of the head began to decrease but the sides remained swollen and high. A peacock's egg could fit into the center of my head. The pain was excruciating. I took tranquilizers to relax. My condition did not improve.

Meanwhile, the doctor told my husband, "I have to drop the case. I've done everything I can to cure your wife. There's nothing more I can do. Take her to another doctor." I begged him not to abandon me, and in spite of everything did not lose hope.

I asked the current chairman of the Vladika John Fund to submit my name for commemoration. She was shocked at my condition and immediately sent a telegram to France, to Vladika John. Soon we received a telegram in reply from Vladika himself: "I'm praying." This convinced me that I would be cured.

Four days later we were at the doctor's. After examining me the doctor informed my husband, "I must tell you that there was no hope for your wife; the pus was on the verge of entering the cerebellum, and death was imminent. Now your wife is saved! Someone was praying very, very hard."

Nina Makovaya

The healing of a boy

When I was ten years old, I became seriously ill with mononucleosis. My temperature rose to 106 and I felt extremely weak. More than a week passed without any change. The doctors tried everything to cure me but finally told my mother that we must hope that the illness would pass of itself. I later learned that this illness frequently lasts several weeks and, in extreme cases, can even result in death.

My father decided to call New York, where Vladika John was taking part in a meeting of the Synod of Bishops, and tell him of my condition. Vladika calmly assured my father that I would soon recover, not to worry but to trust in God's mercy. The next morning my temperature had dropped to 100 and I remember feeling much better; I even got out of bed. When the doctors heard of this, they had a hard time believing how quickly my condition had improved. They cautioned my parents that I would still have to spend a long time in bed recuperating before I regained enough strength to go to school. Before the week was over, however, I had completely recovered and returned to school.

It turned out that after the conversation with my father, Vladika John had gone to the Synod church and served a moleben for my health. Knowing that nothing in life happens by chance, I attribute my quick recovery to the prayers of holy Vladika John.

Priest Alexander Krassovsky, Santa Rosa, CA

1. Oil from Vladika John's sepulchre gives hope for recovery, and 2. Vladika protects from danger during military duty

On Bright Week, 1991, an acquaintance, a Greek Orthodox woman, Cleopatra Nargais, phoned to tell me that her mother, Magdalena Petropoulos, was in the hospital. She had been there already two months after a heart operation. She was no longer able to breathe on her own and her kidneys were no longer functioning. Day by day she was failing. Both the doctors and the Greek priest told her daughter that there was scant hope for her mother's recovery.

I offered Cleopatra some oil from the sepulchre of our beloved Vladika John. She was overjoyed. I explained that she should anoint her mother's head, heart, lungs and kidneys in the form of a cross, in the name of the Father and the Son and the Holy Spirit, with a prayer to Vladika John for help.

When on Bright Saturday Cleopatra anointed her mother with the oil, the latter began to cry. That evening the nurse told Cleopatra that when she went to turn Magdalena on her side, the sick woman for the first time grabbed the crossbar over the hospital bed and tried to help the nurses.

On Sunday I visited Magdalena in the hospital and likewise anointed her with oil from the sepulchre. Again she cried and asked Archbishop John's help. A week has gone by since Magdalena began to be anointed with oil from the sepulchre. She is already sitting up and for the first time in two months is beginning to eat.

The doctors and nurses in the hospital cannot understand what happened; they were already preparing the family for the worst, when suddenly, unexpectedly, Magdalena's health began to improve.

This change in Magdalena's condition in connection with the anointing affected her entire family. Even her son asked for some oil to anoint his head, in hopes of relieving his severe headaches.

I pray that Vladika John continue to help and heal Magdalena completely.

In June 1988 my son, Alexander Logunov, was informed that he was being sent on assignment to the Persian Gulf for six months. I was very anxious; the situation in that part of the world was so volatile. As a mother I could only pray and commit everything into God's hands. When I was in Vladika John's sepulchre I prayed to Vladika and lit a candle. There I spoke to the Troyans, who placed a commemoration slip with my son's name under Vladika's mitre, where it stayed until my son's return home.

On the eve of his departure on an aircraft carrier, I prayed to Vladika John that he protect my son. That night I dreamed that Vladika John was standing on the nose of the carrier, covering it with his mantia. . .

My son returned safely. On the carrier everyone spoke about what an unusual expedition it was. Despite the fact that there were 6,000 men aboard, there were no accidents: no one was wounded and no one drowned at sea. I believe that it was through the prayers of Vladika John that my son and his carrier's entire crew returned home safely.

Marina Logunov, Sacramento, CA

1. A wound heals, and
2. Vladika helps find the true Faith

I was baptized into the Church in 1980. I believe that it was in 1984 that this healing took place. It was on the Feast of Pentecost. I had received the Mysteries and had returned to my parents' home. My parents and I were about to go to my sister's for a family celebration when I was asked to change the windshield wipers on my parents' car. In removing the second wiper, the clip which held it in place broke and sliced a long, wide and deep gash into my right thumb. This was of concern as I had just received Holy Communion and I was bleeding profusely. I quickly bound the wound with a tissue that I had in my pocket. It was very painful, and the cut was so wide that it was clearly going to require stitches. But I couldn't worry about that now. As my mother hunted for something which could serve as a bandage, it occurred to me that I should anoint the wound with oil that I had from the tomb of Vladika John. I did so, and the pain immediately disappeared. After binding the wound, we went to my sister's home and had a pleasant afternoon. Upon returning, I opened the bandage to check on the cut. I had never seen anything like it. Skin had formed over the gash; the blood, visible under the transparent skin, was still liquid and moved freely. Not knowing what to make of this, I bound up the thumb again. In the days that followed a scab formed under the skin, gradually decreasing in size until it was tiny, and finally came to the surface and fell off. As a reminder of this miracle I have a small scar, really no more than an interruption in the fingerprint, on the side of my thumb, the size and shape of the scab when it came off.

I believe it was the next year, or perhaps two years later, when another healing occurred. I was doing some seasonal work with some friends. By the end of the day, one of them, Patrick, was feeling quite sick. A nasty influenza had been going around, and it appeared that he was coming down with it. It was doubtful that he would be back on the job soon, and I was concerned about his long drive home. Pat was a Lutheran, and I didn't know how he would respond to the idea, but I told him of my healing, and suggested that, if he were willing, I would anoint him with oil from Vladika's tomb, which I had on hand. He consented, and with it I drew the sign of the Cross on his forehead. Much to our astonishment, he showed up the next day. He reported that when he arrived home he had a high fever. He just managed to get into bed when sleep overtook him. In the morning, to his surprise, he was completely well.

Over the years I have been convinced of the concern and protection of Vladika John, even when my prayers were not answered as I would have wished. I was eventually blessed by being given a relic of a hair of Vladika John, which I keep against the day when it can be encased in an icon of Vladika with a halo.

After moving to Erie, to join the vibrant Old Rite parish here, I was told a story by Bishop Daniel, which you may wish to check to make sure my facts are correct. When he was a seminarian and deciding about his future, he asked the blessing of Vladika John and another hierarch (it may have been Metropolitan Philaret) to become an Old Rite priest. Vladika John gave his blessing and added something to the effect: "Stay with the Old

101

Rite. The Old Believers need you to protect them." Bishop Daniel, of course, was influential in the Old Ritualists here joining with the New Ritualists under the Russian Orthodox Church Abroad, and eventually he was consecrated Bishop of the Old Rite, with Erie as his cathedra. So one can see even here the blessing hand of Vladika John.

Lastly, I have been praying for some years for a friend of mine, James, a conservative Lutheran who was very dismayed at what he was seeing in the church world. I had hopes that he would eventually convert to Orthodoxy, but not any time soon—especially now that he had a pious Lutheran wife and a new son, and we had moved to virtually opposite sides of the country.

In November 1990, I received a letter from Jim in which he told me that he had contracted a virus which left him with partial paralysis on one side of the face (Bell's palsy). Concerned, I wrote back asking if he would like me to send him a bottle of oil from Vladika's tomb. To my pleasant surprise, a few weeks later Jim wrote that although his health problems were more of a nuisance than a major trial, he would nevertheless appreciate the oil. When I called to be sure the oil had arrived safely, he reported that nothing miraculous had happened; he realized of course that the oil was not some magic charm with a guarantee, but a plea for God's mercy. But something miraculous *had* happened! As I talked with him it became obvious that the prodding of the Holy Spirit was at work. This was borne out in Jim's next letter: "I am doing quite well at the moment, thank you. As I mentioned, nothing immediately spectacular, but have been on an upward trend for me in general lately. I am happy to attribute some of the credit to Vladika John." In the same letter he requested that I paint an icon for his son, and asked for information of what Synod parish and priest might be in his area. I encouraged him to attend Pascha services—which he did. He wrote afterwards: "To say I was moved would be an understatement. I know where I belong, and that is in the Orthodox

Church." He also asked for prayers for his wife, that they could enter the Church together. Clearly, Vladika John is aiding in this conversion. Even years after his repose, Vladika continues to do missionary work to bring converts into the One Holy Catholic and Apostolic Church.

I testify that the above are truthful accounts to the best of my knowledge and memory.

Luke Gehring, Erie, PA

1. Saved through Vladika's prayers, and
2. A case of Vladika's clairvoyance

I was driving with my sister when an oncoming car driven by a young man who was drunk hit us with considerable force, impacting the door where my sister was sitting. An ambulance rushed her to the hospital, where it was discovered that she had a punctured lung and a broken rib. She was in great pain.

The first time Vladika John visited my sister, her face was swollen like a pillow so that her eyes were not even visible, but she was conscious. When she was told that Vladika had come, she opened her eyelid with her finger and, seeing his face, took his hand and kissed it. She was unable to talk, as she had an incision in her throat. Tears of happiness flowed from the fleshy crevices which concealed her eyes. Vladika John visited my sister many times afterwards and she began to improve.

One day Vladika came to the hospital and as soon as he entered the ward, without having spoken to anyone, said to us, "Musya is in a very bad state." He went to her bed, pulled the curtain and prayed there for a long time. While he was still praying two doctors approached us and I asked them, "How serious is my sister's condition? Should we call her daughter to come from Canada?" (We hadn't told her daughter that her mother had been in a car accident in order not to worry her.) "Whether or not you call her relatives," replied the doctors, "is up to you; we can't guarantee that your sister will live until morning."

Glory to God, she not only lived until morning but recovered completely and returned to Canada. My sister and I believe that she was saved through the prayers of Vladika John.

On the anniversary of Vladika John's repose, a pious woman came up to me in church and told me of an interesting incident.

One day she was in church. Vladika John was serving. The service seemed to her to be very long. Feeling tired, she thought to herself, "Such a long service: couldn't Vladika shorten it a bit?" But she continued to stand patiently. At the end of the service, when she went up to kiss the Cross, Vladika said to her, "If you cannot stand for a long time and your legs hurt, you may sit or go home, since your apartment is close by." Besides being rather embarrassed, the woman was astonished that Vladika was able to read her thoughts.

Anna Sheveleva, San Francisco

Vladika warns of a potential disaster

I often go to Vladika John's sepulchre, although I saw him only a few times before his repose. From others I heard how kind he was, what compassion he had for people. For example, on seeing on the street a poor man without shoes, he took off his boots and gave them to the man.

In 1989, before leaving the house one day, I poured some water into the kettle and put it on a hot burner. Later, in passing the cathedral where Vladika's sepulchre is located, I made the sign of the Cross, and that instant the thought struck me: "The

104

teapot!" I felt it came from Vladika John. I jumped out of the bus and ran the ten blocks uphill to my apartment. There on the red-hot burner stood the teapot; it was empty but everything was all right. What a mercy of God! There are nine apartments in the building. . . It's terrifying to think what might have happened.

Alexandra A. Kolicheva, San Francisco

Vladika stops chills

I write this in gratitude to Vladika John by whose intercessions I was made well.

During the winter of 1988-89, I began having violent chills, unaccompanied by any other symptoms. Occurring in the late afternoon or evening, the onset of the chills would be gradual; for several hours I felt as though I were freezing and I would shake uncontrollably, and then the chills would dissipate. The three or four episodes grew progressively worse. Although I felt well between these attacks, I began to fear that I had a brain tumor or some awful disease.

The third or fourth spell was the worst: unable to keep warm and shaking uncontrollably, I was huddled in bed, blankets piled high. My husband tried to warm me but the chills were so violent that I made him shake. I couldn't hold a mug of hot tea without spilling it. My jaws ached from my teeth chattering. I repeated the Jesus Prayer, trying to relax my body, and asked God for relief from the chills. Then I thought to call on Vladika John, and I prayed, asking his intercession to help me, to heal me. All of a sudden the chills stopped. I doubted that such a miracle had occurred and a few minutes later I felt them coming back. I immediately called on Vladika John again to help me and the chills disappeared and never returned.

I firmly believe Vladika John healed me by God's mercy.

Melissa Bushunow, DeWitt, NY

Lessons in faith

I am a [cradle] born Orthodox Christian of Greek descent, baptized in the Greek Orthodox Church.

It was only after joining the Russian Orthodox Church Abroad in 1969 that I heard of Archbishop John of blessed memory. I was told by members of my parish that he had reposed in Seattle, and I read two articles in the periodicals *The Orthodox Word* and *Orthodox America* of the good works he had done for those who were close to him during his life. But as far as I was concerned he was someone from the distant past. Until recently, I knew nothing of the many churches, monasteries, convents and orphanages he helped establish. Nor was I aware that the present Saint Tikhon of Zadonsk Russian Orthodox Church in San Francisco was his home and served also as an orphanage in the early years of his coming to San Francisco from China. It never occurred to me that his spiritual presence would one day powerfully touch me. But in March of 1987, during Great Lent, there were two incidents.

First, my brother George, who lives in Texas, called to inform me he was undergoing surgery the following Tuesday for cancer of the kidney. I immediately called my daughter, who lives outside San Francisco, to ask Father Anastassy at Saint Tikhon Russian Orthodox Church to have prayers said for my brother's health. I then sat down and wrote a letter to Father Anastassy and explained in more detail my brother's illness. The memory of Blessed Archbishop John didn't even cross my mind.

Second, our local parish had been in such turmoil that for almost two years no one had been going to Confession and receiving Communion. Only a small number of us continued attending the Sunday and feast day services. On the Sunday of the Exaltation of the Cross, 1987, after Divine Liturgy, a Russian friend told me she had heard that a priest was coming to our parish to hear confessions and also give Communion to those who were not receiving from the local priest. I responded that I didn't believe rumors and besides, I would have to see it to believe it. While driving home I began musing. Was it possible that our beloved Bishop Nektary of blessed memory was trying to bring the congregation together? I soon dismissed the idea as wishful thinking.

That night, towards morning, I had a dream. Four hierarchs appeared. Among them I was surprised to recognize Archbishop John of blessed memory. His features were so clear, just like his photograph. He said nothing, but in his penetrating eyes I could almost read: "I've got your message; I'm doing something about it." I was so captivated by his presence that I did not pay attention to a voice introducing me to the other three hierarchs. When I finally tried to concentrate on what the voice was saying, the dream vanished and I woke up, stunned for a minute by the dream. In the morning, as I finished my prayers, I remembered that I had a copy of *The Orthodox Word* (1985) with an akathist to Blessed Archbishop John. I began to say the akathist, and at once burst into tears. I could almost feel his presence beside me. I finished by singing the troparion in the Greek chant:

"Like a spiritual daystar in heaven's firmament, thou didst encompass the whole world and didst enlighten men's souls. Hence, thy name is glorified in the East and West, for thou shonest with the grace of the Sun of Righteousness, O John, our beloved shepherd. Wherefore, cease not to entreat Christ, that He may have mercy on our souls."

From that day I have continued to sing the troparion every morning.

My brother George's surgery was successful. He is doing so well that he came and visited me in September, 1989. And before Pascha a priest came from Holy Trinity Monastery and confessed all those who so desired.

I learned a lesson in faith. Not to doubt, but to trust in our Lord Jesus Christ through His chosen servants. . .

Euphrosyne Beck, Summer, WA

107

The doctors were baffled

This happened in San Francisco, on the Friday before Palm Sunday, 1963. We were returning from the store in our new car when we were hit by a drunk driver. For a split second I felt a pain in my head, and that is all I remember until I regained consciousness in the hospital. My head, neck and back were seriously injured. The doctor's diagnosis stated that I had a concussion, cracked skull, injury to the spine and damage to the motor nerves from my waist down into my legs. And I had barely recovered from two other serious operations!

I had to lie on my back, completely immobile. I was put in traction, with heavy weights at my head and my pelvis, pulling in opposite directions. The doctors hoped thereby to free the damaged nerves in the spine. If not, I would have to remain as I was or undergo an operation, which could make things worse. It was a depressing situation. And Pascha was approaching.

Suddenly, two young boys came into the ward followed by a small, elderly, hunch-backed priest with slanting eyes. The nurse pointed at me and the three of them moved towards me. I felt rather awkward in front of the nurse and the others in the ward and I thought, "Why did this Batiushka come, who called him, why did he have to come here?" The priest was already at my bed saying something, but I couldn't make out what it was. He then leaned closer to me and asked my name. I answered. He looked at me and it was as though his gaze seized me from head to foot. Suddenly he placed his hand firmly on my forehead and said, "What happened, were you in a car accident?" "Yes," I answered, thinking to myself, "How does he know?" "Well, let's pray," he said. "All right." Resting his hand on my head (his hand was so warm, so warm!) and closing his eyes, he began to pray. Then he took a bottle of oil from a bag one of the boys was holding and anointed my head, forehead, throat, chest, hands and feet and gave me some wine to drink and a piece of antidoron. Sprinkling me with holy water, he smiled and gave me a paschal egg (not an edible one, but a decorated one wrapped in gold ribbons). Continuing to smile, he reached into his capacious pocket, searched for something and finally pulled out a lilac-blue marble egg which he put into my hand. "Here, hold this; this is no ordinary egg, it's a gold one." Saying this, he blessed me. I kissed his cross and his hand, and they all left.

After he had gone—he had come during the day—I fell asleep holding the egg and awoke when it was already dark. That night a real miracle occurred. I needed a nurse but couldn't call her. Incredibly, I suddenly felt compelled to get up from the bed myself! I took off the various straps, ties, weights, and crawled to the end of the bed and slid onto the floor. The other patients in the ward awoke from all the noise and, seeing me standing by my bed and knowing that I was paralyzed from the waist down, began shouting for the nurse. A nurse came flying in and was stupefied on seeing me. "Help me with this patient!" Two more nurses came and together they tried to put me back in bed, certain that the doctors would reprimand them for what had happened. I insisted on having my way and managed to walk by myself to the bathroom and back! My legs wobbled from weakness, but I wept with joy.

The next day, after many X rays and an examination, my doctor said to me, "I'm completely baffled! From a medical point of view this is impossible! I'm going to call other doctors for a consultation." Other doctors came. . . . They kept me for another nine days before releasing me. No explanation could be found.

Ever since that night, after the visit of that little "priest," I have been walking on my own two legs, without any complications and without any operation. At that time I had no idea who that "priest" was. I didn't know Vladika John, I hadn't even heard about him. Only later did I learn who it was who visited me in the hospital. I understood what mercy I had been granted from the touch of his hands, having received such an incredible healing through his prayers!

At the end of 1963 I experienced a whole series of personal problems. It was an extremely difficult time for me. My mother, having by this time learned about Vladika, invited him to our home. When he came and sat down on the sofa, I simply fell to my knees in front of him, sobbing. He gently stroked my head and quietly prayed. All my troubles disappeared and my whole life took a new direction.

Twice in one year I was granted healing through the prayers of Vladika John. . . My family and I continue to receive mercy and healing, even after Vladika's repose.

Tatiana Estrada, Concord, CA

A serious asthma attack averted

This happened in 1965. I was then eight years old. From the age of two I suffered from asthma, and I had serious attacks rather frequently.

One evening our family were guests at a nameday party and I began having a bad attack. Because of it, my parents decided to leave early and take me home. The hostess, whose nameday it was, persuaded them to stay a bit longer, since Vladika John was expected. Within a matter of minutes Vladika arrived and served a short moleben in honor of the hostess's nameday. Directly after the moleben my parents took me to Vladika and told him about my condition. Vladika blessed us and stroked me on the head, "Never mind, never mind, Natashenka. All will be well." We went home immediately. My parents expected that I would break into a sweat and that I wouldn't sleep all night, as was often the case during such attacks. But this did not happen. The asthma attack subsided and I slept peacefully until morning.

Natalia, née Metlenko, Pacifica, CA

The healing of a Muslim friend

A miracle occurred after I received an issue of *Orthodox Life* containing a photograph of Archbishop John.

I had a friend, a Muslim from Russia, who suffered from cancer of the blood and was losing his sight. He was told by doctors that within three months he would be totally blind. I placed the photo of Vladika John before the vigil lamp in my icon corner and daily prayed for my friend. Within a very short time my friend recovered from the cancer and his normal vision was restored. The eye doctors were stunned. Three years have passed; my friend reads books and leads a normal life.

Truly, Vladika John is a saint.

Victor Boyton, Australia

Spared from an accident

One morning we visited Archbishop John's niece, Mrs. Vera Maximovitch, in Valencia, and she gave us a portrait of Blessed John, which we left in the car. That afternoon we were en route to visit my brother outside Valencia, when we had a terrible accident. The car was demolished, but, miraculously, not only did we all survive, but none of us were even injured. Since that day I always pray to Blessed John.

I have a brother, a drug addict and schizophrenic, who is in a special hospital for addicts in Valencia. Because he doesn't follow the treatment properly they want to evict him. I have been praying to Blessed John, and at home I keep a candle lit for him most of the time. My brother is still at the institution, and it seems he is getting better. I also consider this a miracle, because once the psychiatrists decide to evict a patient there is little chance he can remain.

Grace Lopez, Venezuela

Vladika guides someone to the true Church

There are two incidents in my life, when I feel that Archbishop John greatly helped me. . . . The first happened before I was Orthodox.

I had read a great deal about the Orthodox Church and had come to believe that it was the true Church. After many difficulties, I made contact with a priest and started attending the Russian Church at Emperor's Gate in London. After I had been attending for some time, an elderly priest (actually from the Greek Church) said to me very forcefully, "It is not enough to believe that the Orthodox Church is the true Church; you must always remember that every Liturgy in the Orthodox Church is celebrated on the relics of martyrs, and before being received you must be prepared to die for Orthodoxy." This rather frightened me and even confused me a little because I did not see how I could be sure of such conviction. In theory, yes, I could die for it—but what would happen when they started to interrogate me or torture me?

Several weeks later at the Sunday Liturgy, I was kneeling at the "Our Father"—I did not know yet that this was wrong,* but God reaches even the ignorant—when I was flooded with the conviction that I should become Orthodox and that conviction left me with a feeling of peace and joy. After the Liturgy, I was anxious to tell the priest that I now felt at peace about becoming Orthodox, but a memorial service followed immediately, with the bishop and all the clergy serving. I had no understanding of Slavonic and was rather irritated that another service was going to begin. I turned and asked an old lady who the panikhida was for, and she replied, "For Archbishop John." I remember clearly thinking, "These Russians always have some old archbishop or other to pray for." At the end of the panikhida,

---

* Church canons proscribe kneeling in church on Sundays, for the sake of the honor of Christ's Resurrection.

there was no opportunity to speak with the priest alone. He lived out of town and spent Sunday afternoons visiting members of his flock. Just before leaving, however, he came to the house where I was staying to see the elderly couple who lived there. I thought that I would have no opportunity to speak to him, and felt shy, wondering how to express it in any case. Then, as he was about to leave, he turned and asked, "Isn't it about time you became Orthodox?" I had not needed to prepare a speech or think what to say. I became Orthodox on Saint Marina's day, 1967. Several months passed and only then in *The Orthodox Word* did I read a life of Vladika John. Immediately I realized that the Sunday on which I had felt such conviction was the first anniversary of the repose of Blessed Archbishop John, and I understood that it was through his intercessions that this mercy was granted me.

Years later, when I was living in a monastery in the States, I was told that I was to be made an archimandrite and sent back to England. I had grave misgivings about this, but they were overruled. Only a date had to be fixed. I read somewhere that becoming an archimandrite was likened unto the special ministry with which the Apostles entrusted Saint Barnabas, and so I thought perhaps that I might receive some consolation if the prayer of elevation [to the rank of archimandrite] was read on his feast day, but that did not happen. At the last moment it was decided that the elevation would take place on the anniversary of the repose of Blessed Archbishop John, and again I felt assured of his loving care, especially as I was being appointed to a church which he had blessed and in which he had celebrated when in Europe.

To the outsider these instances are not striking miracles perhaps, but through them my darkened soul experienced the love of Vladika John. I earnestly hope that Vladika will be glorified by the Church on earth, as I believe that he has been by the Church in heaven.

A.A., England

113

"Let go . . . and let God"

After seven disappointing years of infertility studies and medication, we finally realized that we really hadn't let go of our problems and let God do His Will in our lives. We knew we needed to muster up enough trust to let God do His job. That's when we first learned about the holy life and miraculous intercessions of the late Archbishop John Maximovitch. In China he had been a care-giver of orphans. We prayed, asking him to intercede with our Lord Jesus Christ in directing our lives and hopefully sending us a child to love and care for as our own. Several months of prayer passed and things began to happen. After two and a half years of waiting, my husband received word that a U.S.A.F. active duty Orthodox chaplain job slot was open. What's more, the wife of the chaplain he was replacing was the president of the adoption association in their area. She put us in touch with a social worker who filed our homestudy for adoption, and just five and a half weeks after its approval we became parents of fraternal twins, a boy and a girl!

We write this account with prayerful gratitude, asking Archbishop John that he continue to help us and direct our lives closer to the Lord.

Papadija Roberta B. Yonitch, Texas

Help in finding the true Faith

In 1968 I was a Roman Catholic and altogether disillusioned with the Church of Rome, particularly the radical changes instituted by Vatican II. Something inspired me to visit an Orthodox church in Seattle, Washington. Thereafter I began to make inquiries about the Orthodox Faith, and from correspondence with Father Alexey Young (then still a layman) and reading certain publications I learned about the struggler and wonderworker, Archbishop John Maximovitch, and I determined to visit his sepulchre in San Francisco at the first opportunity. At that time I was interested in Orthodoxy, but had not taken any definite steps in that direction.

In January of 1973 I was able to make that visit. Standing in that crypt-chapel and praying, my heart was warmed and moved toward actively seeking Orthodoxy. Father Vladimir Anderson—also a layman at that time—and his family had come to guide me around the cathedral, and to talk with me. The next morning they took me to Liturgy at the convent on Fell Street, and in the afternoon to visit the Vladimir Icon Convent and the miraculously renewed icons. I had some time to be alone in that church, time to venerate the Mother of God in those icons, and this brought me great peace and joy.

Returning home, I told my wife that sooner or later I would be Orthodox, regardless of the fact that we lived over a hundred miles from the nearest Orthodox temple! She had never been Roman Catholic, although she had usually accompanied me to church, and I didn't know how she would react to my decision. She told me that during my absence she had been struck by a keen sense of her mortality, and would not oppose my becoming Orthodox. In fact, we were baptized together at Pascha, 1973, with two of our three children. All of this has been at the intervention of Archbishop John.

Then, in February of 1990, I found myself in the hospital awaiting surgery for colon cancer. In spite of my lifelong devotion to Christianity, I was frightened and upset at the prospect facing me. During the night before surgery, I half awoke in great anxiety over my sins and attachment to this world: I cried out in prayer to the Saviour and to the Mother of God and other saints, although not to Archbishop John, and I received such comfort that several people afterwards commented on my optimistic attitude.

Four days after surgery I awoke at night and saw at the foot of my bed the profile of Archbishop John. He was looking to his left and standing quite still. I blinked, and he looked straight into my eyes, perhaps somewhat sternly. He said nothing, but the thought came to me that he was thinking I should have called for his help earlier, and that I should have been more zealous in acquiring Christian virtue. Again I blinked, and he was gone. Comforted, I fell soundly asleep.

In the morning I remarked to the nurse on the number of visitors I'd had the previous day. She said, "Yes. And you had one during the night, too." I was so astonished at this confirming coincidence that I could think of nothing to say and didn't even have the presence of mind to ask the nurse to describe the nighttime visitor. But there is no doubt.

Four days later I received in the mail from Father Peter Perekrestov a photo icon of Archbishop John, looking exactly as I had seen him in my hospital room. In his accompanying letter, Father Peter said he had only just heard of my illness: the photo icon and letter were mailed the morning after my first experience of comfort, the same morning as my surgery.

At this writing there is no indication of any cancer, but even if it should recur, there is within me the assurance that the Lord does indeed nourish those who cast their care upon Him, as David the Psalmist says. Through Archbishop John, God made known His strength in my weakness.

Joseph Miller, Indianola, WA

Vladika saves from death

Living in Shanghai, I fell seriously ill with an inflammation of the kidneys. The best doctors attended me, but there was no improvement, and after two months all hope was gone for my recovery. I simply lay drugged, no longer taking any medicine, not even water. I was expected to die any day.

116

My mother had very strong faith. One day the poor exhausted lady went to church at Saint Olga's Orphanage, which was under the care of Abbess Ariadna. At the end of the service Vladika John came up to her: "Don't cry," he said. "I know all about it. Julia is near death; I'll come in an hour to give her Unction." He didn't say anything else; he didn't ask for the address, nothing. Within half an hour Vladika was at my bedside, where I lay unconscious.

When he left, my mother later told me, I fell asleep. I slept for a long, long time. Early in the morning I opened my eyes and asked for some water. The pains in my stomach were gone and my temperature had dropped. Within two weeks I was completely well. Abbess Ariadna knows all about this case and can testify to the accuracy of my account.

Sister Julia, Montreal, Canada

Vladika eases pain

There have been many instances in my life when Vladika helped me. Until now I didn't think it was worth paying particular attention to them, but my conscience has been nagging me.

Yesterday I was at the doctor's. I suffer from allergies and often have problems with my nose. After checking my nose the doctor detected a small polyp which he decided to remove then and there. He cut it away and the nose began to bleed profusely—a problem I'd had several years earlier. Mentally I promised Vladika John that if the bleeding stopped I would notify the diocesan commission that was gathering information about the prayerful help of Vladika John. After the operation the doctor left me in the office for a while and then I went home. My nose continued to bleed a little. I then anointed my nostril with oil from Vladika John's sepulchre and lay down to rest. When I woke up, the flow of blood had stopped.

Constantine Youmin, Monterey, CA

The strength of Vladika's faith

Two days ago I brought my grandson to the local church to be baptized. A young woman come up to me and said she thought it wasn't hygienic that all the children were baptized in the same font. I tried to reassure her by relating an incident that I myself had witnessed.

At the Russian hospital in Shanghai, a mental patient, in a moment of lucidity, asked for Holy Communion. Vladika John arrived at once. The sick one was given Communion, but, no longer in his right mind, he forgot about his request and spit out the Body and Blood of our Lord onto the floor. Vladika John did what every true priest ought to do—he licked up every drop and crumb from the floor! And although this mentally deranged man had some dreadful infectious disease, Vladika suffered no ill effects whatsoever. I'm not sure the young woman understood what I was talking about, but I felt compelled to tell her of this incident with Vladika John. I saw this myself; it's not the fruit of someone's imagination.

G. G. Egorov, Moscow

God-pleasers will not be mocked

About eleven or twelve years ago my acquaintances, the Petrovs, offered to give me a ride home from church. This was a middle-aged couple, energetic and well-to-do. As he was driving, Mr. Petrov did nothing but sharply malign Vladika John in a most disrespectful manner.

My husband and I left for Italy the next day, and when I returned to Paris a month later I was shocked to find Mr. Petrov so changed: he had lost at least twenty pounds, and his face was ashen. When I asked what had happened, he answered that his wife was ill and in the hospital. She had undergone an operation but they had found nothing and she was getting weaker virtually by the minute. Very soon she died and was cremated. Mr. Petrov promptly remarried; his second wife was French, a Roman Catholic, and he converted to her faith. They soon left for the south of France. No sooner had they arrived than Mr. Petrov died; he, too, was cremated. What a tragic ending to this couple's earthly existence!

For me it was and is only too evident how the Lord defends His faithful servants, and how careful one must be not to criticize and judge people, especially hierarchs.

I.S., B-na

Vladika heals and strengthens

This happened in January 1966. Suffering from excruciating pain, I was rushed to the hospital, where I learned that an immediate operation was necessary. Gangrene was spreading and my life was threatened. During the operation, on the Feast of our Lord's Theophany, a complication developed; my blood was clotting poorly and I lost a lot of blood. After the operation I was so weak that it was a wonder my soul was still in my body. The Greek woman who shared my room told me later that while I was still unconscious, "a hierarch came to see you; he was quite short and entered with rapid steps; he prayed at your bedside, sprinkled you with holy water, blessed you and left." Hearing this I thought, who could it be? I later learned that it was Vladika John. By the prayers of dear Vladika for me, a sinner, I began quickly to recover. I recall this with gratitude and firmly believe in Vladika's power of prayer.

As a boy in Shanghai, my uncle fell seriously ill with a fever. My grandmother told me that after Vladika came to him and prayed, my uncle immediately became completely well.

Here is another case. My mother was going through a lot of internal unrest. Once she was reading and singing on cliros.

After the Divine Liturgy she sat down at a small table near the cliros and began copying out the Old Testament lessons. Vladika John came out of the altar and, seeing my mother, began telling her the life of Saint Eustratius Placides. He afterwards anointed himself and then my mother with holy oil. My mother soon noticed that all her troubles had disappeared, and she experienced an inner calm and strengthening. Again Vladika John helped!

Irina Trubetskoy, Burlingame, CA

The healing of a child

My godson Adam was born January 6, 1989, and was adopted a few days later by Father Andrew and Ruth. He was healthy until the fall of 1989 when he developed infantile spasms that cause seizures. In October 1989 he was put on Phenobarbitol and in November he began receiving ACTH injections. A month later the medication Klonopin was added and in January—Diamox. The effects of these drugs ranged from lethargy to extreme irritability. Adam rarely slept through the night and his development was arrested.

I wrote asking Father Peter to pray for Adam at the tomb of Archbishop John, which he did, placing Adam's name under his mitre. Father Peter also sent us oil from the sepulchre, with which we anointed Adam daily. Shortly thereafter, Adam's mother reported that he had begun to be less agitated and, following three months of inactivity, finally began responding to his parents.

In March of 1990 Adam was weaned from Klonopin and that same month, on the feast of the Annunciation, his seizures stopped! Adam was slowly taken off ACTH and in June he was also weaned from Phenobarbitol. In August Adam began walking, and by September 8, the Feast of the Nativity of the Theotokos, he was totally drug- and seizure-free.

Because the illness had retarded his development Adam had been receiving physical, occupational and speech therapies. Several months ago, however, he was discharged from the therapy program as he was functioning at an age-appropriate level.

Adam's parents, relatives, and friends consider his recovery a miracle and believe that Archbishop John Maximovitch's prayers and holy oil are responsible for this healing.

I feel fortunate to have learned of Archbishop John from my father who was his student at the Serbian seminary in Bitol, Yugoslavia, and from another student, Father Spiro, who gave me a book of his miracles to read.

I have referred several people for prayers at Archbishop John's tomb and will continue to tell others about this holy man.

Mileva Savich, Chicago

Pains cease through the prayers of Vladika

In early October 1989, I began having sharp pains in my back, caused by my work. In spite of my condition, I continued to work and tried to do as much as I could. I did not consult any doctors, knowing that they cannot always help. I confided to a friend my misfortune.

On getting out of bed in the morning I had made a habit of making a prostration. The pain in my back made this very difficult and for about a week I was unable to make a full prostration. The morning of October 9, a Monday, I got up and, as usual, made an effort at making a prostration. I was stunned! I felt absolutely no pain. It was as though I had never experienced any pain at all. Glory to God!

Only later did I learn that the kind soul to whom I had confided my trouble had gone to Vladika John's sepulchre in San Francisco and had prayed for me. Wondrous is God in His saints.

Alexandra Kiritis, Los Angeles, CA

Vladika helps a family

I would like to detail the intercessions of Blessed Archbishop John on behalf of my family. Perhaps these do not sound like miraculous occurrences to some people, but Father Svetislav and I know that before we sought Vladika's prayers, we were without aid.

The first episode in this related set of events began when, in 1982, the parish council of Saint Nicholas Church in Endicott, New York, invited us to live in the vacant rectory. We had been hoping to move a little closer to Jordanville and to a parish with the Russian Church Abroad. (Father had been a cleric of the Serbian Church since his ordination in 1974.) Until we began daily to entreat Vladika John for intercession, we could find no new home.

There in Endicott, Father Svetislav was able to secure employment in a hospital—again, through the prayers of Archbishop John. Previously he had tried many hospitals in several locations, but since he had no experience in health care he had been unable to find work, and he needed a secular job because he was not to be the rector of the Endicott parish. Vladika John likewise enabled Father Svetislav to be accepted into nursing school, when previously he had been unable to enroll in any school.

Finally, not two years after our first visit to Endicott, we adopted our son, John, giving him the name of our constant intercessor. After ten years of marriage, many visits to doctors, multiple encounters with domestic and foreign adoption agencies, which in fact would only allow us to be placed on a list of people awaiting formal applications for adoptions, we were granted, by God's mercy, the child we had prayed for. John was born in a nearby hospital on that very day when we first visited the parish of Saint Nicholas in Endicott. Our decision to call him John was confirmed when, the day before we were to see the child for the first time, Vladika's prayers sustained Father Svetislav's brother, Predrag, through a life-threatening situation.

Hieromonk Hilarion (now Bishop of Manhattan) baptized John at Holy Trinity Monastery on July 2, 1984, the anniversary of the repose of Blessed Archbishop John. John's godfather, Father Adam Yonitch, and his wife, also childless after many years of marriage, obtained a portrait of Vladika John while they were at the monastery and likewise began to beseech his intercession. A little more than a year later, which was like no time at all after having been on an adoption waiting list eight years, Father and Popadija (Matushka) Roberta adopted twins, Damian and Mira, who were less than two weeks old. Two days later, we adopted our second child, Natalie. Although we had stopped our intense prayers, being grateful for the son God had given us, He did not forget our hope of having a family. We are certain Vladika John, a protector of orphans since his days in China, continued to intercede with God for the sake of our little family.

Father Svetislav and I continue to pray to Vladika John daily. Our children are also very much aware of the impact his care has had on our lives. We hope that our story will help others to know of the powerful intercession of Vladika John before our Heavenly Father. Glory to God, Who is wondrous in His saints!

Matushka Nancy Mirolovich, Buffalo, NY

Vladika pities a young girl

In 1988 my daughter developed a rare condition, *alapecia aniversalys*, causing a complete loss of hair on the head and the entire body. There is no known cause of this illness and no cure.

My daughter liked to pray at Archbishop John's sepulchre, and one Sunday she went there and begged Vladika with tears to give her eyebrows, eyelashes and hair on her body. She couldn't stop weeping. She told Vladika that she could live without hair on her head, but, "please, give me eyebrows, eyelashes and hair on my body."

And there was a miracle. Her eyebrows, eyelashes and body hair began to appear. She is so grateful to Vladika and only regrets that at the same time she hadn't asked for hair on her head as well. . .

A mother, California

Vladika's clairvoyance

Of the two following episodes from the life of Vladika John, the first was told me by a clergyman from Shanghai, the second by a Shanghai merchant, the late Dimitri Mikhailovich Azovtsev.

Vladika was asked to bring the Holy Mysteries to a dying man in the Russian hospital in Shanghai. He was accompanied by a member of the clergy. Arriving at the hospital they saw a young man of about twenty, full of vitality, playing a harmonica. He was waiting in line to be discharged. Vladika called him: "I want to give you Holy Communion." Then and there the young man had Confession and partook of the Holy Mysteries. The astonished clergyman asked Vladika why he hadn't gone straightway to the dying man and instead had delayed with this obviously healthy young man. Vladika replied bluntly, "Tonight he will die, whereas the man who is seriously ill will live for many more years." And indeed, this is just what happened.

A friend of Dimitry Mikhailovich Azovtsev, also a merchant, had a car. While driving one day, he caught sight of Vladika John, stopped and got out of the car to ask his blessing. It was late evening and it was raining. Blessing the merchant, Vladika asked him to give him a ride and gave him an address. They stopped at an apartment. The door was opened by the lady of the house. When Vladika asked to see her husband he was told that the man, feeling tired, had had dinner and had already gone to bed. Vladika asked that the man be awakened.

After confessing him, Vladika gave him Holy Communion. On the way back the merchant asked Vladika what need there was for such haste to commune a perfectly healthy man. "He is going to die tonight," answered Vladika. He was right.

Michael P. Biriukov, Stratfield, Australia

Vladika appears in the sepulchre

Early in the morning of July 2, 1984, the anniversary of Vladika John's repose, Mr. I. Ma made his way to the sepulchre for the Divine Liturgy. He had been cautioned that there would be a lot of people and he therefore arrived early, at 5 A.M.

The clergy were already preparing for the Liturgy when suddenly I. Ma saw Vladika John in white apparel. Vladika walked through the clergy towards I. Ma. I. Ma bowed low to ask Vladika's blessing, but when he raised his head Vladika had disappeared.

It should be noted that I. Ma had just arrived from China in December 1983. There, thanks to the Communists, he had spent seventeen years in prison and for thirty-five years was persecuted because, at Vladika John's request, he had assisted some Russians.

L.N.I., San Francisco

By virtue of necessity and clarity we had to shorten and edit some of these testimonies of Archbishop John's prayerful assistance In doing so we made every effort to preserve the meaning and spirit of what was written. In view of the fact that a great deal of material has been received concerning Vladika John's wonderworking intercession, we tried for this anthology to choose the most varied testimonies. Those which were not included, as well as materials still coming in, will, God willing, appear in a future volume. — *The compiler*

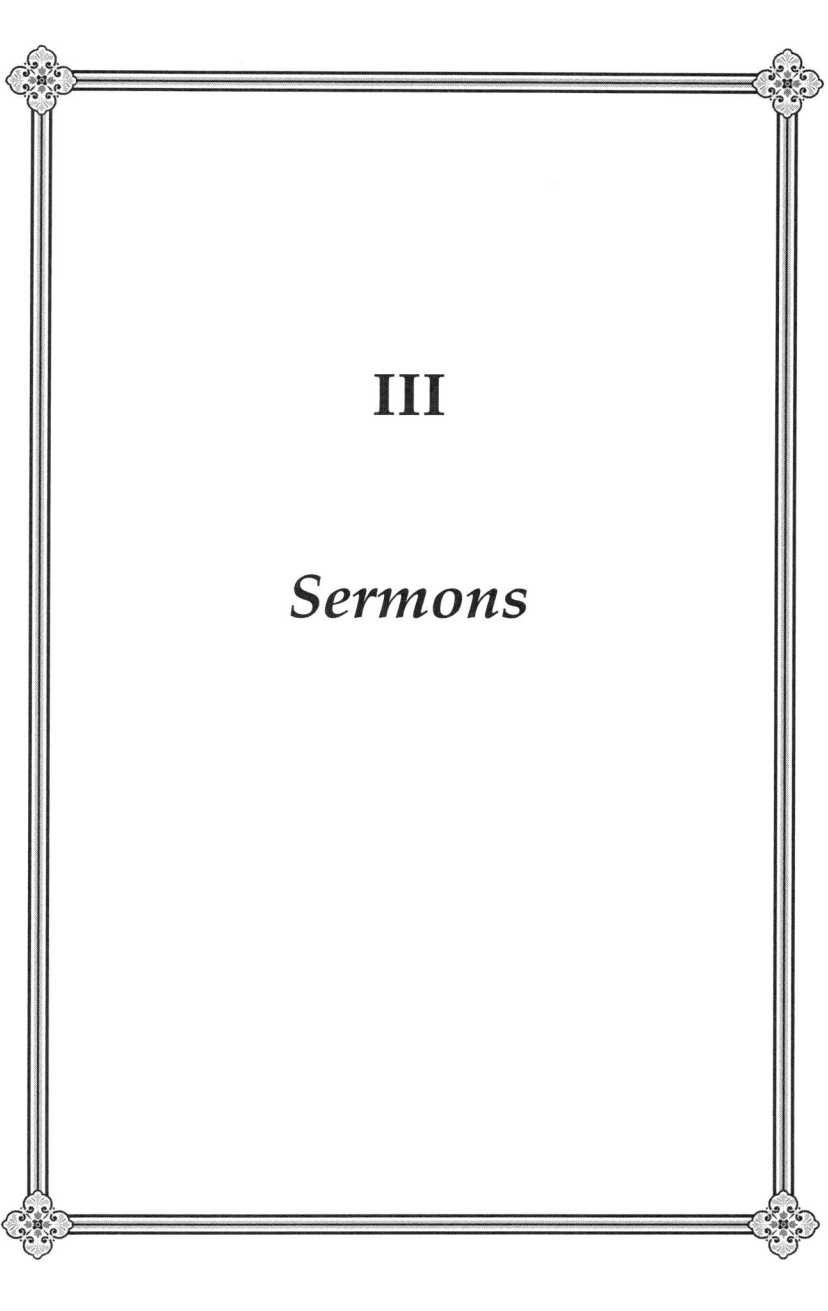

III

Sermons

BEFORE LENT

The DOORS of repentance are opening, Great Lent is beginning. Every year it is repeated, and each time it brings us great benefit—if we spend it as we should. Great Lent is a preparation for the life to come and, more immediately, a preparation for the Bright Resurrection.

Just as a stairway is built into a tall building in order to enable one, by climbing the steps, to easily get to the top, so, too, the various days in the year serve as steps for our spiritual ascent.

This is especially true of the days of Great Lent and Holy Pascha.

By means of Great Lent, we cleanse ourselves of the filth of sin, and at Holy Pascha we experience the blessedness of Christ's Kingdom that is to come. In climbing a high mountain, one tries to eliminate all unnecessary weight. The less a person carries, the easier it is for him to climb and the higher he is able to climb. So, too, in order to ascend spiritually, it is necessary first of all to free oneself from the weight of sin. It is taken from us through repentance, provided that we banish from ourselves all enmity and forgive each person whom we consider to be at fault before us. Once cleansed and forgiven by God, we then greet the Bright Resurrection of Christ.

And what a priceless gift of God we receive then, at the culmination of our lenten struggle. We hear about this already in the first hymns of the daily lenten stichera: "Our food shall be the Lamb of God, on the holy and radiant night of His Awakening: the Victim offered for us, given in communion to the disciples on the evening of the Mystery. . . " (Aposticha sticheron, Sunday of the Last Judgment)

Communing of the Body and Blood of the Risen Christ, unto life eternal—this is the aim of the holy Quadragesima [Forty Days]. Not just on Pascha does one commune. On the contrary, on Pascha those people should commune who fasted, confessed and received the Holy Mysteries during Great Lent. Just before Pascha itself there is little opportunity for a proper and thorough confession; time and the priests are occupied with the Passion services. One must prepare ahead of time.

Each time one receives the Mysteries of Christ, one is united with Christ Himself; each time it is a soul-saving act. Why, then, is such significance attached to receiving Holy Communion on the night of Holy Pascha, and why are we all called to do so?

Then, especially, we are given to experience the Kingdom of Christ. Then, especially, we are illumined with the Eternal Light and strengthened for the spiritual ascent.

This is an irreplaceable gift of Christ, an incomparable good. Let no one deprive himself of this joy and, instead of receiving Holy Communion on Pascha night, hasten to eat meat and other foods. Communing of the Holy Mysteries on that night prepares us for the banquet in the eternal Kingdom of God.

HOMILY BEFORE A MEMORIAL
SERVICE FOR THE TSAR-MARTYR

FORTY YEARS AGO, a single day saw the collapse of the greatness and glory of the Russian State, a bulwark of peace throughout the whole world. The signature of the Sovereign, the Emperor Nicholas Alexandrovich, on the act of abdication from the Throne, is a historical boundary separating Russia's great and glorious past from her present dark and cruel circumstances.

The entire weight of the present regime's evil and its re-ordering of life is aimed at honest, well-intentioned and devout people, and the whole nation lies in oppression and constant fear. People are afraid of their own thoughts, thoughts they have not expressed aloud; they are afraid that what they are thinking might be reflected in their facial expressions.

What happened that day, forty years ago?

Apostasy from God's Anointed, apostasy from an authority submissive to God, apostasy from the oath of fidelity to the Anointed Sovereign, given before God, and the giving over of him to death.

He who had devoted all his strength in God's name to the service of Russia was deprived of authority, and then also of freedom.

For decades the dark forces of evil carried on a struggle against God's Anointed, against the ruling authority faithful to God. These same forces also killed the Emperor Alexander II, the Tsar-Liberator.

This crime sobered the people, it shook the entire country, and that moral upsurge gave Emperor Alexander III, the Peacemaker, the opportunity to rule Russia with a strong arm.

Russia enjoyed two decades of peaceful life and development. Then a new conspiracy arose for the overthrow of the Royal Throne.

It was a conspiracy of Russia's enemies.

Within Russia itself there was a struggle against her very essence, and, having destroyed the Throne, Russia's enemies even obliterated her name.

Now the whole world can see the close connection between the Royal authority, faithful to God, and Russia. When the Tsar ceased to be—Russia ceased to be.

The struggle against the Tsar and Russia was carried out by concealed godlessness, which later revealed itself openly.

Such was the essence of the struggle against the Tsar and Russia, against the foundation of her life and historical development.

Such are the meaning and aim of that struggle, which perhaps not everyone realized — those who were its accomplices.

Everything filthy and paltry and sinful which could be found in the human soul was summoned against the Tsar and Russia. All of this, with all its might, rose up in struggle against the Royal Crown, which was crowned by a cross, for Royal service is a bearing of the Cross.

People always rise up against the Cross by means of slander and falsehood, doing the devil's work, for, according to the word of the Lord Jesus Christ, *When he speaketh a lie, he speaketh of his own: for he is a liar, and the father of it* (John 8:44).

Everything was roused up against the most meek, pure and abundantly-loving Tsar, so that at the terrible hour of the struggle against him he would remain alone. Filthy slanders were spread beforehand against the Tsar and his family, so that the people would grow cool towards him.

Faithless allies took part in the conspiracy. When the Sovereign was in need of moral support, his closest associates did not provide it and violated their oath. Some took part in the conspiracy; others, out of weakness, counseled abdication. The Tsar remained completely alone, surrounded by "treachery, baseness and cowardice."

From the day of the abdication, everything began to collapse. It could not have been otherwise. The one who united everything, who stood guard for the Truth, was overthrown. A sin was committed, and now sin had easy access. In vain do some wish to separate February from October;* the one was a direct consequence of the other.

In those March days, Pskov became the Tsar's Gethsemane, and Ekaterinburg—his Golgotha.

Tsar Nicholas died as a martyr, with unshakeable faith and patience, having drunk the cup of suffering to the dregs.

The sin against him and against Russia was perpetrated by all who in one way or another acted against him, who did not oppose, or who merely by sympathizing participated in those events which took place forty years ago. That sin lies upon everyone until it is washed away by sincere repentance.

In raising up prayers for the repose of his soul, we pray also for Tsars Paul I and Alexander II, who were likewise slain in March. And we pray for the forgiveness of the Russian people of the grave sin of betrayal and regicide. Woe to those who call evil good and good evil. Before us, before the Russian people, lies the path of resurgence—which is the path of consciousness of sin and repentance.

For the rebirth of Russia, all political and other programs of unification are in vain: what Russia needs is the moral renewal of the Russian people.

We must pray for the forgiveness of our sins and for mercy on our homeland, just as the Lord God freed Israel from the Babylonian captivity and restored the ruined city of Jerusalem.

---

* Many attribute the Russian Revolution to the Bolsheviks, who seized power in October (O.S.) 1917. Archbishop John and others point out that the groundwork for the Revolution was laid much earlier, as evidenced by the lack of support given the Tsar at the time of the February uprisings, which precipitated his forced abdication in March. - *pub*.

THE EXALTATION OF THE CROSS

BEFORE THE TIME of Christ, the cross was an instrument of punishment; it evoked fear and aversion. But after Christ's death on the Cross it became the instrument and sign of our salvation. Through the Cross, Christ destroyed the devil; from the Cross He descended into hades and, having liberated those languishing there, led them into the Kingdom of Heaven. The sign of the Cross is terrifying to demons and, as the sign of Christ, it is honored by Christians. The Lord manifested it in the sky to the Emperor Constantine as he was going to Rome to fight the tyrant who had seized power, and the Emperor, having fashioned a standard in the form of a cross, won a total victory. Having been aided by the Cross of the Lord, the Emperor Constantine asked his mother, the Empress Helen, to find the actual Life-giving Cross, and the devout Helen went to Jerusalem where, after much searching, she found it.

Many healings and other miracles were wrought and continue to be wrought by the Life-giving Cross and also by its depiction. Through it the Lord preserves His people from all enemies visible and invisible. The Orthodox Church solemnly celebrates the finding of the Cross of the Lord, recalling at the same time the appearance of the Cross in the sky to the Emperor Constantine. On that and other days dedicated to the Holy Cross, we beseech God that He grant His mercies not only to individual people, but to all Christendom, to the whole Church. This is well expressed by the troparion to the Cross of the Lord, composed in the eighth century, when Saint Cosmas, Bishop of Maiuma, a friend of St. John Damascene, wrote the service to the Exaltation of the Cross of the Lord.

"Save, O Lord, Thy people, and bless Thine inheritance, granting victory to (right-believing) kings over adversaries, and by Thy Cross preserving Thy community."

134

The beginning of this prayer is taken from the twenty-seventh Psalm. In the Old Testament the word "people" designated only those who confessed the true faith, people faithful to God. "Inheritance" referred to everything which properly belonged to God, God's property, which in the New Testament is the Church of Christ. In praying for the salvation of God's people (the Christians), both from eternal torments and from earthly calamities, we beseech the Lord to bless, to send down grace, His good gifts upon the whole Church as well, and inwardly strengthen her.

The petition for granting "victory to kings," i.e., to the bearers of supreme authority, has its basis in Psalm 143, verse 10, and recalls the victories King David achieved by God's power, and likewise the victories granted Emperor Constantine through the Cross of the Lord. This appearance of the Cross made emperors who had formerly persecuted Christians into defenders of the Church from her external enemies, into "external bishops," to use the expression of the holy Emperor Constantine.

The Church, inwardly strong by God's grace and protected outwardly, is, for Orthodox Christians, "the city of God," God's community, His commonwealth, where the path to the Heavenly Jerusalem has its beginning. Various calamities have shaken the world, entire peoples have disappeared, cities and states have perished, but the Church, in spite of persecutions and even internal conflicts, stands invincible; for *the gates of hell shall not prevail against her* (Matt. 16:18). Today, when world leaders try in vain to establish order on earth, the only dependable instrument of peace is that about which the Church sings:

> *The Cross is the guardian of the whole world; the Cross is*
> *the beauty of the Church, the Cross is the might of kings;*
> *the Cross is the confirmation of the faithful,*
> *the Cross is the glory of angels and the wounding of demons.*

(Exapostilarion of the Exaltation of the Cross)

THE GLORIFICATION OF GOD-PLEASERS

HOLINESS IS NOT simply righteousness, for which the righteous are rewarded with blessedness in the Kingdom of God; rather, it is such a height of righteousness that people are so filled with the grace of God that it flows from them even upon those who associate with them. Great is their blessedness, which proceeds from their direct contemplation of the glory of God. Being filled also with love for men, which proceeds from love of God, they are responsive to men's needs, and at their entreaties they act as mediators and intercessors for them before God.

Such, first of all, were the righteous ones of the Old Testament, those whom Christ freed from hades and led into Paradise, and John the Baptist, *the greatest of those born of women.* Then came the Apostles and their immediate successors. None of the Christians had any doubt of their sanctity, and after their decease—the majority were martyred—they began immediately to venerate them and to call on them in prayer. Such also were the martyrs in the first centuries of persecution, when spiritual fervor abounded. A martyr's death was itself a door to the mansions on high, and Christians began to invoke them as holy men pleasing to God. Miracles and signs confirmed this faith of the Christians and gave evidence of their holiness. In the same way Christians later began to venerate the great ascetics. No one decreed that Anthony the Great, Macarius the Great, Basil the Great, Gregory the Theologian, Nicholas the Wonderworker, and many others like them should be venerated as saints, but they are revered by East and West alike, and their sanctity can be denied only by those who do not believe in sanctity.

The assembly of God-pleasers grew continually; wherever there were Christians new ascetics appeared. Overall, however, the life of the Christians began to decline; spiritual ardor began to cool; no longer was there a clear sense of what Divine righteousness is. For this reason the collective consciousness of the faithful could not always recognize who was a genuine ascetic and God-pleaser. In some places there appeared dubious persons who, by means of spurious ascetic feats, deceived some of the flock. Therefore the ecclesiastical authority began to oversee the veneration of saints, taking care to guard the flock from superstition. They began to examine the lives of those ascetics venerated by the faithful, and to verify accounts of their miracles. Towards the time of the Baptism of Rus' it was already established that recognition of a new saint was to be given by the ecclesiastical authority. The decrees made by the ecclesiastical authority were binding in that region under its jurisdiction; however, usually other local Churches also recognized a glorification performed elsewhere, although they did not necessarily enter it into their own menology. After all, the ecclesiastical authority merely attested to sanctity. The righteous became saints not through any decree of the earthly ecclesiastical authority, but by the mercy and grace of God. The ecclesiastical authority merely approved the extolling of the new saint in church and his invocation in prayer.

Just what authority ought and could do this was not precisely determined; it was, in any case, an episcopal authority.

There were glorifications performed by the higher ecclesiastical authority of an entire local Church; the names of the newly glorified were then entered into all the church menologies of that Church; others were glorified more locally, and their veneration gradually spread to other places. Usually the glorification was performed in the locality where the saint had lived or died. But this was not always the case. For example, the youth George from the Serbian town of Kratov, who suffered in 1515 at the hands of the Turks in Sofia (Sredets, Bulgaria), was glorified fourteen years later in Novgorod. Although his compatriots also venerated him as a New Martyr and a service had even been composed to him by his spiritual father, fear of the Turks prevented them from revealing this openly. For this reason the archbishop in Novgorod, which had commercial ties with those places, ordained that a service be composed, and the memory of the martyr George the New began to be venerated there, whence it spread throughout all Russia. Later, when Serbia and Bulgaria were liberated from the Turks, they began using the service composed in Russia, while the original service composed in Sofia remains to this day a treasured property of the library.

In the course of the last two centuries, when Russia lived in glory and prosperity, the glorifications of new saints were celebrated with great solemnity by decree of the Higher Authority, sometimes (but not always) taking place all over Russia, and especially in the locality where the wonderworking relics were found. This does not, however, alter the general order in the Church, and if, under the scourge of the godless authority, the Russian people cannot openly extol and invoke a saint of God, glorified by God, it is the duty of that part of the Russian Church which is free from the scourge of the godless to extol and invoke that Wonderworker, like unto the holy Hierarch Nicholas, who today is praised throughout the world, and to pray to the holy, righteous John [of Kronstadt] for our personal amendment and for an end to the calamities which, as he prophesied, have befallen our homeland.

May the Lord grant the coming of that longed-for day when, from the Carpathians to the Pacific Ocean, will thunder out:

> We magnify thee, O righteous Father John,
> and we honor thy holy memory,
> for thou dost pray for us to Christ our God!

COME, O YE PEOPLE

GOD IS A HOLY Trinity. A Trinity consubstantial and indivisible. Consubstantial, that is, one essence, one nature. A Trinity indivisible: the Son has never been divided from the Father, nor the Holy Spirit from the Father or the Son, and never will be divided.

The Father, Son, and Holy Spirit are not three gods, but one God, since They have one nature. But not only because of this. People also have one nature, one essence. But with people one cannot say that two or three persons are one person, no matter how close and amicable they may be. People not only have separate bodies, but each one also has his own will, his own tastes, his own moods. No matter how similar people may be in body and character, it still never happens that everything is in common or that everything is the same.

With the Three Persons of the Holy Trinity everything is in common. The boundless love of the Father for the Son, of the Son for the Father, and the same love between them and the Holy Spirit make Their will and all of Their actions to be common. They have one will, and everything is performed by Them together. Whatever pleases the Father also pleases the Son and the Holy Spirit. Whatever displeases the Holy Spirit also displeases the Father. Whatever the Son loves, the Father and the Holy Spirit love also.

Everything is accomplished jointly by the Holy Trinity. At the creation of the world it says in the Bible: *And God said, Let there be light: and there was light* (Gen. 1:3). What does "said" mean? It means that God the Father created by His Word, by that Word of which the Gospel says, *In the beginning was the Word, and the Word was with God, and the Word was God* (John 1:1) and which is the Only-begotten Son of God.

God the Father created everything by His Word; in other words, He accomplished everything through His Son. The Father does not create anything without the Son, just as the Son does not create anything without the Father, and the Holy Spirit always assists the Father and the Son. It is said in the Bible about the creation of the world: *And the Spirit of God moved over the waters* (Gen. 1:2). It "moved" over creation, but did not merely move over it—the word in the Hebrew original, which lacks an exact equivalent in Slavonic, signifies "to cover," "to warm," just as a brood-hen sitting on her eggs gives life to them by her warmth, and from them come forth living creatures.

By the Word of the Lord were the heavens established, and all the might of them by the Spirit of His mouth (Ps. 32:6). All that exists was created by God the Father through the Son and was brought to life by the Holy Spirit. Or in other words, everything the Father wanted or wants, immediately was or is fulfilled by the Son and is animated by the Holy Spirit. Thus was the world created, thus was all accomplished by the providence of God concerning the world and mankind.

In order to save man, who through sin had fallen away from God and become mortal, the Son of God, in accordance with the pre-eternal counsel of the Holy Trinity, obeying the will of the Father, came down to earth, was born of the Ever-Virgin Mary through the action of the Holy Spirit, proclaimed to the people the True God the Father and His Divine will, and taught the true worship of God; having suffered for our sins, He descended in soul into hades, and, having freed the souls of the dead, He rose from the dead.

Even before His sufferings, Christ promised His Apostles, chosen by Him from among His disciples, to give them the power to loose and to bind—to remit people's sins or to leave them in their sins. After His Resurrection the Lord bestowed this gift of grace not on any of the Apostles separately, but on all of them together: He established His Church, the repository of that grace, and united in her all those who believe in Him and love Him.

Having promised His Apostles to invest them with power from on high, having sent them the Holy Spirit, and having accomplished all for which He came to earth, the Lord Jesus Christ ascended to heaven, receiving in His humanity that glory and honor which He had as the Son of God since before the creation of the world.

In descending upon the disciples of Christ, according to the promise, the Holy Spirit confirmed them in the faith of Christ and through His grace poured out upon them the gifts of God. He strengthened them for the preaching and fulfilling in life of Christ's teachings, for the building up of the Church established by Christ and put into action by the Holy Spirit.

The Church, standing on her foundation on earth and headed by the Son of God seated at the right hand of the Father, is mysteriously guided by the Holy Spirit. She inwardly links together all of her children and unites them with God. Through the Church, God's gifts of grace are poured out on those striving to follow the way of Christ; they sanctify and fortify all good in them, cleanse them from sin and every defilement, making them able to become receptacles of the radiance of the glory and power of God.

Through the Church man is made a partaker of the Divine nature, and he enters into the closest relationship with the Holy Trinity.

Not only the soul, but also man's body is sanctified and communes with God by partaking of the Body and Blood of Christ, through which he is united with the entire Holy Trinity. Through Divine grace, with the participation of his own will and effort, man becomes a new creature, a participant in the eternal Kingdom of God.

Nature, too, is being prepared for the coming Kingdom of God, for the coming purification by fire of the consequences of man's sin and the curse that lies on her. She receives the first fruits of sanctification through the descent of the Holy Spirit on her at Theophany in the blessing of the waters and in many other Church rites, so that she may later become a new earth and a new heaven.

This will be accomplished at the time appointed by God the Father, and the Son of God will come in glory to pronounce judgment on the world.

Then those who have loved God and have been united with Him will shine with the rays of Divine light and will eternally delight in the uncreated light of the Triune Godhead of the Consubstantial, Life-creating, and Indivisible Trinity.

To God, our Creator and Saviour, be glory, honor, and worship unto everlasting ages:

"Come, O ye people, let us worship the Godhead in Three Hypostases: the Son in the Father, with the Holy Spirit; for the Father timelessly begat the Son Who is Co-ever-existing and Co-enthroned, and the Holy Spirit was in the Father, glorified together with the Son; One Might, One Essence, One Godhead. In worshipping Whom let us all say: O Holy God, Who madest all things by the Son, through the cooperation of the Holy Spirit; Holy Mighty, through Whom we have known the Father, and through Whom the Holy Spirit came into the world; Holy Immortal, the Comforting Spirit, Who proceedest from the Father, and restest in the Son: O Holy Trinity, glory be to Thee." (Dogmaticon of Great Vespers of Pentecost)

I BELIEVE IN THE RESURRECTION OF THE DEAD

OUR GRIEF OVER the death of our close ones would be inconsolable and boundless if the Lord had not given us eternal life. Our life would be meaningless if it ended with death. What benefit, then, would there be from virtue or good deeds? They would be right who say, "Let us eat and drink, for tomorrow we die!" But man was created for immortality, and by His Resurrection Christ opened the gates of the Heavenly Kingdom, of eternal blessedness, to those who believe in Him and who live righteously. Our earthly life is a preparation for the future life, and this preparation ends with our death. *It is appointed unto men once to die, but after this the judgment* (Heb. 9:27). Then a man leaves behind all his earthly cares; his body disintegrates to rise again in the general resurrection. His soul, however, continues to live; not for a moment does it cease its existence.

Many appearances of the dead have given us to know in part what happens with the soul when it leaves the body. When it no longer sees with its bodily eyes, its spiritual vision is opened. This frequently occurs even before actual death; while seeing and even conversing with those around them, the dying see that which others do not. Leaving the body, the soul finds itself among other spirits, good and evil. Usually it strives towards those which are more akin to it, but if while still in the body it was under the influence of certain spirits, it remains dependent upon them when it leaves the body, no matter how unpleasant they might prove to be at the encounter.

For two days the soul enjoys relative freedom and can visit its favorite places on earth, but on the third day it makes its way towards other realms. At this time it passes through a horde of wicked spirits, who obstruct its path and accuse the soul of various sins by which they themselves had deceived it. According to revelations, there are twenty such barriers, so-called "toll-houses." At each stop the soul is tested as to a particular sin. Passing through one, the soul comes upon the next, and only after successfully passing through them all can the soul continue its way, and not be thrown straightway into gehenna. These demons and their trials are so horrendous that the Mother of God herself, when informed by Archangel Gabriel of her imminent repose, entreated her Son to deliver her from those demons and, in fulfillment of her prayer, the Lord Jesus Christ Himself appeared from Heaven to take the soul of His Most Pure Mother and carry it up to Heaven. The third day is terrifying for the soul, and it is especially in need of prayer.

Once having safely passed through the toll-houses and having bowed down before God, the soul spends the next thirty-seven days visiting the heavenly habitations and the chasms of hades, not knowing where it will find itself, and only on the fortieth day is it assigned its place of waiting until the resurrection of the dead. Some souls find themselves with a foretaste of eternal joy and blessedness, while others—in fear of eternal torments, which will begin in earnest after the Dread Judgment. Until that time, changes in the state of the soul are still possible, especially through offering for their sake the Bloodless Sacrifice (commemoration at the Divine Liturgy), and likewise through other prayers.

The importance of commemoration at Divine Liturgy is demonstrated by the following incident. Before the opening of the relics of Saint Theodosius of Chernigov (1896), the priest who had re-vested the relics sat down exhausted near the relics and dozed off. As he was sleeping the hierarch appeared to him and said, "Thank you for laboring on my behalf. I also ask that when you serve the Liturgy, you commemorate my parents," and he gave their names, Priest Nikita and Maria. "How is it that you, a holy hierarch, are asking my prayers, when you stand at the throne of Heaven and grant people God's mercy?" asked the priest. "That is true," replied the Saint. "But the offering at the Divine Liturgy is more powerful than my prayers."

The departed likewise benefit from memorial services and prayers at home on their behalf, and also from good deeds performed in their memory, as, for example, alms-giving and donations to churches. But they benefit most especially by being commemorated at the Divine Liturgy. There have been many appearances of the dead and other occurrences which confirm what great benefit lies in commemorating the departed. Many who died repentant but were unable to manifest this during their life, were released from torment and received repose. In church prayers are always offered for the repose of the departed, and even on the day of the descent of the Holy Spirit, in the kneeling prayers at Vespers, there is a special petition for those "who are held in hades." Each of us, desiring to show his love for the departed and to be of real help to them, can best do this by praying for them, and especially by commemorating them at the Divine Liturgy, when those particles taken out [cf the Lamb] for the living and the dead are placed into the Blood of the Lord with the words, "Through the prayers of Thy saints, wash away, O Lord, with Thy precious Blood the sins of those commemorated here." We can do nothing greater, nothing better for the departed than to pray for them, offering their names for commemoration at the Divine Liturgy. They are always in need of this, but especially during those forty days, when the soul of the deceased makes its way to the eternal mansions. The physical body no longer feels anything, it does not see its close ones who have gathered, it does not smell the fragrance of the flowers, it does not hear the graveside soliloquies. But the soul senses the prayers offered in its behalf, and it is grateful to those who offer them and is spiritually close to them.

Relatives and dear friends of the departed! Do what is needful for them and what lies in your power. Rather than expending money on the external adornment of the coffin and grave, spend it on helping the poor, in memory of your close ones who have fallen asleep, and on churches, where prayers are offered on their behalf. Show mercy to those who have fallen asleep; attend to the good of their soul. That path awaits all of us. How great will be our desire then to be remembered in prayer! Let us be merciful to the departed. As soon as someone passes away, straightway call a priest, so he can read "The Office at the Departure of the Soul," which is appointed to be read over every Orthodox Christian immediately after his repose. Make every effort to arrange for the funeral to be served in a church and, until the funeral, to have the Psalter read over the deceased. The funeral need not be elaborate, but it must not be abbreviated; think not of yourself and your own comfort, but about the deceased, with whom you are parting forever. If in the church there are several deceased at the same time, do not object to having a joint funeral service. It is better that a funeral be served for two or more deceased at once, for the prayers of all their close ones gathered together will be yet more fervent than if the services were conducted in succession and the services abbreviated owing to lack of time and energy; because each word of prayer is for the departed like a drop of water to a thirsty man. Likewise, it is essential to make immediate arrangements for the forty-day memorial, that is, the daily commemoration of the departed at the Divine Liturgy during the first forty days. Usually, in churches where there are daily services, those whose funerals were served there are commemorated over the course of these forty days and longer. But if the funeral is served in a church which does not have daily services, those close [to the deceased] must arrange for a forty-day memorial in a church which does. It is good likewise to send for commemoration the name of the departed to monasteries and to Jerusalem, where there are constant prayers at the holy places. But it is important that the forty-day memorial begin immediately after the person dies, when the soul is particularly in need of prayer, and for that reason to begin the commemoration in the nearest place where there are daily services.

Let us look after those who precede us into the other world, and do for them all that we can, remembering that *Blessed are the merciful, for they shall obtain mercy.*

IN THE BEGINNING
WAS THE WORD

At THE LITURGY on the day of the Bright Resurrection, we read the beginning of the Gospel of Saint John, concerning the Divine Word. When all is filled with the light of Christ's Resurrection, when the heavens are united with the earth in the glorification of the Vanquisher of death, the Gospel proclaims Who He is: *In the beginning was the Word*.

Mention of the Word is made already in the Old Testament: *By the Word of the Lord were the heavens established, and all the might of them by the Spirit of His mouth* (Ps. 32:6); *He sent forth His Word and He healed them* (Ps. 106:20). The book of the Wisdom of Solomon speaks especially clearly and expressively about the mighty acts of the Word of God.

However, the Old Testament people understood the Word of God to mean simply the manifestation of God's will and activity. Now Saint John announces that the Word of God is verily the Only-begotten Son of God Himself, the Second Person of the Holy Trinity.

Why is the Son of God also called "the Word"?

Because through Him the Father expresses His will.

The Word of God is not the same as a human word. Man uses words to express his thoughts and desires. But the words man utters fall silent and disappear. The desires they express are sometimes fulfilled, but often they remain unfulfilled.

The Word of God is eternal and omnipotent. He is always with God. A man's word is his servicing faculty. The Word of God is the Second Person of the Holy Trinity. He Himself is God.

God the Word is the Son of God, and He loves the Father and willingly does everything according to His will. More precisely—They have one will.

God the Father loves His Son and creates everything through Him. Nothing is created by Him without the Son, "by Whom all things were made." Everything has its beginning through Him and without Him nothing began to exist that exists: *All things were made by Him; and without Him was not any thing made that was made* (John 1:3) (as it is expressed by the second article of the Symbol of Faith). When in the book of Genesis it says that at the creation of the world God said, *Let there be light. . . let there be a firmament. . ,* this means that God the Father desired to create light, the firmament, and the rest, and that the Word, His Son, brought this to fulfillment.

The Word of God gives life. He is the source of life: *In Him was life, and the life was the light of men.*

The Word of God is light. Through Him God the Father reveals Himself and makes known His divine will: *That was the true Light, which lighteth every man which cometh into the world* (John 1:9). No darkness can conceal that Light: *the Light shineth in darkness; and the darkness comprehended it not* (John 1:5).

After the Fall, the darkness of sin took hold of mankind, but it could not conceal the Divine Light.

In accordance with the will of the Father, the Son of God, having descended to earth and become incarnate, sanctified the world. *And the Word was made flesh and dwelt among us* (John 1:14).

To prepare the way for Him in men's hearts, God sent John the Forerunner. He preached about Christ and called all to believe in Him, for He was the Son of God.

Long before that time, the Law was given through Moses. But the Law, which restrained evil, could not save men. While outwardly fulfilling the Law, men remained full of evil within. For this reason the world did not recognize its Creator, the Son of God, when He came to earth: *He was in the world, and the world was made by Him, and the world knew Him not. He came unto His own, and His own received Him not* (John 1:10-11). The guardians of the Law did not accept the incarnate Word, for His light was unbearable to them.

148

But the Source of Life, Whom they gave over to death, descended to hades, destroyed it, and dispersed the darkness with His Divine Light.

Having risen from the dead, Christ opened the gates of the Kingdom of His glory to all those who believe in Him. Those who believe in the incarnate Son of God and accept Him into their heart and soul become children of God. The grace of God spiritually regenerates them, dwelling in them and giving them power to love the Truth and to do the Lord's will. *As many as received Him, to them gave He power to become the sons of God, even to them that believe on His name* (John 1:12).

Those regenerated by grace—if they continue in it to the end of their earthly life, and follow that path indicated by Christ, the True Light—will be deemed worthy of receiving from Him a new gift: they will delight eternally in the Kingdom of the Heavenly Father through beholding the glory of His Only-begotten Son, a glory surpassing everything in the world, and they will experience ineffable joy and blessedness.

This same pre-eternal Word of God, by Whom the world was made, saved and regenerated the human race unto a new and joyous life through His Incarnation and Resurrection.

The Bright Resurrection is the triumph of God the Word, the day of His victory over hades and death, the beginning of a new life and of eternal gladness—His gift.

Let us, O ye faithful, praise and worship the Word, Who with
the Father and the Spirit is without beginning, and Who was
born of the Virgin for our salvation; for He was pleased
to ascend the Cross in the flesh and to endure death,
and to raise the dead by His glorious Resurrection.

(Resurrection Troparion, Tone 5)

O Only-begotten Son and Word of God, Who art immortal, . . .
trampling upon death by death, Thou Who art One of the Holy Trinity,
glorified with the Father and the Holy Spirit, save us.

149

AN INSTRUCTIVE LESSON FOR YOUTH FROM THE PARABLE OF THE PRODIGAL SON

And the younger of them said to his father, Father,
give me the portion of goods that falleth to me.
(Luke 15:11-32)

THE PARABLE of the Prodigal Son is a most instructive lesson for youth. We see in the prodigal son the true character of flighty youth: light-minded, thoughtless, thirsting for independence; in short, everything that usually distinguishes the majority of youths. The younger son grew up in his parents' house. On reaching adolescence, he already began to imagine that life at home was too restrictive. It seemed unpleasant to him to live under his father's rule and his mother's watchful eye. He wanted to imitate his comrades, who had given themselves up to the noisy pleasures of the world. "I am the heir of a rich estate. Would it not be better," he reasoned, "if I received my inheritance now? I could manage my wealth differently than my father does." Thus the light-minded youth was carried away by the deceitful glitter of the world's pleasures and decided to throw off the yoke of obedience and to depart from his parents' home.

Are not many inspired by similar impulses today, and, while they may not leave their parents' home, do they not depart from the home of their Heavenly Father, that is, from obedience to the Holy Church?

The yoke of Christ seems difficult for immature minds, and His commandments burdensome. They think that it is not really necessary to keep that which God and His Holy Church command us. To them it seems possible to serve God and the world at the same time. They say, "We are already strong enough to withstand destructive temptations and seductions. We can hold on to the truth and sound teachings by ourselves. Allow us to perfect our minds through acquiring many kinds of knowledge. Let us strengthen our wills ourselves amid temptations and seductions. Through experience our senses will become convinced of the vileness of vice!" Are such desires any better than the ill-considered request of the younger son to his father, "Father, give me the portion of goods that falleth to me" ?

And so, a light-minded youth ceases to heed the commandments and admonitions of the Holy Church. He ceases to study the Word of God and the teachings of the Holy Fathers, and listens intently to the sophistries of those who are falsely-called teachers, and in these pursuits he kills the best hours of his life. He goes to church less frequently or stands there inattentively, distracted. He does not find the opportunity to devote himself to piety and to exercise himself in the virtues, because he spends so much time attending shows, public entertainments, etc. In a word, with each day he gives himself up more and more to the world, and, finally, he goes off to "a far country."

What is the result of such an estrangement from the Holy Church? It is the same as the result of the prodigal son's leaving his parents' house. Light-minded youths very quickly waste their excellent energies and talents of soul and body, ruining for time and eternity all the good they have done. Meanwhile, there appears "a mighty famine in that land": emptiness and dissatisfaction—the inevitable result of wild pleasures. A thirst for enjoyments appears, which intensifies with the gratifying of wanton passions, and finally becomes insatiable. It often happens that the unfortunate lover of the world, in order to gratify his passions, resorts to base and shameful pursuits, which do not bring him to his senses like the prodigal son and do not return him to the path of salvation, but complete his ruin, both temporal and eternal!

A WORD ON REPENTANCE

Open to me the doors of repentance,
O Giver of Life!

REPENTANCE IS EXPRESSED by the Greek word, *metanoia*. In the literal sense, this means a change of mind. In other words, repentance is a change of one's disposition, one's way of thinking; a change of one's inner self. Repentance is a reconsideration of one's views, an alteration of one's life.

How can this come about? In the same way that a dark room into which a man enters is illumined by the rays of the sun. Looking around the room in the dark, he can make out certain things, but there is a great deal he does not see and does not even suspect is there. Many things are perceived quite differently from what they actually are. He has to move carefully, not knowing what obstacles he might encounter. When, however, the room becomes bright, he can see things clearly and move about freely.

The same thing happens in spiritual life.

When we are immersed in sins, and our mind is occupied solely with worldly cares, we do not notice the state of our soul. We are indifferent to who we are inwardly, and we persist along a false path without being aware of it.

But then a ray of God's Light penetrates our soul. And what filth we see in ourselves! How much untruth, how much falsehood! How hideous many of our actions prove to be, which we fancied to be so wonderful. And it becomes clear to us which is the true path.

If we then recognize our spiritual nothingness, our sinfulness, and earnestly desire our amendment—we are near to salvation. From the depths of our soul we shall cry out to God: "Have mercy on me, O God, have mercy according to Thy mercy!" "Forgive me and save me!" "Grant me to see my own faults and not to judge my brother!"

As Great Lent begins, let us hasten to forgive each other all hurts and offenses. May we always hear the words of the Gospel for Forgiveness Sunday: *If ye forgive men their debts, your heavenly Father will also forgive you; but if ye forgive not men their debts, neither will your Father forgive your debts* (Matt. 6:14-15).

A BRIEF SERMON ON THE DAY OF THE HOLY SPIRIT

IN THE OLD Testament there are only obscure indications of the Divine Mystery of the Holy Trinity. The Holy Bible says that before the creation of man, God said, *Let us make man according to our image and likeness,* which indicates that God is not one Person. But there is no indication as to how many persons are in the Godhead and who these conversers and co-creators are.

Elsewhere [in the Old Testament] the Divine Trinity is revealed somewhat more clearly, in the story of the Righteous Abraham, but again, only in the visible form of three angels.

In the New Testament the mystery of the Holy Trinity is manifest three times: at the Baptism, at the Transfiguration, and at the descent of the Holy Spirit.

At the Baptism the Divine voice was heard: *This is My Beloved Son,* when the incarnate Son of God, the God-man, set out on His exploit of saving man. Here is the glory of God the Father, and His exultation at seeing this feat of love. God the Son stands in the streams of the Jordan in the form of a servant, while God the Holy Spirit, in the form of a dove, confirms the word of the Father, which testifies to the Divinity of the Son, Who humbly bows His head beneath the right hand of the Forerunner.

SERMON ON THE SUNDAY OF ORTHODOXY

In the midst of two thieves, Thy Cross was found to be
a balance of justice; for the one was borne down to hades
by the weight of his blasphemy; the other was raised up
from his sins to the knowledge of theology.
O Christ our God, glory be to Thee.

(Hymn on the Glory of Ninth Hour for Great Lent)

THIS IS WHAT is said about the Cross of the Lord. A balance of justice was found between two thieves. Pilate erected three crosses on Golgotha—two thieves and one Life-giver. But only the Cross of the Saviour provided salvation for all mankind, that Cross which stood in the center; it is a weapon of peace, an invincible victory—victory over the devil and victory over death. As for the two remaining crosses, one was soul-saving for the one who hung on it, while the other was for the second thief a ladder to hades.

Two thieves hung on crosses next to the Lord Jesus Christ; one never stopped reviling Him; the other began by reviling but then came to his senses and, becoming aware of his sins, cried out to the Lord: *Remember me, O Lord, when Thou comest into Thy Kingdom!* And the Lord replied, *This day shalt thou be with Me in Paradise!* So it was that through the Cross, through suffering, the wise thief came to believe in the crucified Christ; he believed, as it is said, "to the knowledge of theology." But when the Lord forgave him his sins, he recognized Him to be the Very Son of God; he understood that the Man hanging in disgrace and dishonor was the glorious King of Glory; he understood that He, Who at that moment appeared weak and powerless, was the Very omnipotent Creator and Ruler of the entire universe. Through repentance, through humility, the thief who hung on the right side came to understanding; the eyes of his mind, the eyes of his soul were opened. Christ abased Himself more than all men, He abased Himself in order to wipe out, to annihilate the sin of Adam's pride. So too, the thief, humbly acknowledging his sins, asked the Lord's forgiveness, and through this the Lord appeared to him in all His glory. But that other thief, hanging on the left, constantly mocked Him; he mocked Him because he realized that he was a sinner, that he was a criminal, that he had violated the laws of both man and God, but he did not want to repent, he did not want to humble himself, and he reviled those very laws which he had transgressed; he reviled the Lawgiver Himself, Who had given the laws of nature, Who had endowed men with a conscience, according to which they write their own human laws, although they do not always agree with it; and he continued reviling Him until his soul went down to hades.

Here are two paths placed before man. Before us lies the Life-creating Cross of the Lord. The Lord said, *If any man will come after Me, let him. . . take up his cross and follow Me.* Follow where? At first through sufferings, just as Christ also suffered; then he will also enter with Christ into the Eternal Kingdom, the Kingdom of Heaven, where the Lord Jesus Christ sits on His throne. There is no other path except to follow the Lord. The thief who hung on the right recognized Him to be God and, in his soul, followed after Him. He could not, of course, become miraculously transformed, and this was not necessary; he followed Christ in his soul, recognizing Him to be God Who had humbled Himself for the sake of saving mankind. The thief humbled himself likewise, acknowledged his transgressions, and went with Christ into Paradise.

Before us lie the paths of the two thieves. Which path shall we take? Mankind has always taken one or the other path. The Cross of the Lord was to the Jews a stumblingblock; to the Greeks—that is, to the pagans—it was foolishness: how could anyone bow down before an instrument of humiliation, an instrument of torture? They did not understand that by means of this instrument the Lord saved all of mankind from the dominion of the devil, from the dominion of sin, from eternal perdition.

For the Jews also, the Cross of the Lord was an offense; they wanted to see their messiah as a king of glory, as an earthly king who would exalt the Jewish race. The Cross on which Christ was crucified was for them a stumblingblock; Christ's crucifixion was perceived as an offense, as something senseless, and yet, as the holy Apostle Paul tells us, this stumblingblock unto the Jews, this foolishness unto the Greeks is for us *Christ the power of God, and the wisdom of God* (I Cor. 1:24). What for some spelled perdition, for others became a source of salvation.

The Cross of the Lord separates men into two parts. We see that some believed in Christ, while others stumbled at that stumblingstone (Rom. 9:32) and persecuted Christ's Church, the Body of Christ, whose Head is the Lord Jesus Christ Himself. The Church of Christ is the Body of Christ; He Himself is its Head, and with His Divine Body and Blood He nourishes the faithful, He nourishes the children of His Church, making us one with Himself. And we should be one with Christ, bodily and spiritually. We unite ourselves with Christ in body through Divine Communion; spiritually we must also join with Him and eagerly follow His commandments.

We all sin, but some sin and repent, while others mock the laws which they violate. So it was in ancient times, when Arius and other heretics repudiated the dogmas of the Holy Church. And then the faithful often suffered. They suffered when there were impious rulers who sent them into banishment. Saint Athanasius the Great spent twenty of his forty-seven years as a hierarch in exile. And other hierarchs suffered similarly for the truth, as did many of the faithful. But within the purity of Orthodoxy they found salvation and opened the gates of eternal life, the gates of the Kingdom of Heaven. There were times when the unbelievers triumphed, when they trampled the Church of Christ; but then came their demise, and their souls were sent—not to the Kingdom of Heaven but into everlasting torments in the nethermost depths, just as Christ once sent to hades the soul of Herod and others who had sought His life.

We have before us the path of salvation, or the path of perdition. Even to some Christians the Cross proved a stumblingblock during the iconoclast period, when they began to persecute holy icons, when they began to defame other sacred objects, including the Cross of the Lord. And these were those who called themselves "right-believing," who considered themselves to be Orthodox. The iconoclast heresy prevailed for a hundred and fifty years before it was finally eradicated.

On the day of the Triumph of Orthodoxy we celebrate Christ's victory over iconoclasm and over all demons. The Cross of the Lord separated believers from unbelievers, those who followed the path of salvation from those who followed the path of perdition. Today's iconoclasts—Protestants and others who reject holy icons—likewise reject the Cross of the Lord. They allow pretty pictures of various biblical events to hang in their homes, but they repudiate the veneration of icons, which remind us that salvation is attained by following a difficult path, a narrow path, such as the Lord Jesus Christ Himself followed, a path of battling one's sins and vices, a path of fasting and prayer. Those who want to see Christianity only as something rosy and attractive, who think it possible to enter the blessedness of eternity without any particular effort, without forcing themselves, without warring with their passions—they deny all this. They follow the path taken by the thief who hung on the left: they reject all the laws which the Lord Himself delivered and which He sent the Apostles to preach throughout the world; they reject those statutes and writings which are sacredly preserved by the holy Orthodox Church.

And so, through the Cross some are being saved unto the knowledge of theology, the knowledge of eternal Truth, while others are being pulled down by the weight of blasphemy into the torments of hades. Such a broad path lies before us Orthodox, and here are temptations which separate believers if they desire to follow that path which Christ has indicated to them.

We all sin, we all transgress Christ's commandments and the laws of the holy Church, but some acknowledge themselves to be sinners and repent of their transgressions, while others, instead, reject the very laws and do not want to submit to them; they say that these laws are out-dated, that they are no longer needed; as if we are smarter than those who gave us the Church laws, which the Lord Himself gave through His Apostles and hierarchs. Here before you are two paths: the path of the wise thief, and the path of the one who was pulled down to hades by the weight of his blasphemy.

We also have here before us eternal [iconographic] creations. Some are prepared to recognize icons if they are well executed, if they are aesthetic and pleasing to the eye. Others venerate those icons in which saints are depicted in their sufferings, where their martyric exploits are reflected, their fasts and vigils; these sacred depictions portray an inner nobility rather than any external comeliness. Here, brethren, is the path of the two thieves. Some desire salvation, others desire only enjoyment in this world, and when they do not succeed in obtaining it they blaspheme those laws which are given for our salvation.

Even today various divisions can spring up among us. The laws of Christ's Church are immutable; a Christian must submit to them irrespective of what others think, of how society regards these laws—whether favorably or unfavorably. Those faithful to Christ follow after Him along the path of those laws, those ordinances which the holy Church sacredly preserves. Those who desire unnecessary comforts and pleasures in this temporal world—which sooner or later will perish—these people prefer other laws, not the laws of the Church but those which allow them to live as they want, to think what they want, to place their own will above the spirit of the Church, that spirit given by the Lord God Himself; and they invite others to follow this same path.

It may be, brethren, that soon you will again experience a time of turmoil, and some of you will be called to take the path of denying those sacred laws and to submit to laws established by mere human authority. Beware of such a path! Beware of the path taken by the thief on the left, for by the weight of blasphemy, by the weight of reviling Christ he went to his eternal perdition. Those who revile the laws of the Church revile Christ Himself, Who is the Head of the Church, for the laws of the Church were given by the Holy Spirit through the Apostles. And the laws of local Churches are based on those same laws and canons of the Church. Let us not consider ourselves wiser than those saints and hierarchs who established the rules of the Church; let us not imagine ourselves to be great sages. Rather, let us humbly call out together with the wise thief, *Remember me, O Lord, in Thy kingdom!*

Pray for the forgiveness of sins. If we transgress the laws of the Church, if we constantly violate them, pray that the Lord have mercy and lead us together with the wise thief into the Kingdom of Heaven. Then we will not follow the path taken by the ungodly thief, who remained ungodly to the end and descended into the nethermost depths. From which may the Lord deliver us all. Amen.

CONCERNING TALENTS AND ICONOGRAPHY

THE LORD SPOKE a parable about a master who distributed talents to his servants, each man according to his abilities. After a certain time had passed, he demanded an accounting from each and rewarded those who earned as much as they had received. But the one who did nothing and simply returned the talent he had been given was punished severely. The master is the Lord God, the talents are His gifts, the servants are men. The Lord grants spiritual gifts; He grants them to individuals, and also to entire nations.

Until the Coming of Christ, God's words were entrusted to Israel. When Israel wavered in faith, when Judea began to fall, the Prophet Baruch, a disciple of the Prophet Jeremiah, called out, *This is the book of the commandments of God, and the law that endureth for ever: all they that keep it shall come to life; but such as leave it shall die. Turn thee, O Jacob, and take hold of it: walk in the presence of the light thereof, that thou mayest be illuminated. Give not thine honor to another, nor the things that are profitable unto thee to a strange nation. O Israel, happy are we; for things that are pleasing to God are made known unto us* (Baruch 4:1-4).

Israel, however, did not keep God's commandments and, rejecting the Son of God, fell away from God. The Lord founded His New Testament Church, into which many formerly pagan peoples entered. After Christianity's victory over paganism, Byzantium became the special guardian of Orthodoxy. There the Ecumenical Councils and Holy Fathers of the Church established a precise exposition of the dogmas of the Faith and Orthodox teaching. After the fall of Byzantium, the Orthodox Faith was preserved best by the Russian people, who by that time had thoroughly absorbed it. Their way of life, the country's civil laws, its customs—all were grounded in the Orthodox faith or conformed to it.

One representation of the Orthodox Faith is the temple, and the Russian land was covered with them. The Orthodox temple itself is an image of the invisible universal Church, of which we speak in the Symbol of Faith: "In One Holy, Catholic [meaning "universal"] and Apostolic Church." This is why our temples are also called churches. Rising aloft, the cupola symbolizes for us a striving towards Heaven and reminds us of the heavenly vaults beneath which our prayers ascend to God. It reminds us of the invisible heavens, God's kingdom on high.

Churches are adorned with icons. Icons are not simply pictures of certain people or events. An icon is a symbol of the invisible. It depicts not only the outward, visible countenance of the Lord and His saints, but also their inner likeness, their sanctity.

Even secular paintings often personify certain ideas. Let us take, for example, the famous statue of Peter the Great in Petrograd; here he is represented high up on a rearing horse, symbolic of how high, in many respects, he raised up Russia. Many other statues similarly convey certain ideas. If this is true of secular art, it should be true all the more of religious art, which portrays the sublime, the heavenly, the spiritual. An icon is not a portrait; a portrait depicts only a person's earthly aspect, while an icon depicts also his inner state. Even if only the external features are depicted, at different times the subject will have a different expression. Blessed Metropolitan Anthony related how, as a student at the Theological Academy, he and some classmates attended services in Kronstadt celebrated by righteous Father John. When Father John ended the Liturgy he appeared radiant, just like Moses when he came down from Mount Sinai. Shortly afterwards Father John received them in his cell and was his usual self. Our Lord Jesus Christ Himself once showed us His divine glory on Mount Tabor, while at other times He looked like an ordinary man, and people wondered, amazed, at the source of His power and miracles.

An icon ought to depict not only the outward but also the inner life, holiness and closeness to heaven. This is depicted primarily in the face and its expression, and the rest of the icon should conform to this. Our Orthodox iconographers directed all their attention to conveying the state of the soul, concealed beneath the flesh. The more successful this attempt was, the better the icon was. The execution of other parts of the body was frequently inadequate, not because this was done consciously by the iconographers but because the attainment of their principal goal did not always allow them to pay sufficient attention to secondary aspects. One might add that even in taking ordinary photographs, especially candid ones, many would undoubtedly show unnatural positions of the body, which ordinarily we would not notice. One cannot paint an icon by depicting the external aspect alone; this external representation must reflect the unseen struggles and must radiate with heavenly glory. This can be achieved most successfully by the person who himself leads a spiritual life, and who understands and deeply reveres the lives of the saints. Our ancient iconographers, in engaging in this art, always prepared for it with prayer and fasting. To many icons executed in this manner the Lord granted wonderworking power.

Of course, every icon, after it is sanctified, should be revered and must not be treated with disdain or disrespect. We should therefore refrain from passing judgment on icons which have already found a place in churches, but we must always strive towards what is better, and, what is most important, our attention should be directed not so much towards the aesthetic appeal of icons as to their spirituality. Icons that do not satisfy the requirements of Orthodox iconography ought not be placed in churches or in homes. Icons cannot be painted by simply anyone who has a talent for art and who is capable of their artistic execution. Often the state of the person painting an icon and a desire to serve God are of greater significance than artistic skill. In Russia, after the reign of Peter the Great, along with the good which arrived from the West, many novelties foreign to the spirit of Orthodoxy entered into Russia. A significant portion of Russia's educated class fell under this influence, which injected much that was unhealthy and bad into their literary and artistic works. This tendency was also reflected in iconography. Instead of emulating the ancient Russian iconographers, they began to emulate artists of the West, who were unfamiliar with Orthodoxy. The new images, although they were very beautiful, did not correspond to the spirit of iconography. This spirit, foreign to Orthodoxy, began to take root in Russia and gradually unsettled her. The words of the prophet are addressed to us today: *Give not of thy glory to another, and what is beneficial to thee to an alien people.* Just as in life, so, too, in church traditions we must return to those firm and pure foundations on which Russia was built and secured herself. One reflection of these foundations is our iconography. Icons for our churches must not be painted in a spirit foreign to Orthodoxy. Some think this means icons must be painted in dark colors, with unnatural positioning of the bodies. This is not true. Ancient icons were painted with bright colors and darkened over time with the accumulation of dust. At the same time, it must be remembered that many saints were in fact dark-complexioned, having spent their lives in hot deserts, and many had bodies that were indeed emaciated with long years of ascetic struggle. Theirs was not an earthly but a heavenly beauty. Through their prayers may they help our churches become reflections of heavenly glory and help our flock to unite in seeking the Kingdom of God and to preach—not only through the church but also through life—the truth of Orthodoxy.

A SERMON ON THE DAY OF THEOPHANY

TODAY THE nature of the waters is sanctified. Today the Son of God is baptized in the waters of Jordan, having no need Himself of cleansing, but in order to cleanse the sinful human race from defilement.

Now the heavens open and the voice of God the Father is heard: *This is My beloved Son.* The Holy Spirit descends upon the Saviour of the world, Who stands in the Jordan, thereby confirming that this indeed is He Who is the incarnate Son of God. The Holy Trinity is clearly made manifest and is revealed to mankind.

The waters of the Jordan are sanctified, and together with them all the waters of creation, the very nature of water. Water is given power to cleanse not only the body, but also man's whole soul, and to regenerate the whole man unto a new life through Baptism.

Through water all of nature is cleansed, for out of water the world was made, and moisture penetrates everywhere, giving life to everything else in nature. Without moisture neither animals nor plants can live; moisture penetrates into rocks, into every place in the world.

The waters are sanctified and through them the whole world, in preparation for renewal and regeneration for God's eternal Kingdom which is to come.

Every year on this day the glory of God is revealed, renewing and confirming what was accomplished at Christ's Baptism. Again the heavens are opened; again the Holy Spirit descends. We do not see this with our bodily eyes, but we sense its power. At the rite of blessing, the waters which are thereby sanctified are transformed; they become incorruptible and retain their freshness for many years.

Everyone can see this—both believers and unbelievers, both the wise and the ignorant.

Whence do the waters acquire this property?

It is the action of the Holy Spirit.

Those who with faith drink these waters and anoint themselves with them receive relief and healing from spiritual and bodily infirmities. Homes are sanctified by these waters, the power of demons is expelled, God's blessing is brought down upon all that is sprinkled with these waters. Through the sanctifying of the waters God's blessing is again imparted to the whole world, cleansing it from the sins we have committed and guarding it from the machinations of the devil.

Today the Holy Spirit, descending upon the waters when the Cross of Christ is immersed into them, descends upon all of nature. Only into man He cannot enter without his will.

Let us open our hearts and souls to receive Him and with faith cry from the depth of our souls: "Great art Thou, O Lord, and marvelous are Thy works, and there is no word which sufficeth to hymn Thy wonders."

164

THE CHURCH AS
THE BODY OF CHRIST

> *And He [Christ] is the head
> of the body, the Church (Col. 1:18),
> which is His body, the fulness of Him
> that filleth all in all. (Eph. 1:22)*

IN THE HOLY Scripture, the Church is repeatedly called the Body of Christ.

Who [Paul] *now rejoice in my sufferings for you, . . . for His Body's sake, which is the Church* (Col. 1:24), the Apostle Paul writes about himself.

Apostles, prophets, evangelists, pastors and teachers, he says, are given by Christ . . . *for the work of the ministry, for the edifying of the Body of Christ* (Eph. 4:11-12).

At the same time, bread and wine are made into the Body and Blood of Christ during the Divine Liturgy, and the faithful partake thereof. Christ Himself ordained it, in communicating His apostles at the Mystical Supper with the words, *Take, eat; this is My Body; . . . Drink ye all of it; For this is My Blood of the New Testament* (Matt. 26:26-28).

How is the Body of Christ at the same time both the Church and the Holy Mystery?

Are the faithful themselves both members of the Body of Christ, the Church, and also communicants of the Body of Christ in the Holy Mysteries?

In neither instance is this name, "Body of Christ," used metaphorically, but rather in the most actual sense of the word. We believe that the Holy Mysteries, while keeping the appearance of bread and wine, are the very Body and the very Blood of Christ. We likewise believe and confess that Christ is the Son of the Living God, come into the world to save sinners; that He became true man, and that His flesh, taken from the Virgin Mary, was actual human flesh; that in body and soul Christ was a true man, like other men in all respects except sin, while remaining at the same time true God. In this incarnation, the Divine nature was neither diminished nor changed in the Son of God; likewise the human nature was not changed at this incarnation, but retained in full all human qualities.

Unchanged and unconfused forever, indivisibly and inseparably, Godhead and manhood were united in the One Person of the Lord Jesus Christ.

The Son of God became incarnate to make people partakers of the Divine nature (II Peter 1:4), to free them from sin and death, and to make them immortal.

Uniting ourselves with Christ, we receive Divine grace which gives human nature strength for victory over sin and death. By His teaching, the Lord Jesus Christ has shown people the way to victory over sin, and He grants them eternal life, making them partakers of His eternal Kingdom by His Resurrection. In order to receive from Him that Divine grace, the closest possible contact with Him is necessary. Drawing all to Himself by His divine love, and uniting them unto Himself, the Lord has united to each other those who love Him and come unto Him, uniting them into one Church.

The Church is unity in Christ, the closest union with Christ of all who rightly believe on Him and love Him, and their union is through Christ.

Now the Church consists of both her earthly and heavenly parts, for the Son of God came to earth and became man that He might lead man into heaven and make him once again a citizen of Paradise, returning to him his original state of sinlessness and wholeness and uniting him unto Himself.

This is accomplished by the action of Divine grace granted through the Church, but man's effort is also required. God saves His fallen creature by His own love for him, but man's love for his Creator is also necessary; without it he cannot be saved. Striving toward God and cleaving unto the Lord by its humble love, the human soul obtains power to cleanse itself from sin and to strengthen itself for the struggle to complete victory over sin.

The body also partakes in that struggle; now it is a receptacle and instrument of sin, but it is foreordained to be an instrument of righteousness and a vessel of holiness.

God created man, breathing divine breath into the animate body He had created earlier from the earth. The body was to have been an instrument of the spirit, subject to God, for through it the human spirit manifests itself in the material world. Through the body and its separate members, the spirit reveals its properties and qualities which God gave it, as to His own image, which is why the body also, as a manifestation of the image of God, is both called and is indeed "our beauty created in the image of God" (sticheron from the Funeral Service).

When the first-created people fell away in spirit from their Creator, the body, hitherto subject to the spirit and obtaining its directions through the soul, ceased to be subordinate to it and began to strive to dominate it. In place of the law of God, the law of the flesh began to rule man.

Sin, having cut man off from the source of life—God, rent man asunder. The union of spirit, soul, and body was violated, and death entered into him. The soul, no longer surrounded by the streams of life, could not transmit them to the body, which became corruptible, and the soul began to languish.

Christ came to earth to restore the fallen image and return it to union with Him Whose image it is. Uniting man unto Himself, God thus restores him to his original goodness in all its fulness.

Granting grace and sanctification to the spirit, Christ also purifies, strengthens, heals, and sanctifies the soul and the body.

But he that is joined unto the Lord is one Spirit [with Him] (I Cor. 6:17). The body, then, of the man who has been united unto the Lord, must be an instrument of the Lord, must serve for the fulfillment of His will, and become a part of the Body of Christ.

For a man's complete sanctification, the body of the servant of the Lord must be united with the Body of Christ, and this is accomplished in the Mystery of Holy Communion. The true Body and the true Blood of Christ which we receive become part of the great Body of Christ.

Of course, for union with Christ, the mere conjoining of our body with the Body of Christ does not suffice. The consumption of the Body of Christ becomes beneficial when in spirit we strive toward Him and unite ourselves with Him. Receiving the Body of Christ, while turning away from Him in spirit, is like the contact with Christ which they had who struck Him and mocked and crucified Him. Their contact with Him served not for their salvation and healing, but for their condemnation.

But those who partake with piety, love and readiness to serve Him, closely unite themselves with Him and become instruments of His Divine will.

He that eateth My flesh and drinketh My blood, dwelleth in Me, and I in him, said the Lord (John 6:56).

Uniting with the Risen Lord, and through Him with the entire Eternal Trinity, man draws from It power for eternal life and himself becomes immortal.

As the living Father hath sent Me, and I live by the Father: so he that eateth Me, even he shall live by Me (John 6:57).

All who believe in Christ and unite themselves unto Him by giving themselves to Him and by the reception of Divine Grace, jointly comprise the Church of Christ, whose Head is Christ Himself, and they who enter into her are her members.

Christ, invisible to the bodily eye, clearly manifests Himself on earth through His Church, just as the invisible human spirit manifests itself through its body. The Church is the Body of Christ both because her parts are united to Christ through His Divine Mysteries, and because through her Christ works in the world.

We partake of the Body and Blood of Christ, in the Holy Mysteries, so that we ourselves may be members of Christ's Body: the Church.

This is not accomplished instantly. To fully abide in the Church is already a state of victory over sin and complete purification therefrom. Everything sinful estranges us from the Church to some degree, and keeps us out of the Church. This is why, in the prayer read over every penitent at Confession, we hear, ". . . reconcile and unite [him/her] unto Thy Holy Church." Through repentance a Christian is cleansed and he is united closely to Christ in partaking of the Holy Mysteries. Later, however, the dirt of sin again settles upon him and estranges him from Christ and the Church, and therefore repentance and Communion are again necessary.

Until man's earthly life finishes its course, up to the very departure of the soul from the body, the struggle between sin and righteousness continues within him. However high a spiritual and moral state one might achieve, a gradual or even headlong and deep fall into the abyss of sin is always possible. Therefore, communion of the holy Body and Blood of Christ, which strengthens our contact with Him and refreshes us with the living streams of the grace of the Holy Spirit flowing through the Body of the Church, is necessary for everyone. The great importance of partaking of the Holy Mysteries is seen in the life of Saint Onuphrius the Great to whom, as well as to other hermits living in the same desert, angels brought Holy Communion; and in the life of Saint Mary of Egypt, whose final wish after many years in the desert was to partake of the Holy Mysteries. And there are similar examples in the lives of Saint Sabbatius of Solovki and many others. Not in vain did the Lord say, *Amen, amen, I say unto you, except ye eat the Flesh of the Son of Man, and drink His Blood, ye have no life in you* (John 6:23).

To partake of the Body and Blood of Christ is to receive in oneself the Risen Christ, the Victor over death, Who grants to those with Him victory over sin and death.

Preserving in ourselves the grace-filled gift of Communion, we have a guarantee and foretaste of the blessed, eternal life of the soul and body.

Up to the very "Day of Christ," His Second Coming and the Judgment of the whole world, the struggle of sin with righteousness will continue, individually in each person, and collectively in all mankind.

The earthly Church unites all who are reborn through baptism and who have taken up the cross of the struggle with sin, and who follow after Christ, the contest-master of this struggle. The Divine Eucharist, the offering of the bloodless sacrifice and partaking thereof, sanctifies and strengthens its partakers and makes those who receive of the Body and Blood of Christ true members of His Body, the Church. But only with death is it determined whether a man remained a true member of the Body of Christ to his last breath, or whether sin triumphed in him and drove out the grace which he received in the Holy Mysteries and which bound him to Christ.

He who, as a member of the earthly Church, has reposed in grace, goes over from the earthly Church into the heavenly Church; but he who falls away from the earthly Church will not enter into the heavenly, for the Church in this world is the way into the heavenly.

The more one is found to be under the influence of the grace of communion and the more tightly one has united himself to Christ, the more one will find pleasure in communion with Christ in His coming Kingdom.

It is important to partake of the Mysteries of Christ just before death, when the lot of a man is determined forever. It is necessary to try to receive just before death, if there be even the slightest possibility of this, to beseech the Lord to find us worthy of this and to take thought for others, so that they may not be deprived of Communion before the end.

Inasmuch as sin continues to operate in the soul until death, so the body is liable to its consequences, bearing in itself the seeds of disease and death from which it is freed only when it decays after death, and then rises at last free of them in the general resurrection. He who unites himself in spirit and in

170

body with Christ in this life will be with Him in spirit and in body in the life to come. The grace-filled streams of the life-creating Mysteries of the Body and Blood of Christ are the wellspring of our eternal joy in converse with the risen Christ and in the contemplation of His glory.

The same consequences of sin, not yet completely driven out from the human race, operate not only in individual people, but through them they are manifested in the earthly activity of entire parts of the Church. Heresies, schisms, and disputes arise constantly, tearing away part of the faithful. Misunderstandings between local Churches or parts of them have troubled the Church since antiquity, and prayers for their cessation are repeatedly heard in the Divine services.

"We pray for the unity of the Churches," "unity to the Churches" (Triadic, Resurrection Canon, Tone 8), "Set aright the dissensions of the Church" (service to the Archangels, 8 November, 26 March, 13 July), and similar prayers have been offered by the Orthodox Church through the centuries. Even on Holy and Great Saturday, before the *epitaphion* of Christ, the Church pronounces: "O most blameless, pure Virgin, who didst bring forth the Life, stop the scandals of the Church, and grant peace as thou are good" (last verse of the second stasis of the Lamentations).

Only when Christ appears on the clouds will the tempter be trampled down, and all scandals and temptations disappear. Then the struggle between good and evil, between life and death will cease, and the earthly Church will merge with the Church Triumphant, in which God will be *all in all* (I Cor. 15:28).

In the Kingdom of Christ to come, there will no longer be a need to receive the Body and Blood of Christ, for all who have been vouchsafed it will be in closest converse with Him and will enjoy the pre-eternal light of the Life-originating Trinity, experiencing that blessedness which no tongue can express, and which is incomprehensible to our feeble mind. For this reason, after partaking of the Holy Mysteries at Liturgy, in the altar there is always said the prayer which we sing during the Paschal season: "O Christ, Thou great and most sacred Pascha! O Wisdom, Word and Power of God! Grant us to partake of Thee more perfectly in the unwaning day of Thy Kingdom" (Ninth Ode, Paschal Canon).

HOMILY ON THE TWO BANQUETS

IN THE NAME of the Father and the Son and the Holy Spirit.

Today's Gospel readings present before us a mental image of two banquets. One banquet, described in the parable, was arranged by a king full of benevolence and mercy. When, however, the banquet was ready, those invited did not come. They preferred to occupy themselves—one with buying, another with his domestic affairs; others seized and insulted those who were sent to call them and even killed some of them. The incensed king, having severely punished the guilty, again sent forth his servants—to invite to the banquet whomever they should meet. Many gathered, and when the king came to see them, he noticed one who was not in proper festive attire. The king asked why it was he had not come suitably dressed. The man was silent, indicating disdain for the king and a lack of desire to participate in the festivities, and for this reason he was made to leave. And so, at this banquet there were many who had been called, but few turned out to be chosen, who took part in the supper.

The other banquet belonged not to a parable but to reality. It was a banquet of the iniquitous Herod. It seems that in this case none of those invited refused to come, all were dressed as befitted the occasion, and they enjoyed themselves immensely. The evening passed in drunkenness, in revelry uninhibited by shame or conscience, and it concluded with a monstrous crime, the murder of John the Baptist.

These two banquets are images of two ways of life, two kinds of enjoyment. The first is an image of the spiritual banquet, of spiritual enjoyment. It is arranged by the Lord. This is the banquet of Christ's Church. We are invited to this banquet when we are called to participate in the Divine services, especially the Divine Liturgy and the Communion of the Divine Body and Blood of Christ; when we are called to good works, to vigilance and sobriety. We refuse to go to that banquet when we do not go to church services, when instead of good we do evil, when we prefer life's cares and pleasures to godly life. We come without a wedding garment when we bring an alien, sinful disposition into that life. Each of us is invited to that banquet many times a day, and we refuse each time we prefer what is carnal and sinful to what is spiritual and divine.

Every day we are likewise invited to Herod's banquet. Often we do not immediately realize that we are being tempted by evil. Sin always begins with a small thing. Herod at first even delighted in listening to John the Baptist; inwardly he realized the sinfulness of his conduct, but he did not war against sin and he ended up murdering the great Saint. We go to Herod's sordid banquet each time instead of good we choose carnal, sinful pleasures and hardheartedness; each time we choose to disregard our souls, and so forth.

Once having begun with what appears small or trivial, it is difficult to stop, and if afterwards we do not catch ourselves in time and do not forcefully take ourselves in hand, we can fall into grave sins and crimes, for which eternal torments await us.

Even now John the Baptist calls to each of us: *Repent, for the Kingdom of Heaven is at hand.* Repent, in order to enjoy the supper of the Lamb, slain for the sins of the whole world, in the bright, eternal mansions, and not to share with the devil the banquet of malice and torment in Tartarus (in the nether regions) and outer darkness.

A TALK ON THE
DREAD JUDGMENT

TODAY IS THE Sunday of the Dread Judgment, and it is natural for us to speak of the Dread Judgment and of the signs of the end of the world. No one knows that day; only God the Father knows; but the signs of its approach are given in the Gospel and in the Revelation [Apocalypse] of the holy Apostle John the Theologian. Revelation speaks of the events at the end of the world and of the Dread Judgment principally in images and in a concealed manner; but the Holy Fathers have explained it, and there is an authentic Church tradition that speaks to us both about the signs of the approach of the end of the world and about the Dread Judgment.

Before the end of life on earth there will be confusion, wars, civil strife, famine, and earthquakes. Men will suffer from fear; they will expire from the expectation of calamities. There will be no life, no joy of life, but a tormenting state of falling away from life. There will be a falling away not only from life, but from faith as well: *when the Son of Man cometh, shall He find faith on the earth?* [Luke 18:8]

Men will become proud and ungrateful, denying the Divine Law: together with a falling away from life there will be also a dearth of moral life.

There will be an exhaustion of good, and a growth of evil. The holy Apostle John the Theologian, in his divinely-inspired work, the Revelation, also speaks of this time. He himself says that he "was in the Spirit," which means that the Holy Spirit Himself was in him when the fate of the Church and the world was revealed to him in various images, and that is why it is God's Revelation.

He represents the fate of the Church in the image of a woman who, in those times, hides in the wilderness: she does not show herself in public life, just as in Russia today.

Those forces that are preparing the appearance of Antichrist will have a leading significance in public life. Antichrist will be a man and not the devil incarnate. "Anti" is a word meaning "old," or it means "in place of" or "against." That man wants to be in place of Christ, to occupy His place and possess that which Christ ought to possess. He wants to possess the same attraction and authority over the whole world.

And he will receive that authority before his own destruction and that of the whole world. He will have a helper, a Magus, who, by the power of false miracles, will fulfill his will and kill those that do not recognize the authority of Antichrist. Before the destruction of Antichrist, two righteous men will appear who will denounce him. The Magus will kill them and their bodies will lie unburied for three days, and Antichrist and all his servants will rejoice exceedingly. Then suddenly, those righteous men will resurrect, and the whole army of Antichrist will be in confusion and horror, and the Antichrist himself will suddenly fall dead, slain by the power of the Spirit.

But what is known about this man, Antichrist? His precise ancestry is unknown. His father is completely unknown, while his mother is a defiled, pretended virgin. He will be a Jew from the tribe of Dan. There is an indication of this, in that Jacob, when dying, said that [Dan], in his posterity, would be *a serpent by the way...biting the heel of the horse (and the rider shall fall backward).* [Gen. 49:17] This is a figurative indication that he will act with craftiness and evil.

In Revelation, John the Theologian speaks of the salvation of the sons of Israel, that before the end of the world a multitude of Jews will be converted to Christ; but the tribe of Dan is not included in the enumeration of the tribes that are saved.

Antichrist will be very intelligent and gifted with the ability to deal with people. He will be charming and affectionate.

The philosopher Vladimir Soloviev worked extensively on this subject in order to present the advent and the personality of Antichrist. He made careful use of all relevant materials, not only Patristic, but also Muslim, and produced a very striking picture.

Before the advent of Antichrist, his appearance is already being prepared in the world. "The mystery is already at work" [cf. II Thess. 2:7], and the forces preparing his appearance struggle above all against lawful royal authority. The holy Apostle Paul says that Antichrist cannot appear until "he that restrains" is removed. John Chrysostom explains that "he that restrains" is the lawful, godly authority.

Such an authority struggles with evil. The "mystery" working in the world does not want this; it does not want an authority that wars against evil; on the contrary, it wants an authority of iniquity, and when it succeeds in bringing this about, then nothing will stand in the way of the coming of Antichrist. He will be not only intelligent and charming: he will be compassionate, he will be charitable and do good, for the sake of consolidating his power. And when he will have strengthened it sufficiently, so that the whole world acknowledges him, then he will show his real face.

176

He will choose Jerusalem as his capital, because it was here that the Saviour revealed His Divine teaching and His Person, and the whole world was called to the blessedness of goodness and salvation. But the world did not accept Christ and crucified Him in Jerusalem; while under Antichrist, Jerusalem will become the capital of the world that has recognized the authority of Antichrist.

Once having attained the summit of power, Antichrist will demand that men acknowledge his attainment as something to which no other earthly power and no other man could possibly attain, and he will demand that men bow down to him as to a superior being, a god.

Soloviev describes well the character of his activity as Supreme Ruler. He will do what pleases men, on the condition that they recognize his Supreme Authority. He will let the Church function, and allow her to hold Divine services, he will promise to build magnificent temples—provided he is recognized as the "Supreme Being" and that he is worshipped. He will have a personal hatred for Christ. He will live by this hatred and will rejoice at seeing men apostatize from Christ and the Church. There will be a mass falling away from the faith; even many bishops will betray the faith, justifying themselves by pointing to the splendid position of the Church.

A search for compromise will be the characteristic disposition of men. Straightforwardness of confession will vanish. Men will cleverly justify their fall, and an endearing evil will support such a general disposition. Men will grow accustomed to apostasy from the truth and to the sweetness of compromise and sin.

Antichrist will allow men everything, if only they "fall down and worship him." This is not something new. The Roman emperors were similarly prepared to grant the Christians freedom, if only they recognized [the emperor's] divinity and divine supreme authority; they martyred Christians only because they professed: "Worship God Alone and serve Him Alone."

The whole world will submit to him, and then he will reveal his hatred for Christ and Christianity. Saint John the Theologian says that all who worship him will have a mark on their forehead and right hand. It is not clear whether this will be an actual mark on the body, or if this is a figurative expression of the fact that men will acknowledge in their minds the necessity of worshipping Antichrist, as well as submit their wills to him. And when the whole world manifests such a complete submission—of both will and conscience—, then the two righteous men [already] mentioned will appear and will fearlessly preach the faith and expose Antichrist.

Holy Scripture says that before the coming of the Saviour two "lamps," will appear, two "burning olive trees," "two righteous men." Antichrist will kill them by the power of the Magus. Who are these men? According to Church tradition, these are the two righteous who never tasted of death: the Prophet Elias and the Prophet Enoch. There is a prophecy that these saints, who had not tasted of death, will taste it for three days; but after three days they will resurrect.

Their death will be a great joy for Antichrist and his servants. Their rising three days later will bring them unspeakable horror, terror and confusion. And then will come the end of the world.

The Apostle Peter says that the first world was created out of water and perished by water. "Out of water" is also an image of the chaos of the physical mass, while "perished by water" is [an image] of the Flood. And now the world is *reserved unto fire. . . . . The earth also and the works that are therein shall be burned up* (II Peter 3:7, 10). All the elements will melt. This present world will perish in a single instant. In an instant everything will change.

And the sign of the Son of God will appear, that is, the sign of the Cross. The whole world, having willingly submitted to Antichrist, "will break out in lamentation." Everything is

178

finished. Antichrist is slain. The end of his kingdom, the end of the war with Christ. The end, and accountability for one's whole life, an account to the True God.

Then, from the mountains of Palestine, the Ark of the Covenant will appear. The Prophet Jeremiah hid the Ark and the Holy Fire in a deep well. When they took water from that well, it burst into flame. But the Ark itself they did not find.

When we look at life today, those able to see, see that everything foretold about the end of the world is being fulfilled.

Who then is this man—Antichrist? Saint John the Theologian figuratively gives him the name 666; but all attempts to understand this designation have been futile.

The life of the contemporary world gives us a fairly clear understanding of the possibility of the world burning up, when all *the elements shall melt with fervent heat.* Atomic fission gives us that understanding.

The end of the world does not signify its annihilation, but its transformation. Everything will be changed, suddenly, in the twinkling of an eye. The dead will resurrect in new bodies—their own, but renewed—just as the Saviour arose in His Body, and on it were the traces of the wounds from the nails and the spear; but it possessed new properties, and in this respect it was a new body. It is unclear whether this will be an altogether new body or that with which man was created.

And the Lord will appear on the clouds with glory. How will we see Him? With our spiritual eyes. Even now, at death, righteous people see that which other people around them do not see.

The trumpets will sound, loud and powerful. They will trumpet in men's souls, in their conscience. Everything in the human conscience will become clear.

The Prophet Daniel, speaking of the Dread Judgment, relates how the Ancient of Days, the Judge, is on His throne, and before Him is a river of fire. Fire is a purifying element. Fire scorches sin, it burns it up, and woe also burns it up; if sin has become natural to a man, then it burns up the man himself as well.

That fire will flare up inside a man: on seeing the Cross, some will rejoice, while others will fall into despair, confusion, terror. In this way, men will immediately be separated. In the Gospel narrative, some stand to the right of the Judge, some to the left—their inner consciousness separated them. The very state of a man's soul casts him to one side or the other, to the right or to the left.

The more consciously and persistently a man strives toward God in his life, the greater will be his joy when he hears the words: "Come unto Me, ye blessed"; and conversely, those same words will call forth the fire of horror and torment on those who did not want Him, who fled or fought or blasphemed Him during their life.

The Dread Judgment knows no witnesses or charge-sheets. Everything is recorded in men's souls, and these records, these "books" are open. Everything becomes clear to all and to oneself, and the state of a man's soul assigns him to the right or to the left.

Some go to joy, others to horror.

When the "books" are open, it will become clear to all that the roots of all vices are in man's soul. Here is a drunkard, a fornicator; some may think that when the body dies the sin dies as well. No; the inclination was in the soul, and to the soul the sin was sweet.

And if [the soul] has not repented of that sin and has not become free of it, it will come to the Dread Judgment with the same desire for the sweetness of sin and will never satisfy its desire. In it will be the suffering of hatred and malice. This is the state of hell.

The "fiery Gehenna" is the inner fire; this is the flame of vice, the flame of weakness and malice; and *there will be* [the] *wailing and gnashing of teeth* of impotent malice.

180

ZACCHAEUS

And Jesus entered and passed through Jericho. And behold, there was a man named Zacchaeus, which was the chief among the publicans, and he was rich. And he sought to see Jesus Who He was; and could not for the press, because he was little of stature. And he ran before, and climbed up into a sycamore tree to see Him: for He was to pass that way. And when Jesus came to the place, He looked up and saw him, and said unto him, Zacchaeus, make haste and come down, for today I must abide at thy house. And he made haste, and came down, and received Him joyfully. And when they saw it, they all murmured, saying that He was gone to be guest with a man that is a sinner. And Zacchaeus stood and said unto the Lord: Behold, Lord, the half of my goods I give to the poor; and if I have taken away anything from any man by false accusation, I restore him fourfold. And Jesus said unto him, This day is salvation come unto this house, forsomuch as he also is a son of Abraham. For the Son of Man is come to seek and to save that which was lost. (Luke 19:1-10)

WHO WAS Zacchaeus? He was a leader of publicans, "the chief among the publicans." The common comparison between the humble publican and the proud Pharisee often obscures a correct characterization of these two images in our minds. In order to understand the Gospel correctly, one must have a clear picture of just who they were.

The Pharisees were actually righteous men. If our calling someone a "pharisee" sounds like a condemnation, in the days of Christ and during the first decades of Christianity this was not so. On the contrary, the Apostle Paul emphatically confesses before the Jews, *I am a Pharisee, the son of a Pharisee. . .* (Acts 23:6) And later on, to the Christians, to his spiritual children, he writes, *I am of the stock of Israel, of the tribe of Benjamin, an Hebrew*

181

of the Hebrews, as touching the law, a Pharisee (Phil. 3:5). Beside the holy Apostle Paul, many other Pharisees became Christians: Joseph, Nicodemus, Gamaliel. Pharisees (in ancient Hebrew *perusim;* in Aramaic, *pherisim,* which means "other"—those who were separate, different) were zealots of the law of God. They "rested upon the law"; in other words, they meditated upon it continually, they loved it and strove to fulfill it exactly, they preached and interpreted it. The reason for the Lord's denunciations against the Pharisees is to warn them that all their struggle, all their really good efforts, they render worthless in the eyes of God, they turn them to naught, and acquire for themselves not a blessing from the Lord, but condemnation, by pridefully exalting themselves on account of their righteous deeds and, mainly, by judging their neighbors. A striking example of this is given by the Pharisee of the parable, who says, *God, I thank Thee, that I am not as other men* (Luke 18:11).

By contrast, publicans were unmistakable sinners, who broke the most fundamental laws of the Lord. Publicans were collectors of taxes from the Jews on behalf of the Romans. One must remember that the Jews, conscious of their exclusive position of being divinely chosen, gloried in the fact that they were *Abraham's seed, and were never in bondage to any man* (John 8:33). But now, as a result of well-known historical circumstances, they found themselves in subjection, in bondage to a proud, coarse, "iron" people, the pagan Romans. And the yoke of this bondage was being pulled tighter and tighter and was becoming increasingly painful.

The most tangible and obvious sign of this bondage and subjection of the Jews to the Romans was the payment of all kinds of taxes—tributes—by the Jews to their enslavers. For the Jews, as for all ancient peoples, bringing tribute was for the most part a symbol of subjection. And the Romans, not in the least inhibited before a subjugated people, roughly and imperiously exacted of them both customary and supplementary taxes.

Naturally, the Jews paid back with hatred and disgust. Not without reason did the Scribes, desiring to compromise the Lord in the eyes of His people, ask Him, *Is it lawful to give tribute to Caesar?* (Matt. 22:17). They knew that if Christ were to say that one should not give tribute to Caesar, it would be easy to accuse Him before the Romans, while if He said it is necessary to pay tribute, He would be hopelessly compromised in the eyes of the people.

While the Romans ruled Judea by means of local kings, such as Herod, Archelaus, Agrippa, and others, this bondage to Rome—and especially the necessity of paying taxes—was mitigated somewhat for the Jews in that they were only indirectly subject and paid tribute to their kings, who in turn were subject to and paid Rome. But just before Christ began His preaching ministry, there was a change in the system of governing Judea. The universal census connected with the Nativity cf Christ was the first step towards the establishment of a head tax upon all Roman subjects in that locale.

In A.D. 6 or 7, after the removal of Archelaus, when a personal tax upon all inhabitants of Palestine was introduced, the Jews retaliated with revolts led by the Pharisee, Sadduc, and Judas the Galilean (cf. Acts 5:37). It was only with great difficulty that the High Priest Joazar was able to calm the people. Instead of local kings, Roman procurators were appointed as rulers of Judea and neighboring provinces. For a more successful levying of taxes by the Romans, the institution of publicans was then introduced. This had existed in Rome from ancient times, but while in Rome and throughout Italy publicans were recruited from a respected class of knights [*equites*], in Judea the Romans had to engage publicans from among moral outcasts, from among Jews who agreed to go over to work for them and force their brothers to pay tribute.

The acceptance of such a position was bound up with a most profound moral fall. It was bound up not only with a national but, above all, a religious betrayal; in order to become a tool for the enslavement of the divinely-chosen people by coarse pagans, one had to renounce the hopes of Israel, everything holy to it, its expectations. What is more, a publican, upon accepting a position, had to swear a pagan oath of fidelity to the emperor, and perform a pagan sacrificial offering to his spirit, the "genius" of the emperor. (The Romans did not take into account the religious sensibilities of their agents.) Not only did the publicans serve Rome's interests by levying taxes upon their own countrymen, but, by pursuing their own mercenary goals and enriching themselves at the expense of their enslaved brothers, they made the yoke of Roman oppression still more onerous. This is what the publicans were. This is why they were surrounded by well-founded hatred and scorn: they were betrayers of their people, betraying not only their own but a divinely-chosen people, God's instrument in the world, the only people through which rebirth and salvation could come to mankind.

Everything said here applies to Zacchaeus to the highest degree, because he was not an ordinary publican but a *chief* among publicans—an *architelonis*. Without doubt he had done everything: offered pagan sacrifices and sworn a pagan oath, ruthlessly extracted taxes from his brothers, increasing them to his own advantage. And he became, as the Gospel testifies, a rich man. Of course, Zacchaeus understood clearly that the hopes of Israel were lost for him. Everything proclaimed by the prophets and beloved from childhood, that which caused every believing Old Testament soul "that knoweth jubilation," to tremble joyfully, was not for him. He was a traitor, a betrayer, an outcast. He had no part in Israel. And now rumors reached him that the Holy One of Israel, the Messiah announced by the prophets, had appeared in the world and, together with a small group of disciples, was walking the fields of Galilee and Judea, preaching the Gospel of the Kingdom and performing great miracles. In believing hearts, joyous hopes were ignited. How will

Zacchaeus react to this? For him personally, the coming of the Messiah is a catastrophe. The rule of the Romans must come to an end, and triumphant Israel will undoubtedly take revenge for the damage suffered because of him, for the offences and oppressions caused by him. But even if this is not so—for the Messiah, as the prophet testified, comes as a righteous one, bringing salvation, as a meek one (cf. Zech. 9:9)—the triumph of the Messiah must bring to him, to Zacchaeus, only the greatest disgrace and the loss of all the wealth and of the position he acquired at the terrible price of his treachery before God, his own people, and all the hopes of Israel.

But perhaps this is not so, not yet. Perhaps the new preacher is not really the Messiah. Not everyone believes in Him. The Pharisees and Sadducees—the greatest foes of the publicans and of him, Zacchaeus, in particular—do not believe in Him. Perhaps all this is just the idle talk of the populace. In that case, one can calmly continue living as one has until now. But Zacchaeus does not want to be confirmed in such thoughts. He wants to see Jesus, in order to know, to really know: Who is He? Zacchaeus wants the preacher passing by to truly be Christ the Messiah. He wants to say with the prophets, *Oh, that Thou wouldst rend the heavens, that Thou wouldst come down!* (Is. 64:1). Let this be so, even if it entails a ruinous catastrophe for him, Zacchaeus. In his soul, it seems, there are such depths that he himself has not sensed up to now; there is in him a burning, flaming, consuming, completely unselfish love for the "Expectation of the Nations," for the image of the meek Messiah described by the prophets, *Who hath borne our griefs and carried our sorrows* (Is. 53:4). And when an opportunity comes to see Him, Zacchaeus does not think of himself. In the triumph of the Messiah, for him personally, for Zacchaeus, there lies catastrophe and ruin. But he does not think of this. He wants to glimpse, at least from the corner of his eye, Him Whom Moses and the prophets had foretold.

And now Christ is passing by. He is surrounded by a crowd. Zacchaeus, being short of stature, cannot see Him. But the thirst, the utterly unselfish thirst of Zacchaeus to see Christ, at least from afar, is so boundless, so overwhelming, that he—a wealthy man, invested in status, an official of the Roman Empire, in the midst of a hostile crowd that hates and scorns him—pays no attention to anything and, consumed by the burning desire to see Christ, disregards all convention and outward decorum, and climbs up a tree, a sycamore growing along the way. And the eyes of this great sinner—leader of traitors and betrayers—meet the eyes of the Holy One of Israel, Christ the Messiah, the Son of God. Jesus sees that which is inaccessible to an indifferent or hostile glance. Selflessly loving the image of the Messiah, Zacchaeus is immediately able to recognize Christ the Lord in the passing Galilean Teacher; and the Lord, filled with Divine and human love, sees this in Zacchaeus, who is peering at Him from the branches of the sycamore; He sees those spiritual depths of soul hitherto unknown even to Zacchaeus himself. The Lord sees that the burning love for the Holy One of Israel in this heart of a traitor, a love not in the least blemished by any sort of self-interest, could regenerate and renew him. The Divine voice sounds: *Zacchaeus, make haste and come down, for today I must abide at thy house.* And moral regeneration, salvation, and renewal came to Zacchaeus and his entire house. The Son of Man truly came to seek and to save the lost.

O Lord, O Lord, we too have betrayed Thee and Thy work, as once did Zacchaeus; we have deprived ourselves of a portion in Israel; we have betrayed our hope! But even if it is to our shame and the shame of those like us, let Thy kingdom come! and Thy victory and Thy triumph! Even if, deservedly according to our sins, Thy coming will bring us ruin and condemnation, come, O Lord, come quickly! But grant us, at least from afar, to see the triumph of Thy righteousness, even if we cannot be participants in it. And have mercy on us beyond hope, as once Thou hadst mercy on Zacchaeus!

(Saint Clement of Rome testifies that Zacchaeus subsequently became a companion of the holy Apostle Peter, and, together with the holy Pre-eminent Apostle, preached in Rome, where under Nero he accepted a martyr's death for Christ. In a Christian manner, he repaid the Romans with the greatest good for the greatest evil that was all but perpetrated upon him by them. To the proud capital of the Romans who had once tempted and enslaved him, forcing him to renounce all that was holy to his soul, he came, liberated and regenerated by the grace of our Lord, the Lover of man, and he brought Rome not curses, but the Good News, for which he gave his very own life.)

WHY THE WISE THIEF WAS PARDONED

And one of the malefactors which were hanging railed on Him, saying, If thou be Christ, save thyself and us. But the other rebuked him, saying, Dost thou not fear God, seeing thou art in the same condemnation? And we indeed justly; for we receive the due reward of our deeds: but this man hath done nothing amiss. And he said unto Jesus, Lord, remember me when Thou comest into Thy kingdom. And Jesus said unto him, Verily I say unto thee, Today shalt thou be with Me in paradise. (Luke 23:39-43)

THIS IS HOW the holy Evangelist Luke relates the edifying and moving incident concerning the conversion and the Lord's pardoning of the thief who hung on the cross next to Him on Golgotha.

How did the thief deserve such mercy? What prompted such a quick and definitive response from the Lord? All the righteous figures of the Old Testament, including Saint John the

Baptist, were still shut up in hades. The Lord Himself was preparing to descend into hades, not, of course, to suffer there, but to bring out the prisoners.

The Lord had not yet promised anyone to lead them into the Kingdom of Heaven; even the Apostles were promised to be taken into His mansions only after He had prepared them.

How is it that a thief was granted such mercy before anyone else? Why were the gates of Heaven opened so quickly for him? Let us examine the soul of the thief and the attendant circumstances.

His whole life had been one of theft and crime. But evidently his conscience had not died, and in the depths of his heart something good remained. Tradition even holds that he was that very thief who, during Christ's flight into Egypt, took pity on the beautiful Baby and forbade his accomplices to kill Him, when they attacked the holy family. Did he perhaps recall the face of that Child when he looked upon the face of the One hanging next to him on the Cross?

Whether or not this actually occurred, when the thief looked upon Christ his conscience was awakened. There he was hanging next to the Righteous One, next to Him Who was *comely in beauty more than the sons of men* (Ps. 44:2), Whose form at that time was ignoble, and inferior to that of the children of men. . . , *having neither form nor comeliness* (Is. 53:2-3).

Gazing upon Him, the thief awoke as it were from a deep sleep. He saw clearly the difference between Him and himself. That One was without doubt a Righteous One, Who forgave even His tormentors and prayed for them to God, Whom He called His Father; while he was the killer of many victims, one who had shed the blood of people who had done him no harm.

Gazing upon the One hanging on the Cross, he saw as in a mirror his moral downfall. All the good concealed within him was awakened and surfaced. He came to a realization of his sins, he understood that it was his own fault that had brought him to this bitter end; he had no one to blame. Like the thief crucified on Christ's left, he too had been gripped by hatred for the executioners, but this gave way to a feeling of humility and compunction. He felt fear at God's coming judgment.

Sin became loathsome, dreadful. In his soul he was no longer a thief. There awakened in him feelings of love for mankind, merciful kindness. With his fear over the fate of his soul there was united a revulsion to the outrage being heaped upon the innocent Sufferer.

He had undoubtedly heard about the great Teacher and Wonderworker from Nazareth. What had occurred in Judea and in Galilee was the subject of many conversations and debates throughout the country. Previously, he had paid scant attention to any of this. Now, finding himself together with Him and in the same situation, he began to understand His moral greatness.

Christ's lack of malice, His all-embracing forgiveness, His prayer, astonished the thief. He understood in his heart that beside him was no ordinary man. To turn to God as to One's own father, in the hour of death, was possible only for Someone who truly knew Himself to be the Son of God. Not to waver in One's teaching about love and unconditional forgiveness, to bear the humiliation of men's slander and malice on the part of those to whom one has done good, was possible only for One who had the most intimate relationship with the source of Love, or Who was that Love.

The thief recalled all the remarkable things he had heard about the One now crucified with him, and a warm feeling of faith was kindled in his heart. Yes, He was without doubt the Son of God, incarnate on earth while existing in uninterrupted communion with His Father; the Son of God, Whom the earth did not receive and Who was returning to Heaven; the Son of God, Who was able and powerful to forgive men their sins! That gave hope that the thief would escape condemnation at the Dread Judgment. If Jesus prayed to His Father for His hangmen,

He would not refuse to do the same for the one crucified with Him. The thief need only turn to Him, Who now shared with him the same bitter suffering, and He would receive him into His blessedness.

True, his turning to Christ with words of love and sympathy would be met with jeers on the part of the angry crowd. To acknowledge Him as a holy man and the Son of God would mean drawing upon himself the attention and anger of the Hebrew elders. Although they could not cause him greater physical agony than he already endured, it would be painful to be surrounded by malice; how much more grievous his sufferings would be when they began to revile him likewise.

But what did he care now about the anger of earthly authorities, about men's taunts. As painful as it was to be abandoned by men at the threshold of death, it would be still more painful to be abandoned by God. He was nearing God's judgment, and it was God alone he need fear! In the final moments of life, he had to do whatever was still in his power to gain God's good will.

Perhaps he could say something to ease His suffering even just a little, perhaps even just one of the blasphemers would be ashamed and stop slandering Him. Christ had promised to give a reward for a cup of water offered in His name; surely He would not leave him without recompense. Let those reviling Christ revile him also! This would tighten his bond with Christ! He was going to share Christ's lot here; Christ would surely remember him when He came into His glory!

There, amidst the clamor of slander, blasphemy and derision, he began exhorting his companion hanging to the left of Christ to stop slandering Him. *Dost not thou fear God, seeing thou art in the same condemnation? And we indeed justly: for we receive the due reward of our deeds: but this man hath done nothing amiss.* And then from his lips came a humble voice: *Remember me, O Lord, when Thou comest into Thy kingdom* (Luke 23: 40-42).

This was the cry of a former thief—now Christ's new disciple—who came to believe in Christ at a time when His other disciples had abandoned Him.

"A thief blessed Him, while I denied Him" (Sedalion, Tone 5), Saint Peter lamented afterwards. At that time all the other Apostles likewise doubted the Lord. Even Saint John the Theologian, who had followed inseparably after his Teacher and was standing at the Cross on Golgotha, although he continued to be faithful to his beloved Jesus, even he did not then have complete faith in the Divinity of his Teacher. It was only after the Resurrection, after entering the empty tomb where lay the napkin and grave clothes which had wrapped Christ's dead Body, only then did he "see and believe" that Christ had truly risen and was indeed the Son of God.

The Apostles wavered in their faith in Jesus as the Messiah, because they anticipated and desired to see in Him an earthly king, in whose kingdom they could sit at the right and the left hand of the Lord.

The thief understood that the Kingdom of Jesus of Nazareth, despised and given over to a shameful death, was not of this world. And it was precisely this Kingdom that the thief now sought: the gates of earthly life were closing after him; opening before him was eternity. He had settled his accounts with life on earth, and now he thought of life eternal. And here, at the threshold of eternity, he began to understand the vanity of earthly glory and earthly kingdoms. He recognized that greatness consists in righteousness, and in the righteous, blamelessly tortured Jesus he saw the King of Righteousness. The thief did not ask Him for glory in an earthly kingdom but for the salvation of his soul.

The faith of the thief, born of his esteem for Christ's moral greatness, proved stronger than the faith of the Apostles, who, although captivated by the loftiness of Christ's teaching, based their faith to a still greater extent on the signs and wonders He wrought.

Now there was no miraculous deliverance of Christ from His enemies—and the Apostles' faith was shaken.

But the patience He exhibited, His absolute forgiveness, and the faith that His Heavenly Father heard Him so clearly, indicated Jesus' righteousness, His moral superiority, that one seeking spiritual and moral rebirth could not be shaken.

And this is precisely what the thief, aware of the depth of his fall, craved. He did not ask to sit at the right or the left hand of Christ in His Kingdom, but, conscious of his unworthiness, he asked in humility simply that he be remembered in His Kingdom, that he be given even the lowest place.

Before everyone he openly confessed the Crucified Christ as Lord, and asked of Him the mercy of forgiveness.

His humble faith in Christ made him a confessor. By his own volition he was even a martyr, for he did not fear to recognize as his Lord the rejected "King of the Jews"—on Whom was concentrated the hatred of the multitude who had gathered in Jerusalem from all corners of the world for the Passover, and who, together with their elders and priests, were blaspheming Christ. The thief would not have feared even to suffer for Him.

Thus, the earnest repentance of the thief gave birth to humility, and together with this turned out to be a solid foundation for a strength of faith which at that time not even Christ's closest disciples possessed. The converted thief performed a spiritual feat which not one of them was then capable of doing.

Whoever shall confess Me before men, him will I confess also before My Father which is in heaven (Matt. 10:32).

The thief confessed Christ; he confessed Him before a whole multitude who were railing at Him; he confessed Him then when no one else dared, and when even those few disciples and women who remained faithful to Him manifested their love for Him only with their bitter tears.

The thief did what once the three youths in Babylon did, refusing to bow down before the golden idol which Nebuchad-

Belfort, France, November 1954.

Right: Tunis, 1955.

Below: in Tunis, 1955, with Hieromonk Mitrofan, at the consecration of the Church of the Resurrection.

Archbishop John presides at a meeting of hierarchs.

At the funeral of Bishop Leonty in Geneva, 1956.
Cathedral of the Exaltation of the Cross.

Right: with Archbishop Tikhon in San Francisco.

Below: Archbishop John, Archbishop Tikhon and Bishop Anthony of Melbourne (now Archbishop of San Francisco) in 1956.

In America, early 60s.

1960s. With Bishop Nektary at a Russian scout camp in California .

The raising of the crosses onto the cupolas of the San Francisco Cathedral.
Bishop Savva, Metropolitan Philaret, Archbishop John and Bishop Nektary.

Pascha 1966.

With the Kursk Icon of the Mother of God.

The sepulchre beneath the San Francisco Cathedral of the Mother of God, "Joy of All Who Sorrow," where Saint John's relics lay until his glorification on July 2, 1994.

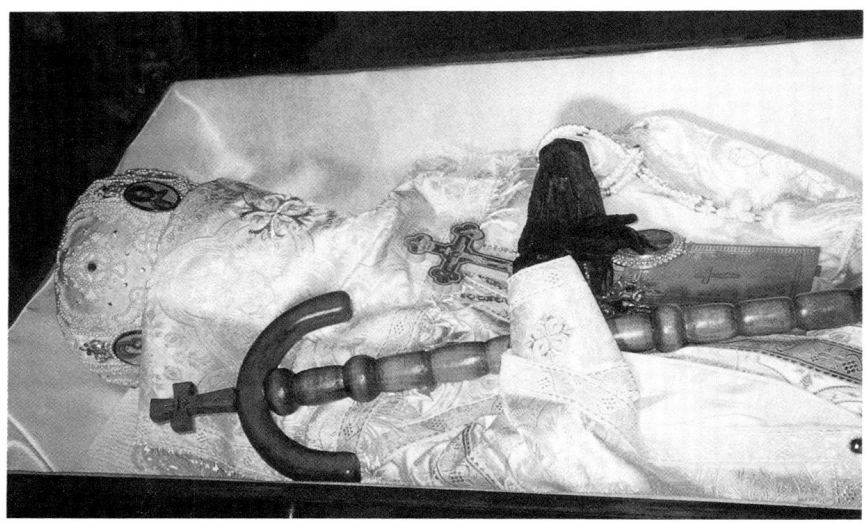

The holy and incorrupt remains of Saint John, after being washed and newly vested on December 14, 1993.

nezzar had set up on the plain of Dura and before which "all nations, tribes and tongues" bowed down (Dan. 3:7).

The thief came to belief in the suffering Lord; confessing Him as "the hidden God," he came to know Him before anyone else, and the power of His resurrection, and participation in His sufferings, *being made conformable unto His death* (Phil. 3:10); he understood before anyone else what constitutes the Kingdom *not of this world*; he came to know *what is truth* (John 18:36-38).

He was the first to comprehend the nature of Christ's Kingdom, and therefore he was the first to enter it.

He was the first to see *Jesus Christ and Him crucified* (I Cor. 2:2), the first to preach *Christ crucified, to the Jews a stumblingblock, to the Greeks foolishness, But unto them which are called, both Jews and Greeks, Christ the power of God and the wisdom of God* (I Cor. 1:23-24).

For this reason he was also first to personally experience the power and wisdom of God, the power of Christ's co-suffering and regenerating love; he was first to hear "the sound of the power of the Cross, for through it Paradise was opened." (Fourth Ode, Ascension Canon)

His thorough repentance of his sins and transgressions, his profound humility, his firm faith in the Crucified Lord Jesus Christ Who gave Himself over to suffering, and his confession, made at a time when the whole world was against Christ—these are the strands which wove the crown that adorned the head of the former thief, this is the substance of which the key was forged that opened to him the gates of Paradise!

Many people sin, trusting to repent just before death; they point to the example of the wise thief. But is anyone capable of what he did? "The Lord pardoned the thief at the final hour so that no one would despair. But it was a single instance, that no one should have immoderate hope in His mercy." (Blessed Augustine)

"Such was his end! What ours will be we do not know—neither do we know by what death we will die: whether it will

193

come suddenly or with some sort of forewarning." (Saint Theodore Studite, "Lesson on the occasion of a monk's sudden death")

Will we then be capable of a moral transformation and rise up spiritually like Christ's "fellow traveler," "who let out a small voice and gained great faith? Will a sudden death not carry us away, deceiving our hope of repentance at the last minute?" (Saint Cyril of Alexandria, "On the Dread Judgment," printed in *The Great Horologion*)

For this reason, "sinner, do not postpone repentance, that your sins not accompany you into the other life and weigh you down with an intolerable burden." (Blessed Augustine, in *The Sunflower* of Saint John of Tobolsk, Book 4, chap. 5)

May the example of the wise thief prompt us not to postpone repentance but to crucify ourselves with Christ (Gal. 2:19) and more earnestly repent, that we too might experience upon ourselves the mercy of co-suffering. (Prayer of Saint Symeon the New Theologian) *They that are Christ's have crucified the flesh with its affections and lusts* (Gal. 5:24). Let us be zealous for our speedy and complete inner amendment, wholly giving ourselves over to the will of God and asking of Christ mercy and grace.

"Do Thou, Who alone lovest mankind, grant us the repentance of the thief as we serve Thee with faith, O Christ our God, and cry to Thee: Remember us also in Thy kingdom" (verse on the Beatitudes, Tone 4).

"O Lord, this very day hast Thou vouchsafed the Good Thief Paradise. By the Wood of the Cross do Thou enlighten me also and save me" (Exapostilarion, Matins of Holy Friday).

RUSSIA

THE DAY commemorating the saints who have shown forth in the Russian land points to that spiritual heaven beneath which the Russian land was founded and lived.

Before the holy Prince Vladimir, there lived on the Russian land separate, pagan tribes that warred with one another. The holy Prince Vladimir brought them a new faith, a new consciousness and meaning of life, a new inner spiritual state; he gave them a new spirit of life that united everyone, and thus a single nation was formed.

The very existence of the Russian nation is tied to the begetting of spiritual life within it, with the assimilation of the fundamentals of a Christian world-view. It is senseless to seek the meaning and purpose of life in earthly life, which ends with death. One must strive to acquire the Divine, grace-filled, eternal life, and then this temporal, earthly life will arrange itself as well: *Seek ye first the Kingdom of God and his righteousness; and all these things shall be added unto you* (Matt. 6:33).

Faith and the Orthodox Church united the separate tribes into one nation. Faith in the Kingdom of God and the search for it, the search for righteousness [*pravda* *] became the most salient characteristic of the Russian people.

For the sake of the Kingdom of God, for the sake of participation in it, for the sake of prayer, Russian ascetics left the vanity of the world and went into the forests, onto uninhabited islands. They sought only the Kingdom of God. They did not want to found or build anything; they went away from people, but people followed after them for the sake of the Kingdom of

---

* Translator's note: *pravda* covers a wide range of meanings, including "truth," "justice" and "righteousness". Unless otherwise indicated, *pravda* has been translated herein as "righteousness."

195

God, which was present on those islands and in those forests around the righteous ones, and thus lavras and monasteries grew up.

The search for righteousness is a basic thread in the life of the Russian people, and it is not by chance that the first written code of laws, which was designed to regulate life, was called "Russian Justice" [*Russkaya Pravda*].

It was not only those who withdrew from the world and from the company of men, who thought about heaven and the Kingdom of God; all believing Russian people understood the meaning of life. All who truly contributed to the development of Russia as a nation, likewise considered that their primary concern was to be faithful to the Divine Kingdom and to Divine Truth [*Pravda*].

In Russia there were princes, military leaders, landowners, people of all ranks and occupations; and all had in common a fundamental understanding and striving, which were the acquisition of the Kingdom of God and participation in it. This was the meaning of life.

Saint Alexander Nevsky spent his entire life in struggles on behalf of the military and the State; he rode on horseback through the whole of Siberia to the Tartar khan in order to establish peace in Russia, and became renowned for his military victories. But when he fell ill and death came, he accepted it as liberation from the labors of earthly life and gave himself over to that which was dearer than everything to his soul and became a monk, in order to enter the longed-for Kingdom of God, not as an earthly warrior, but as a warrior of Christ.

Prince Theodore of Smolensk likewise accepted monasticism before his death. In their striving for the Kingdom of God, such spiritual leaders of the Russian people were the best exponents of the fundamental trait of the nation's spiritual life, of the basic force which guided its historical life.

The assimilation of the Christian faith regenerated the Russian princes as well. Authority is always an expression of

196

consciousness and will. Authority is always guided by one or another philosophy, by one or another understanding of the meaning and purpose of life and its activity. Before Saint Vladimir, Russian princes were leaders of warring tribes and waged wars for the sake of military spoil and glory. Having become Christians, they became the heads of separate parts of one nation. With the acceptance of Christianity came a sense of unity. Righteousness was in the brotherhood of princes, and internecine war became unrighteous.

Prince Vladimir gave the Russian people a new meaning of life and a new vitality. Calamities, failures and defeats are powerless before the main force of life, powerless before spiritual life. The Kingdom of God, the spiritual joy of participating in it remain untouched. The terrible storm passes, and again a man lives. Thus, during the most cruel tortures, the martyrs rejoiced, sensing God's grace.

This is the source of Russia's vitality. Calamities do not strike her heart. The Tartars burned the whole of Russia. Kiev fell, and in the same year Novgorod arose; and that great commander and leader of the Russian people, the Right-believing Prince Alexander Nevsky, roused the Russian people for a struggle, not with the Tartars, who had racked Russia's body, but with the Catholic Swedes, who, taking advantage of Russia's misfortune, wanted to seize the soul of the Russian people and kill the spiritual might of the Russian nation and Russia. For Alexander Nevsky it was necessary above all to preserve that spiritual might.

The history of Moscow's ascendancy is a clear confirmation of this same idea. In its nascence, Moscow was a not very large, local amalgamation. But at its head stood right-believing princes, who had assimilated this Orthodox understanding of righteousness; and therefore, when the holy hierarch, Metropolitan Peter, told the prince that Moscow would rise to prominence and that the hierarch himself would live and be buried there if the prince built a home in Moscow for the Most Holy Mother of

God, the prince fulfilled this covenant. In other words, the holy hierarch Peter told him, "If thou wilt be faithful to Orthodoxy to the end and wilt first of all seek the Kingdom of God and His righteousness, then all these things—everything earthly, everything of this life, everything pertaining to the state—will be added unto thee."

Such was Moscow's intent, and it was faithful to Saint Peter's testament; the night muster of the military watch on the Kremlin's walls took place with the words: "O Most Holy Theotokos, save us!"

This does not mean that Russia's life and people were holy. No! Men are always sinful; but when there is an awareness of good and evil, when there is a striving towards righteousness, restoration is possible. This is what is important and soul-saving.

In its historical life, sinful Moscow, the capital of sinful Russia, fell to the bottom, but it arose again because the consciousness of righteousness did not die.

During the Time of Troubles, Russia fell so low that all her enemies were convinced that she was mortally stricken. In Russia there was no tsar, no authority, no army. In Moscow, foreigners were in power. People became "fainthearted" and weak, and they awaited salvation from the foreigners with whom they ingratiated themselves. Destruction was inescapable, and Russia would inevitably have perished had the consciousness of righteousness been completely lost. But the holy hierarch Germogen saved Russia and the Russian people. The enemies of Russia held him in a cellar in the Kremlin, mocked him, tortured him, and tried to force him to submit to them, thereby betraying the Russian understanding of righteousness. Saint Germogen was tortured to death, but spiritually he did not surrender, and he called Russia to her historical path as a Christian state with a Christian authority; he called her to remember the truth and to be faithful to it.

In faith and confession, Saint Germogen spiritually and morally regenerated the Russian nation, and it again started on the path of seeking the Kingdom of God and His righteousness, the righteousness of subordinating the earthly life of the state to spiritual principles. And Russia rose up. In history there is no other example of such a profound fall of a state and such a rapid, miraculous resurgence, within a year's time, when spiritually and morally the people rose up. Such is the history of Russia, such is her path.

After Tsar Peter I, public life turned aside from this path. It did not turn aside completely, but it lost the clarity of the consciousness of righteousness, the clarity of faith in the Gospel Truth, "Seek ye first the Kingdom of God and His righteousness".

The heavy sufferings of the Russian people are the results of the betrayal of Russia herself, her path, her calling. But those heavy sufferings and the melancholy of life under the cruel atheists' authority indicate that the Russian people has not completely lost the consciousness of righteousness, that it feels spiritually and morally weighed down by the unrighteousness of the godless state and the godless authority.

Russia will arise, just as she arose before. She will arise when faith will flame up, when people will arise spiritually, when a clear, firm faith in the truth [*pravda*] of the Saviour's words, *Seek ye first the Kingdom of God and His righteousness and all these things will be added to you,* will again be dear to them. Russia will arise when she will come to love the Faith and the confession of Orthodoxy, when she will see and come to love the righteous and the confessors.

Today, on the day of All the Saints Who Have Shown Forth in the Russian Land, the Church points to them, and the faithful spiritually exult on seeing what a multitude of them there are in the Kingdom of God. And there are countless numbers of those not yet glorified! Here Metropolitan Vladimir of

Kiev goes to his death, quietly, fearlessly. The murderers lead him out from the gates of the Lavra, in order to kill him outside the city, as they killed the Lord and Saviour, and in silence, like a lamb for the slaughter, the hierarch accepts death for Christ, for the Faith, for the Russian Church, because he sought first of all to acquire the Kingdom of God and eternal life.

There is a multitude of martyrs and confessors; and again we see God's blessing on their struggle of faith, and again the manifestation of incorrupt relics: the bodies of the righteous, who already live according to the laws of the future life, where there is neither suffering nor corruption, and the incorruption of their relics testify of this. Thus, the incorrupt remains of the Grand Duchess Elizabeth, which rest in the Gethsemane convent, testify to us of her righteousness in the eyes of God.

Russia will arise when she will lift up her gaze and see that all the saints who have shown forth in the Russian land are alive in the Kingdom of God, that the spirit of eternal life is in them, and that it is necessary for us to be with them and spiritually touch and communicate of their eternal life. Herein lies the salvation of Russia—and of the whole world.

In Russia today there is no spirit of life, no joy of life. Everyone is afraid of it, as they are afraid of demons. Russia also was terrible to other powers, but because she drew peoples to herself.

Russian humility created faithfulness to the commandment, "Seek ye first the kingdom of God and His righteousness." It humbled authority as well, and in the days of its greatest earthly glory, Russian authority, by the lips of Tsar Alexander I, confessed itself as a Christian authority, and on the monument of its glory wrote: "Not unto us, not unto us, but unto Thy Name."

The Russian heaven, the Russian saints call us to be with them, as they are with us. They call us to commune of the spirit of eternal life, and the world thirsts for that spirit.

The restoration of Russia is needed by the whole world, from which the spirit of life has departed, and it all shakes in fear, as in the face of an earthquake.

Russia awaits a Christ-loving army, Christ-loving tsars and leaders, who will lead the Russian people, not for earthly glory, but for the sake of faithfulness to the Russian Path of Righteousness.

"Not unto us, not unto us, but unto Thy Name."

In repentance, in faith, in purification, may the Russian land be renewed and may Holy Rus' arise.

THE SIN OF REGICIDE

AFTER THE DEATH of Saul, who had fallen on his sword during a battle with the Philistines, an Amalekite ran to inform David, who at that time was being persecuted by Saul.

Supposing that David would be very glad at the news he brought, the messenger decided to pose as Saul's killer, in order to increase the anticipated reward.

However, when David had heard the story made up by the Amalekite about how he, at the request of the wounded Saul, had slain him, he took hold of his garments and rent them, as did also all the people who were with him. They mourned and wept and fasted till evening. *And David said to the young man that told him, Whence art thou? And he answered, I am the son of a stranger, an Amalekite. And David said unto him, How wast thou not afraid to stretch forth thine hand to destroy the Lord's anointed? And David called one of the young men, and said, Go near, and fall upon him. And he smote him that he died. And David said unto him, Thy blood be upon thy head; for thy mouth hath testified against thee, saying, I have slain the Lord's anointed* (II Kings [II Samuel in the Authorized Version] 1:1-16).

Thus the foreigner who posed as Saul's killer was executed. He was subjected to a cruel punishment, even though Saul was the persecutor of the innocent David and had done much evil, for which the Lord had departed from him.

From David's words it is evident that he doubted the veracity of the Amalekite's story and was not convinced that the man was indeed Saul's murderer; nevertheless, he gave him over to death, considering that even calling oneself a regicide and boasting of such a deed was worthy of death.

How many times more grave and sinful was the murder of the Orthodox monarch anointed by God; how many times greater must the punishment be for the murderers of Tsar Nicholas II and his family?!

In contrast to Saul, who had turned away from God and because of this had been abandoned by Him, Tsar Nicholas II was an exemplar of piety and complete devotion to God's will.

Having received not the Old Testament pouring of oil on the head, but the grace-filled "Seal of the gift of the Holy Spirit" in the Mystery of Chrismation, Emperor Nicholas II was faithful to his high calling till the end of his life and was conscious of his responsibility before God.

In his every action, Emperor Nicholas II took his conscience into account; he always "walked before the Lord God." He was "Most Pious" during the days of his earthly well-being, not only in name, but in actual fact. In his time of trial, he displayed patience like that of righteous Job.

Against such a Tsar did criminals raise their hands, and at a time when he had already been purified, like gold in the furnace, by the trials he had endured, so that he was an innocent sufferer in the full sense of the word.

The crime against Tsar Nicholas II is all the more terrible and sinful in that his whole family was killed together with him, including the children, who were not guilty of anything!

202

Such crimes do not remain unpunished. They cry out to Heaven and bring God's wrath down upon the earth.

If the foreigner — the supposed murderer of Saul — underwent death, now the whole Russian nation is suffering for the murder of the defenseless Tsar-Sufferer and his family, because it allowed such a terrible misdeed to take place and remained silent when the Tsar was subjected to humiliation and deprived of his freedom.

God's justice requires of us a profound realization of the sinfulness of what was done, together with repentance before the Tsar-Martyr and his memory.

The memory of the innocent holy princes Boris and Gleb aroused the conscience of the Russian people during the disturbances which upset the appanage principalities, and it shamed the princes who had initiated the strife. The blood of the holy Great Prince Igor brought about a spiritual change in the souls of the Kievans and united Kiev and Chernigov in venerating the slain holy prince. Saint Andrew Bogoliubsky sanctified with his blood the monarchy of Rus', which was confirmed only considerably later, after his death as a martyr. The veneration of Saint Michael of Tver throughout Russia healed the wounds caused by the struggle between Moscow and Tver. The glorification of the holy Tsarevich Dimitri cleared the consciousness of the Russian people, inspired moral strength and led, after severe shocks, to the rebirth of Russia.

The Tsar-Martyr Nicholas II and his much-suffering family have now entered into the choir of these Passion-bearers.

This greatest of crimes, committed with respect to him, must be expiated by fervent veneration of him and by the glorification of his struggle.

Rus' must bow down before its humiliated, slandered and martyred Tsar, just as the Kievans once bowed down before the venerable Prince Igor whom they martyred, and just as the people of Vladimir and Suzdal bowed down before the slain Great Prince Andrew Bogoliubsky!

Then the Tsar-Passion-bearer will acquire boldness before God, and his prayer will deliver the Russian land from the calamities it is enduring.

Then the Tsar-Martyr and his fellow sufferers will become new heavenly defenders of Holy Rus'.

The innocent blood that was shed will regenerate Russia and make it radiant with new glory!

THE SPIRITUAL CONDITION OF THE RUSSIAN PEOPLE IN THE DIASPORA

A CONSEQUENCE OF THE downfall of the Russian Empire was the rise of a "Russia outside Russia," the Russian Diaspora. More than a million Russians were compelled to leave their homeland and were scattered across the face of the globe. Living in new conditions, among other peoples, many of the Russians in the course of these years have managed almost to forget their homeland, their language, and their customs, and to merge with the peoples in whose midst they reside. The overwhelming majority, however, not only have preserved their nationality, but even live with the hope of returning to the homeland on the fall of the present regime. Today there are Russians living in all parts of the world. There is not one corner on earth where there are no Russians, in greater or lesser number. The important question is, "From a spiritual standpoint, what is the state of the Russians abroad?"

A significant portion of the Russians that have gone abroad belong to that intellectual class which in recent times lived according to the ideas of the West. While belonging to the

Orthodox Church and confessing themselves to be Orthodox, the people of that class had strayed far from Orthodoxy in their world view. The principal sin of these people was that their beliefs and way of life were not founded on the teachings of the Orthodox faith; they tried to reconcile the rules and teachings of the Church with their own habits and desires. For this reason they had, on one hand, very little interest in the essence of Orthodox teaching, often even considering the Church's dogmatic teaching completely unessential, and, on the other hand, they fulfilled the requirements and rites of the Orthodox Church but only insofar as this did not interfere with their more European than Russian way of life. This gave rise to their disdain for the fasts, to their going to church for only a short time (and then only to satisfy a more aesthetic than religious feeling) and to a thorough lack of understanding of religion as the principal foundation of man's spiritual life. Many, of course, were inwardly otherwise disposed, but few possessed sufficient strength of spirit and the ability to manifest this outwardly in their way of life.

In the social sphere this class also lived by the ideas of the West. Without giving any room at all to the influence of the Church, they strove to rebuild the whole life of Russia, especially in the realm of government, according to Western models. This is why in recent times an especially bitter struggle was waged against the government. Liberal reforms and the democratic structuring of Russia became, as it were, a new faith. Not to confess this new idea meant that one was behind the times. Seized with a thirst for power and utilizing for their struggle with the monarchy widespread slander against the Royal Family, the intelligentsia brought Imperial Russia to its downfall and prepared the way for the Communist regime. Then, unreconciled to the thought of losing the power for which they had waited for so long, they declared war on the Communists, in the beginning mainly out of their unwillingness to cede them power. The struggle against the Soviet power subsequently involved broad sectors of the populace, especially drawing in the youth in an outburst of enthusiasm to reconstruct a "United, Indivisible Russia," at the cost of their lives. There were many exploits which manifested the valor of the Christ-loved Russian army, but the Russian nation proved itself still unprepared for liberation, and the Communists turned out to be the victors.

The intelligentsia was partially annihilated and partially it fled abroad to save itself. Meanwhile, the Communists showed their true colors and, together with the intelligentsia, large sections of the population left Russia, in part to save their lives and in part because of ideology: they did not want to serve the Communists. Finding themselves abroad, the Russian people experienced great spiritual shocks. A significant crisis occurred in the souls of a majority, which was marked by a mass return of the intelligentsia to the Church. Many churches abroad are filled primarily by these people. The intelligentsia took an interest in questions of spiritual life and began to take an active part in church affairs. Numerous circles and societies were formed for the purpose of religious enlightenment. Members study the Holy Scriptures, the works of the Holy Fathers, general spiritual life and theological questions, and many of them have become clergy.

However, all these gratifying manifestations also had a negative aspect. Far from all of those who returned to the faith adopted the Orthodox teaching in its entirety. The proud mind could not be reconciled to the fact that, until then, it had stood on a false path. Many began to attempt to reconcile Christian teaching with their previous views and ideas. This resulted in the appearance of a whole series of new religious-philosophical trends, some completely alien to Church teaching. Among them Sophiology was especially widespread. It is based on the recognition of man's worth in and of himself and expresses the psychology of the intelligentsia.

As a teaching, Sophiology is known to a comparatively small group of people and very few openly espouse it. Nonetheless, a significant part of the immigrant intelligentsia is spiritually related to it because the psychology of Sophiology is based on the worship of man, not as a humble servant of God, but rather as a little god himself, who has no need for being blindly obedient to the Lord God. The feeling of keen pride, joined with faith in the possibility of man living by his own wisdom, is quite characteristic of many people considered to be cultured by today's standards, who place their own reasonings above all else and do not wish to be obedient in everything to the teaching of the Church, which they regard favorably but with condescension. Because of this, the Church Abroad has been rocked by a series of schisms which have harmed her up till now and have drawn away even a part of the hierarchy. This consciousness of a feeling of personal worthiness is manifested also in social affairs, where each person who has advanced a little among the ranks, or thinks he has, puts his own opinion higher than everyone's and tries to be a leader. As a result, Russian society is split into countless parties and groups irreconcilably at odds with each other, each trying to put forward its own program, which is sometimes a thoroughly developed system and sometimes simply an appeal to follow after this or that personality.

With the hope of saving and resurrecting Russia through the realization of their programs, these social activists almost always lose sight of the fact that besides human activity making history, there moves the hand of God. The Russian people as a whole has committed great sins, which are the reasons for the present misfortunes; namely, oath-breaking and regicide. Civic and military leaders renounced their obedience and loyalty to the Tsar, even before his abdication, forcing the latter upon him, who did not want internal bloodshed. The people openly and noisily greeted this act, without any loud protest anywhere. This renunciation of obedience was a breach of the oath taken to the Emperor and his lawful heirs. On the heads of those who committed this crime fell the curses of their forefathers, [members of] the Zemsky Sobor of 1613, which imposed a curse on those who disobeyed its resolutions. The ones guilty of the sin of regicide are not only those who physically performed the deed but the people as a whole, who rejoiced when the Tsar was overthrown and allowed his degradation, his arrest and exile, leaving him defenseless in the hands of criminals, which itself spelled out the end.

Thus, the calamity which befell Russia is the direct result of terrible sins, and her rebirth is possible only after she has been cleansed from them. However, until now there has been no real repentance; the crimes that were committed have not been openly condemned, and many active participants in the Revolution continue even now to assert that at the time it was impossible to act otherwise.

By not voicing an outright condemnation of the February Revolution, of the uprising against the Anointed One of God, the Russian people continue to participate in the sin, especially when they defend the fruits of the Revolution, for in the words of the Apostle Paul, those men are especially sinful who, *knowing . . . that those who practice such things are deserving of death, not only do the same but also approve of those who practice them* (Rom. 1:32 NKJV).

While punishing the Russian people, the Lord at the same time is pointing out the way to salvation by making them teachers of Orthodoxy throughout the world. The Russian Diaspora has acquainted the four corners of the earth with Orthodoxy, for a significant part of the Russian immigration unconsciously preaches Orthodoxy. Everywhere, wherever Russians live, they build little refugee churches or even majestic cathedrals, or simply serve in premises adapted for this purpose.

The majority of Russian refugees are not familiar with the religious tendencies of their intelligentsia, and they are nourished by those spiritual reserves which they accumulated in the homeland. Large masses of refugees attend Divine services, some of them actively participate in them, helping with the singing and reading on cliros and serving in the altar. Affiliated organizations have been established which take upon themselves the responsibility of maintaining the churches, often performing charitable work as well.

Looking at the faithful who pack the churches on feast days, one might think that in fact the Russian people have turned to the Church and are repenting of their sins. However, if you compare the number who go to church with the number of Russians who live in a given place, it turns out that about one-tenth of the Russian population regularly goes to church. Approximately the same number attend Divine services on major feasts, and the rest either very rarely—on some particular occasions—go to church and occasionally pray at home, or have left the Church altogether. The latter sometimes is a conscious choice under sectarian or anti-religious influences, but in most cases it is simply because people do not live in a spiritual manner; they grow hard, their souls become crude, and sometimes they become outright nihilists.

The great majority of Russians have a hard life full of personal difficulties and material deprivation. Despite the hospitable attitude towards us in some countries, especially in our fraternal Yugoslavia, whose government and people are doing everything possible to show their love for Russia and to ease the grief of the Russian exiles, still, Russians everywhere feel the bitterness of being deprived of their homeland. Their surrounding environment reminds them that they are strangers and must adapt to customs that are often foreign to them, feeding on the crumbs that fall from the table of their hosts. Even in those countries which are very well disposed towards us, it is natural that in hiring practices preference should be given to the country's citizens; and with the current difficult situations of most countries, Russians often cannot find work. Even those who are relatively well provided for are constantly made to feel their lack of rights in the absence of organizations which could protect them from injustices. Although only a comparatively insignificant number have been completely absorbed into local society, it quite often happens in such cases that they become totally alienated from their own people and their own country.

In such a difficult situation in all respects, the Russian people abroad have shown a remarkable degree of patient endurance and self-sacrifice. It is as if they have forgotten about their formerly wonderful (for many) conditions of life, their service to their homeland and its allies in the Great War, their education and everything else that might prompt them to strive for a comfortable life. In their exile they have taken up every kind of work and occupation to make a living for themselves abroad. Former nobles and generals have become simple workmen, artisans and petty merchants, not disdaining any type of work and remembering that no work is degrading, provided it is not bound up with any immoral activity. The Russian intelligentsia in this respect has manifested an ability, whatever the situation, to preserve its vitality and to overcome everything that stands in the way of its existence and development. It has also shown that it has lofty spiritual qualities, that it is capable of being humble and long-suffering.

The school of refugee life has morally regenerated and elevated many people. One has to give honor and credit to those who bear their refugee cross doing difficult work to which they are unaccustomed, living in conditions which previously they did not know or even think of. Remaining firm in spirit, they have maintained a nobility of soul and ardent love for their homeland, and, repenting over their former sins, they endure their trial without complaints. Truly, many of them, men and women, are now more glorious in their dishonor than in the years of their glory. The spiritual wealth which they have now acquired is better than the material wealth they left in the homeland, and their souls, like gold purified by fire, have been cleansed in the fire of suffering and burn like brightly glowing lamps.

With sorrow, however, it must be said that by no means has suffering had such an affect on everyone. Many proved.to be neither gold nor precious metal but reed and straw that perish in the fire. Many were not cleansed and whitened by suffering; they did not endure the trial and became worse than before. Many were embittered, not understanding that, being punished by God, we must be consoled, remembering that there are no children that have never undergone punishment, that in chastening us God looks upon us as sons and daughters who must be corrected by punishment. Forgetting about their previous sins, such people, instead of repenting, compound their sins, asserting that there is no use being righteous, that God either does not look at man's affairs, since He has turned His face away from them, or even that "there is no God." Considering in their imagined righteousness that they are suffering innocently, these people have more pride of heart than the boastful Pharisee, but in their sins they often surpass the publican. In their bitterness against God, they are in no way inferior to the persecutors of the faith in our homeland, and by their way of thinking have become closely related to them.

For this reason some of their fervent opponents have become, here in exile, their friends. They have become their open and secret slaves and try to lure their other brothers into the net. Others see no further purpose of existence and consciously give themselves up to vices, or, finding no satisfaction in anything, end their lives by suicide. Then there are others who have not lost faith in God or awareness of their sinfulness, but their will is completely broken and they have become like reeds shaken by the wind. Outwardly they resemble those just mentioned, although internally they are different in that they recognize the foulness of their behavior. However, not finding strength to fight with their weaknesses, they sink lower and lower, becoming the slaves of alcohol or giving themselves up to drugs, and become incapable of doing anything. It is truly pitiful to see how formerly worthy and respected people have sunk practically to the level of beasts. Now they direct the whole meaning of their existence towards satisfying their weaknesses, their only occupation being to search for means to fulfill this goal. No longer capable of earning a living, they look greedily for a hand out and, having received something, they immediately set out to indulge their passions. Only the faith that seems to be hidden in such fallen souls, if combined with self-condemnation, gives us hope that not all of them are lost for eternity.

There are others who, although better outwardly, are far from being better inwardly. They maintain the outward rules of pious behavior, but their consciences are dull. Sometimes they occupy well-paid positions at work and have managed to acquire some standing in the society where they have relocated. But with the loss of their homeland they have lost the internal law of morality. Penetrated through and through with self-love, they are prepared to bring evil upon anyone who stands in the way of their success. They are deaf to the suffering of their compatriots and sometimes act as if they have no connection with them. They are not ashamed to intrigue and slander others in order to knock them off their path, especially defenseless exiles.

There are some that try to appear as if they have cut all ties with their former homeland in order to gain favor in the eyes of their new fellow citizens. As a rule, these spiritually wasted people have no restraining inner law and are therefore capable of any crime that can be to their advantage, if they feel they will not be caught. We are ashamed to say that in almost all the countries of the Diaspora many crimes are committed by people with Russian names. This is why people have less trust in us and our name is ruined among the nations. The breakdown of morality is especially noticeable among families. Twenty-five years ago no one would have believed what is going on there now.

Marriage as something sacred has ceased to exist; it has turned into an everyday transaction. Many respected couples, happily and inseparably married for years, have dissolved their marriage and entered into a new one. Some have done this because of passions, others for gain. Every imaginable reason is found to dissolve a marriage, some even lying under oath to gain their end.

There is no permanency in marriage among the young or old. It has become quite common to hear of a divorce only a few months after the marriage. The slightest argument or disagreement is grounds today for a divorce. This happens because the consciousness that marriage is holy has been lost. Church authorities have condescended to the weaknesses of the present generation, making it significantly easier to obtain a divorce. After a marriage is dissolved, they quickly enter into another, just as unstable, and sometimes a third.

Unable to satisfy all the demands of their lust by marriage, and paying no attention to any Church or moral laws, many go even further, considering it unnecessary to turn to the Church for a blessing on the marriage. In countries where the civil law allows the registration of a marriage without requiring a church wedding, more and more often we see people living together without the blessing of the Church, or obtaining a civil divorce without the consent of the Church, even when the marriage was performed in the Church. It is easy to forget that a sin is no less sinful because a more "respectable" name is given to it, and that cohabitation not sanctified by the Church is nonetheless fornication or adultery. Many openly live together without the slightest concern about hiding their dissipation. Some are joined together out of passion, others for personal advantage, and, suppressing all sense of shame, appear everywhere in society together with their "partner" and dare to introduce them as their spouse. It is especially deplorable that people have begun to look at such occurrences with indifference, not expressing any disapproval. Thus, the number of such cases is increasing since there is nothing holding them back. According to Church rules, people who fall into this category should be refused Communion for seven years or more; according to civil laws, they should be restricted in their civil rights. That which was despised not long ago by society has now become commonplace even among people who attend church regularly and desire to take part in church functions, which in such cases is forbidden by Church rules. What can we say of those who are even less influenced by the Church! How low has the morality fallen among our countrymen; one part coming to church out of habit and the other turning into the dwelling-place of baser passions. They have given in to a lifestyle worse than the animals; they disgrace the Russian name and bring down the wrath of God on the present generation.

The future generation of children and young people is growing up learning immoral lessons from their elders. Besides this, the present generation sins before the future one in paying so little attention to the upbringing of children. Previously, in Russia, the way of life, the whole atmosphere had a great influence on the upbringing of children. Today, we see the opposite: the upbringing of children receives very little attention not only on the part of parents, who are frequently preoccupied with making a living, but on the part of the entire Russian community abroad as a whole. Although in some places Russian schools have been founded (and these do not always live up to their purpose), the majority of Russian children study elsewhere, without any Orthodox training or study of the Russian language. They grow up as strangers to Russia, never knowing her true wealth. In some places Sunday schools or other types of Russian schools have been established in order to give the children that knowledge which they cannot receive in local schools. However, it must be sorrowfully admitted that the parents show little interest in sending their children to these schools. Rich as well as poor parents are guilty of this.

Over the past years, despite the difficult conditions for Russians, many have been able to acquire a comfortable existence. Among us are also those who were able to bring considerable sums out of Russia or who previously had foreign capital and have kept it to this day. Although there are many among them who generously help their compatriots and generally support Russian affairs, most of them are concerned solely with their personal interests. They relate coldly to the plight of their compatriots, whom they look down upon. They are occupied with increasing their wealth and spend their free time amusing themselves. Frequently their extravagance surprises the native people, who then find it hard to believe that among the Russians there are those in need when there are such rich ones among them, and they become annoyed when Russians ask them for help.

Truly, if there were a greater national self-awareness and understanding of the debt to one's homeland, there great things might be accomplished here abroad. For now we have only a fraction of what we could have, and those few benevolent and educational institutions we do have are maintained more by the gifts of local people than by Russians. Because of this, most of our institutions lack sufficient means. Those Russians who are well-off, instead of coming to their aid, prefer to make use of non-Russian institutions, giving their money to them, while Russian institutions are attended by the less affluent. It is a disgrace that wealthy Russians frequently raise their children in non-Russian schools, which can contribute nothing to the children's Orthodox outlook and appreciation of their homeland, even in the best of circumstances. Meanwhile, they give no assistance to the Russian schools, nor do they make any effort to fill the gaps in the Russian education of their children, although they have the financial means to do so.

Many parents are completely indifferent towards the future worldview of their children. Some, with the help of scholarships, and others, even those who are very well-off, send their children to educational institutions which have as their goal the upbringing of children in a spirit wholly antagonistic to Orthodoxy. Various colleges which have as part of their program some sort of religious, though not Orthodox, education are filled with Russian children, sent there either by rich parents who are interested only in the external aspect of education, or by poor parents who are gratified by the idea of free education for their children, and therefore turn over their children's upbringing to the whims of the institution.

It is difficult to say which children will be more unfortunate in the future: the above or those altogether abandoned—of which there are not a few in the Diaspora. Often not knowing their fathers, abandoned by their mothers, these wander about the big cities begging for food and finally resort to theft. In the end they become professional criminals and fall ever lower morally. Many of them end up in prison or are executed. But in the life to come these unfortunates will not be held to account as severely as those who are educated in magnificent colleges and then become Russia's worst enemies. One can foresee the time when out of the Diaspora will come conscious workers against Orthodox Russia, who will strive either to convert her to Roman Catholicism or to spread sectarianism within her borders. These are people who, while remaining outwardly Orthodox and Russian, will secretly work against her. A significant number of those who are today being educated in native schools, especially convents, though certainly not all, will apostatize and betray Orthodox Russia. Not only will they be guilty, but even more so will their parents who did not guard them from such a path and did not instill in their souls a firm devotion to Orthodoxy.

Striving to provide for their children in this life and therefore choosing schools which in their opinion will give the children more security in the future, these parents pay no attention to their children's souls, and thus they are to blame for their future falling away from Orthodoxy and the betrayal of their homeland. Such parents are greater criminals before Russia than their children, who are won over to a new religion often at an unconscious age and then educated in a spirit hostile to Orthodoxy. Equally bad are those who leave the Orthodox Faith for

216

another in order to assure themselves of a more comfortable lifestyle and a more lucrative job. Their sin is the sin of Judas, and the job or other advantage they received through the betrayal of their Faith may be counted together with the "thirty pieces of silver." Some of them may claim that they did this, convinced that Orthodoxy is not the truth, and that they will try to serve Russia while confessing their new faith. Russia was founded on and flourished through Orthodoxy, and only Orthodoxy will save Russia. Like those who betrayed her in 1612, during the Time of Troubles, the new traitors should not be allowed to rebuild the new Russia or even be admitted into her borders.

Just what will the Diaspora contribute to the future in view of its present degeneration? Will it not become a source of a new spiritual infection when we return to our homeland?

The moral state of the Russian people in the Diaspora would be hopeless if we did not observe, together with the sad facts already set forth, a greatness of spirit and sacrifice. Despite the difficult conditions in which the exiles live, they find the means to build and embellish churches, support priests, and assist the needy. Together with those who have hardened their hearts and who offer nothing towards the general good, there are others who set aside for these needs a significant portion of what they have. Among us are also those who gladly donate to the Church: some—significant sums from their hard-earned labors, while others give smaller amounts but which constitute almost all they have, like the widow's mites. Contributions are reckoned not only in terms of money but also in the tireless labors for the good of the Church and one's neighbor. Many have dedicated themselves to this, eagerly sharing the work in various church and charitable organizations, or working independently. Burdened as they are already by jobs and trying to make a living, they give up needed rest to devote their free time, energy and strength to these activities, the men contributing their good judgment and the women their innate love.

The concerns of Russians abroad embrace not only needs in the Diaspora, but there are courageous fighters for the homeland, preparing for its liberation. Some of these fighters even risk reentering Russia's frontiers, braving almost certain death. Love for the homeland has moved some in the Diaspora as well to deeds for which they have paid bitterly but which history will record as heroic.

Much zeal and fortitude has been shown in the struggle for Church rights. It is especially heartening to see how dedicated some of the youth are to the Church and to our homeland, loving it wholeheartedly without ever having seen it.

These and similar examples, together with the unsilenceable voice of the conscience, give us hope that there will still be found those ten righteous men for whose sake the Lord was willing to spare Sodom and Gomorrah, and who will show the way for the Russian Diaspora.

Russians abroad have been given to shine with the light of Orthodoxy throughout the world in order that other peoples, seeing their good works, might glorify our Father Who is in heaven, and in so doing the Russians will draw nearer to salvation. By not fulfilling this task and even degrading Orthodoxy by its life, the Diaspora has before it two paths: either to turn to the path of repentance and, beseeching God's forgiveness and renewing itself spiritually, to make itself capable of giving rebirth to our suffering homeland, or to be finally cut off by God and remain in exile, persecuted by everyone, until, gradually degenerating, it disappears from the face of the earth.

A report to the Second All-Church Council of the Russian Church Abroad, Belgrade, 1938.

218

950-YEAR ANNIVERSARY
OF THE BAPTISM OF RUS'

"WITH VOICES OF praise the land of Rome extols Peter and Paul, through whom its people came to believe in Jesus Christ, the Son of God. Asia, Ephesus and Patmos likewise laud John the Theologian; India—Thomas; Egypt—Mark; all lands and cities and peoples venerate and glorify their own teachers, who instructed them in the Orthodox faith. Let us also, then, with our feeble voices, but to the best of our ability, praise one who wrought great and wondrous deeds, our teacher and instructor, the great *kagan* (prince) of our land, Volodymer, the grandson of old Igor."

Thus spoke Saint Hilarion, Metropolitan of Kiev, in the middle of the eleventh century, when little more than half a century had passed since the baptism of Rus'. At that time this holy man, with his penetrating vision, already saw the greatness of Saint Vladimir's accomplishments, and called upon Rus' to glorify him in a fitting manner. In what words, then, and with what colors shall we depict what Saint Vladimir accomplished by the baptism of Rus', now that we have lived to see the millennium of this glorious occurrence? Let us recall what Rus' was before Vladimir and what it became after its baptism by Saint Vladimir.

This was Rus' in the days of "old Igor" or of Vladimir's father, Sviatoslav. Each tribe lived its life in isolation. Various clans were often at odds with one another, avenging themselves and often engaging in mutual self-destruction, as they followed the laws of blood vengeance.

Before Vladimir, Russian princes were more like military leaders and conquerors than fathers and benefactors of their people. They were more concerned with attacking and plundering than with the welfare of their subjects. Many of the tribes were still at a very low stage of moral and cultural development; some of them had the custom of abducting or seizing young women to be their wives.

Still, it would be a mistake to think that the Slavs possessed only negative qualities and comprised simply masses of half-savage people. On the contrary, they had much that was good in their character. They were hospitable, courageous and honest. Wives were faithful companions to their husbands, and their loyalty often extended to those who were dead. The Slavic peoples honored the elderly and listened to them concerning personal or social questions. At the same time, however, treachery, cruelty and guile were found among them. Particularly in times of war, they became a terror to all who were around them. The peaceful Slav would turn into a wild beast, and woe to those against whom his rage was directed, for it spared no one! Byzantium trembled before its northern neighbors, while they themselves often lived in fear of one another.

Thus, the Slavic world stood at the crossroads of good and evil, displaying both the virtuous qualities of man, created in the image of God, and the fierce attributes of a beast in human form.

What were the highest ideals among the Slavs? To what could they direct their thoughts and feelings? Whence could they derive inspiration, and to whom could they turn their uplifted eyes?

The gods in whom they believed possessed all the qualities of their good and bad characteristics. The Slavs served gods of their own devising; this fact reinforced their own faults, which found their justification in the attributes of their gods. Thus, as servants of fierce Perun, the Slavs waged cruel warfare and wiped out their neighbors. It is difficult to say what eastern Europe would have become if Saints Cyril and Methodius had not shed the light of Christ upon the Slavs and begun the enlightenment of the Slavic peoples.

Together with their disciples, Saints Cyril and Methodius enlightened some of the Slavs with the teachings of Christ. The

220

influence of Christianity was soon felt among them, and it brought them into the family of Christian nations. Within a short span of time, those countries which accepted Christianity were transformed. Yet the majority of the Slavs, the East Slavs, continued in their old ways. At times there was reason to fear that their militant princes, such as Sviatoslav, would destroy the young shoots, watered by Christianity, which had sprung up on their brothers' fields. The darkness which hung over the East Slavic tribes was so thick and impenetrable that it could not even be dispelled by one who emerged on the princely throne like the morning star on the horizon, the first Russian Christian princess, Olga. It required the rising of the bright sun* itself, and for Rus' this meant Olga's grandson, the Great Prince Vladimir.

Vladimir had learned the rudiments of faith in Christ from his grandmother, but had drowned them in the revelry of youthful passions. Shaken to the depths of his soul by the martyrdom of the Varangian boyars Theodore and John, he decided to change his way of life. After carefully investigating questions of faith, Vladimir, whose life and convictions were closely connected, made a choice. Being by nature straightforward and honest, he did not stop half way along the road, but pursued the best course to the end. He was enlightened by the light of Orthodoxy, and after his baptism became a zealous follower of the commandments of Christ. By his example and his appeals he led his subjects to follow him. A striking change took place in Vladimir; from a pleasure-loving youth of unbridled passions he turned into a man of holiness.

No less striking was the change which came over Rus' after its baptism. The baptism of Kiev, followed by that of the rest of Rus', opened up a new life for the East Slavs; it became the point of departure for their glorious history.

---

*krasnoye solnyshko, lit., "beautiful sun," an appellation given to Saint Vladimir.

The divided Slavic tribes which composed Vladimir's nation began to feel united. This new consciousness of their unity was strengthened by the fact that for several centuries the whole of Rus' constituted, in ecclesiastical terms, one metropolitan district, despite the later division of Rus' into independent principalities.

The Church greatly influenced the unification of Rus' into one state. As Orthodoxy spread among the Slavic and non-Slavic tribes which were living in eastern Europe, they were able to become one with the Russian nation. The Church acted as a peacemaker in times of civil strife, and inculcated an awareness that the Russian nation is one, and should therefore constitute an integral unit in all things. It was under the protection of the Holy Orthodox Church that Rus' was formed, became strong and grew into a great power, occupying one-sixth of the globe. The Russian people, who accepted Christianity not by force but freely, strove from the very first years following their baptism to make their life reflect the teachings of the Gospel. People whose hearts had been brutish were reborn through baptism and changed from within. While retaining those qualities which were good from their past, they were freed from the bad qualities which had also been present. The battle between good and evil did not take place in Vladimir's soul alone, but in the entire nation as a whole, and the result was a great change for the good. The Russian people after baptism were not the same as they had been before baptism. They were a new people, a new nation.

This does not mean that they all became perfect right away, or that evil vanished from every heart and ceased to be found in Rus'. Not at all; evil was still present, and it continued its struggle with good in every man. But the force which motivated the Russian people was Orthodoxy, which embraced all areas of life—personal, social and political. Family and community life was imbued with the spirit of the Gospel; opinions were formed under the influence of the Church's rules, and civil laws were in harmony with the canons. The life of the Russian people had a common direction, to seek God's righteousness.

This striving to attain God's righteousness penetrated legislation, the administration of justice, and decisions of state. The same striving to serve God marked the intellectual and spiritual life of the Russian people. Practically all spheres of their cultural life had their origin in the life of the Church and developed under her influence.

Russian literature and Russian art originated in the monasteries and were so thoroughly penetrated by the Christian spirit that not even those writers of later times whose goal was to combat the Church's teachings could completely escape its influence. The principal rulers of Rus', the grand dukes and the emperors of all Russia, were aware of their responsibility to the King of kings and regarded themselves as servants of God, which is what they were in the eyes of their subjects as well. The tsars of Russia were not tsars "by popular will," but tsars "by the grace of God."

Of course, not everything in Rus' went along with this general direction, not by any means. Over the past centuries much was done that was evil. If *there is no man that liveth and sinneth not*, all the more do sin and evil inevitably occur in the life and history of a nation. However, just as in assessing the character of a person the important thing is to determine which of his qualities are more prominent and outweigh others, so also, in defining the character of a nation one must ascertain what are the chief elements of its spiritual life.

For Rus' and the Russian people, despite all their individual deviations and departures from their ideal, what was of primary importance was to serve righteousness and to stand in the truth. When we call to mind ancient Greece, the words of the Apostle Paul about the ancient Greeks come to mind, *The Greeks seek wisdom*, even though there were certainly many among them who did not seek wisdom. Sparta is linked with the idea of physical development. The name of Phoenicia is connected with trade. Rome was proud of its civic virtue. Just so, the Russian nation became known as a God-bearing nation, and the Russian land was called Holy Rus'.

Rus' was holy in the multitude of saints who shone forth in the Russian land. Beginning with the sons of Saint Vladimir, the holy and right-believing princes Boris and Gleb, who were the first saints glorified by miracles in Rus', from the baptizer of Rus', Saint Vladimir, and his grandmother Olga, a countless multitude of saints have lived in holiness and been glorified by miracles in the Russian land. These saints are the "beautiful fruit" of Orthodox Rus', sharing the very flesh and bones of the Russian people. They were not strangers in their beliefs and way of life; no, they were the clearest expression of the strivings of the people as a whole.

From the baptism of Rus' down to our own times, there has not been a single hour when, somewhere in Russia, there was not living a saint, one who after death became a heavenly protector of the Russian land. All parts of Russia have had their heroes, from Carpatho-Russia (Saint Moses the Hungarian and Ephrem of Novotorzhok) to Alaska, which only belonged to Russia for a short time but produced Saint Herman. Every area of Russia and practically every city of any significance had its shrines. The monasteries were spiritual centers which exercised an influence on the cities and the countryside. Every place, every dialect was sanctified by the service of God. The history of Russia is full of wonderful proofs of God's care for her; it is a history of the divine plan, a new sacred history. The effect of Russia's holy men on the events of its history has been so great that the history of the Russian State cannot be separated from the history of the Church. The whole way of life of the Russian people was steeped in the piety of the Church. Even Russia's foreign policy was frequently an expression of her spiritual make-up.

So it was in the past. But where are you now, Holy Rus'? Do you no longer exist? The throne of Saint Vladimir has fallen, holy things have been desecrated, churches are destroyed. Has the God-bearing nation become a beast? Has the red dragon devoured Holy Rus'? How has a land of spiritual heroism become the site of infamous crimes? How is it that where saints once sought salvation now bandits rule? Is it possible that Holy Rus' is no more and will never again exist, or perhaps that it never did exist, that it merely wore a veil of holiness, which has now fallen once and for all?

No! Holy Rus' is not a mirage or an illusion, but a true reality! In heaven there is no end to the offering of incense which is the prayers of the saints who have shone forth in the Russian land and who now pray for it before the throne of God. Yet Holy Rus' exists not only in heaven; it continues to exist even here on the sinful earth. The rule of God's enemies has but enslaved it, not destroyed it. The council of the ungodly which has taken over the Russian nation is alien to it, having nothing in common with the essence of Russia. An alien international force, calling itself "the International," has imposed its yoke on Russia, but remains her enemy. Those of them who formerly called themselves Russians, because they were of Russian blood, have forfeited the name of Russian, because they have become alien to the spirit of Rus'. Of such it may be said, *They went out from us, but they were not of us* (John 2:19). They have fallen away from the Russian nation, having become oppressors of Rus'. By rejecting God they have also rejected man's likeness to God, and have surpassed the wild beasts in their ferocious cruelty.

But Rus' remains holy. The choir of the Apostles was not diminished when Judas fell away from it; the radiance of the angelic ranks was not dimmed when Satan fell away from them, together with those angels who listened to him.

Just as it happened that the devil came from the ranks of the angels, but after the fall of Lucifer and his adherents the rest of the angels were inflamed with an even greater love for God and shone even more brightly in heaven, so also the godless came from among the Russian people, but their defection made the holiness of Rus' more apparent and caused it to be glorified in heaven and throughout all the earth.

An innumerable multitude of new martyrs have borne witness to their loyalty to Christ. The entire Russian nation has endured with indescribable patience such sufferings as no other nation on earth has yet experienced, and has furnished an incalculable multitude of new testimonies to its steadfastness in faith. In spite of the cruelest persecution the Church remains unconquered. Numerous churches have been destroyed, so that in many cities which were once adorned with majestic churches not a single one of them is left; yet believers gather in secret to pray to the Lord God. Russia has met the age of the catacombs, which it never knew before, because it had never before experienced persecution for the faith.

In the great choir of saints who were pleasing to God and were glorified in Rus' there were many holy hierarchs, monks, righteous men and women, and fools for Christ's sake, but in all of its preceding history there were only a few martyrs in the Russian land. The "radiant army of martyrs," whose blood was the seed of Christianity throughout the world, and which is glorified almost every day by the earthly Church, was practically nonexistent in the heavenly Russian Church. The time came to fill up its ranks. Now an inestimable number of new martyrs and sufferers has been added to the small number of passion-bearers and martyrs who suffered in ages past. Among them is the Tsar, wearing his crown, the descendant and heir of the baptizer of Rus', along with his whole family, as well as that namesake of the baptizer of Rus' who was the chief hierarch of the city of the baptism, and also bishops, princes, noblemen, soldiers, priests, monks, the learned and the illiterate, city dwellers and country folk, the famous and the ordinary. Every age, every class, every corner of Rus' has produced new martyrs. All Rus' has been flooded by martyrs' blood and sanctified thereby.

O wonderful and glorious army of new martyrs! Who can worthily proclaim your glory? Truly, "blessed is the land which has been watered with your blood, and holy are the places which have received your bodies."

Blessed are you, O Russian land, purified by the fire of suffering! You have passed through the water of baptism; now you are passing through the fire of suffering, and you will enter also into your rest. Once Christians would reverently gather the sand of the Coliseum, soaked with the blood of the martyrs. The places where the martyrs suffered and died were regarded as sacred and worthy of special honor. But now all Rus' is the ground where the martyrs contested. Its soil has been hallowed by their blood, its air by their souls' ascent to heaven. Truly sacred are you, O Rus'! That writer of old was right in saying that you are the third Rome, and there will be no fourth. You have surpassed ancient Rome in the multitude of your martyrs' exploits; by your firmness in the Orthodox faith, you have out-shone even that Rome which baptized you, and you will remain unsurpassed till the end of the world. Only that land which was made holy by the earthly life and sufferings of the God-Man is holier than you in the eyes of Orthodox people.

Sons of Russia, shake off the sleep of sloth and despondency! Gaze upon the glory of Russia's sufferings and cleanse yourselves, wash yourselves from your sins! Strengthen yourselves in the Orthodox faith, that you may be worthy to abide in the dwelling place of the Lord and to take up your abode in His holy mountain. Awake, awake, arise, O Rus', who have drunk from the Lord's hand the chalice of His anger! When your sufferings come to an end, your righteousness will be with you and the glory of the Lord will accompany you. Nations will come to your light and kings to the radiance rising over you. In that day, lift up your eyes round about you and behold, for your children will come to you from the west and the north, from the south and the east, blessing Christ in you unto the ages.

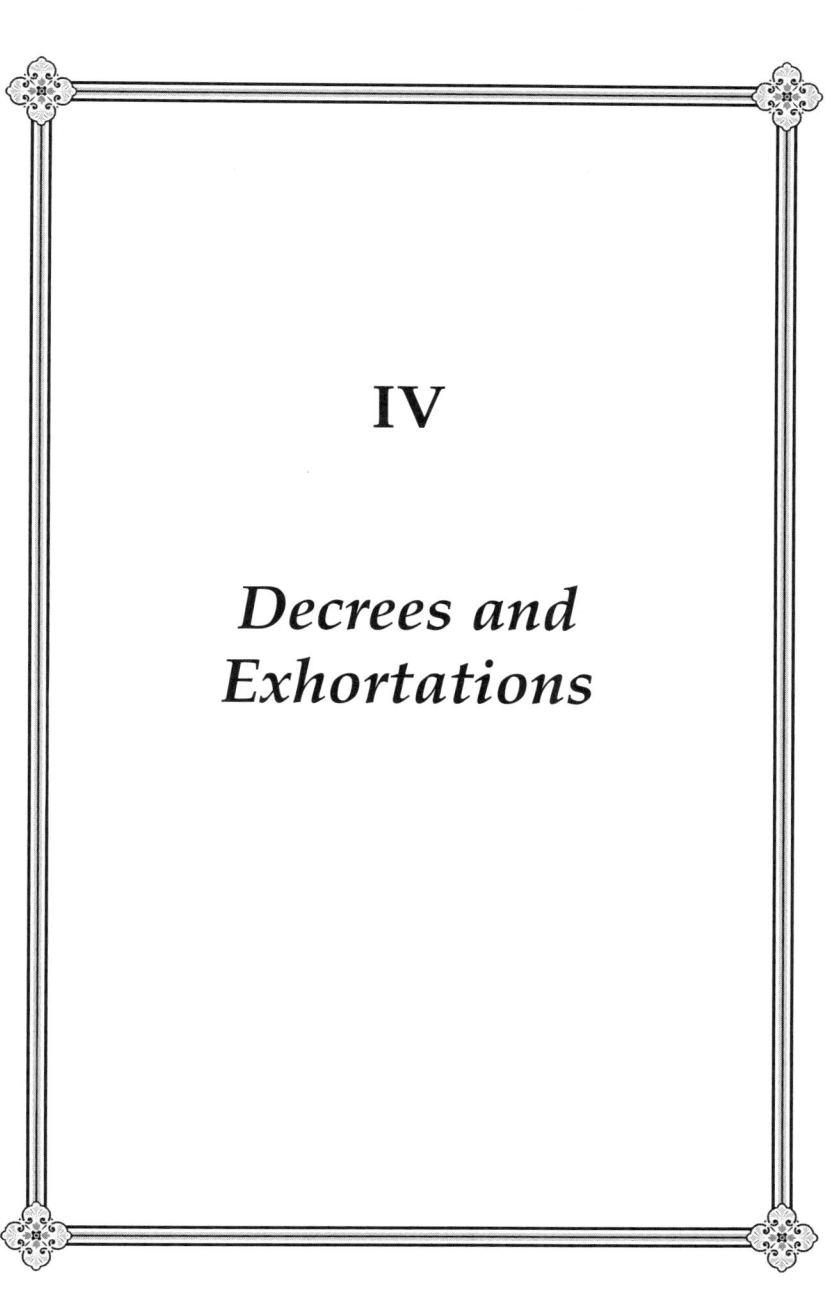

IV

Decrees and Exhortations

Is it permissible for clergy to participate in public life?

Those who have accepted the gift of the priesthood have as their main purpose the regeneration of human souls and leading them to the eternal Kingdom of God. Priests must not be diverted from this apostolic work and waste time in worldly matters. No one else can give the people what the priest gives them, and nothing can be compared to those eternal blessings to which he leads the people. Therefore, a priest must not dare to become distracted from his duties and become occupied with even beneficial worldly affairs; he must bear in mind that he is the guardian of human souls and will give an answer at the Dread Judgment of God for every sheep which perished through his negligence. The Apostles gave an example when disputes rose up among them concerning the distribution of goods, saying, *It is not reason that we should leave the word of God, and serve tables* (Acts 6:2).

The Church canons strictly forbid clergy to be occupied with worldly concerns and undertake public duties. That does not mean, however, that the clergy can completely withdraw from all worldly affairs. People consist of soul and body, and it is impossible, while caring for the soul, to completely forget about the needs of the body. The Lord commanded us to show love for our neighbor through works of mercy, concerning which He will question us at the Dread Judgment. Many hierarchs and saints were active participants in events occurring in their times, and sometimes they even headed governments, but this happened only in cases of exigency. When it is necessary to save people from disaster, when the participation of the pastor is required in order to direct his flock on the right path, the pastor does not dare remain apathetic or neutral. He not only may, but he *must* come to their aid, concerning himself with both personal as well as public matters. It is the duty of the pastor to urge the people to give alms and, if necessary, to become the leader of a charitable organization, directing public affairs according to the spirit of the teachings of Christ.

At the same time, however, he must always remain a priest and a pastor. It is inadmissible for him to join some party and be in submission to its discipline. It is likewise improper for the pastor to be immersed in the purely worldly side of public affairs. He should let the laymen do everything they can, while striving himself to concentrate on spiritual matters, which are the work of a pastor. The priesthood is the light of the world, and its role in public life must be to sanctify the path of personal, public, and civic life. The duty of the clergy is to make clear the moral foundations on which society should be built, and to inspire its activity, filling it with the spirit of Christ's teaching. Without sinking into the squalor of worldly vanity, the pastor must hover over his flock and vigilantly watch over it, support when necessary those who are spiritually or physically weak, cut short and denounce evil, inspire all to good works and spiritual struggles, and strengthen them in the performance of good deeds.

The highest and most important gift of the priesthood, for which the pastor must be especially fervent in prayer, is the calling down of God's blessings and grace upon the people, remembering that he is above all a servant of God, and must be an example to the faithful in word, life, love, spirit, faith, and purity (I Tim. 4:12), leading them by prayer, example, and instruction to the Kingdom of God.

Concerning the reception of
the Holy Mysteries on Pascha

The Lamb of God communicates with us on the holy and light-bearing night of Resurrection. We pray for this when we are just beginning to prepare for Lent, and afterwards many times during the course of the Great Fast: that the Lord would vouchsafe us to partake of the Holy Mysteries on the night of Holy Pascha. At that time the grace of God acts in a special way upon men's hearts. We partake of Christ Resurrected, we become partakers of His Resurrection. Of course, we must prepare ahead of time, and, having already communed during Great Lent, receive again the Holy Mysteries. Before the Paschal Liturgy there is no time for a proper confession; this must be done earlier. And then, on that light-bearing night, having received general absolution, to draw near to the Divine Lamb, the pledge of our resurrection. No one should leave the church prematurely, rushing away to eat the meat of animals instead of receiving the Most Holy Body and Blood of Christ.

Resolution concerning the distribution
of eggs on Pascha night

On April 2 of this year, you asked permission for your Circle to distribute red eggs to the faithful in the Memorial Church after the Paschal Matins, inasmuch as a great many single, elderly, ill and poor people cannot stay to the end of the Divine Liturgy, when they would return to their homes in damp, cold weather. In response, His Eminence Archbishop John has issued the following resolution:

"What is most important on the holy day of Pascha is our communion with the Risen Christ, which is principally manifest in the reception of the Holy Mysteries at the holy service, and for which we repeatedly pray in the services of Great Lent.

233

"Leaving the Paschal service before the end of Liturgy is a sin—or the result of a lack of understanding of the church service.

"If one is compelled to do so by unavoidable necessity, then an egg, which is merely a symbol of resurrection, cannot take the place of actually partaking of the Resurrection in the Divine Liturgy, and the distribution of eggs before the Liturgy would be an act of disdain for the Divine Mystery and a deception of the faithful.

"The Church canons strictly forbid bringing to the altar anything besides the bread and wine which are to be transformed into the Body and Blood of Christ, likewise oil for the lamps and incense. A cleric who violates this canon is deposed according to the third rule of the Apostolic Canons.

"I call upon all to fully participate in the Divine banquet of the Risen Christ—the Holy Liturgy, and then, at its conclusion, to announce the good news of Christ's Resurrection and greet one another with this symbol of the Resurrection."

Ukase concerning the inadmissibility of engaging in entertainments on the eves of feast days

The holy canons dictate that Christians should spend the eves of feast days in prayer and with reverence in preparation for participation or attendance at the Divine Liturgy. If all Orthodox Christians are called to this, then this pertains all the more to those who take an active part in the church service itself. Their participation in diversions on the eve of a feast day is especially sinful. In view of the above, those who attend a dance or similar form of entertainment and diversion may not participate in the choir the next day, may not serve in the altar, enter the altar or stand on the cliros.

An appeal for aid to the Holy Land

If I forget thee, O Jerusalem, let my right hand wither, prophetically exclaimed King David, when Sion was still flourishing. In their grief the Jews sang this song during the Babylonian captivity.

The Lord Jesus Christ loved Jerusalem; He shed tears over the calamities soon to befall it.

Jerusalem, which was sacred for the Old Testament Jews, became yet more sacred for Christians, sanctified as it was by the steps and then also the blood of our Divine Saviour, Jesus Christ.

As soon as the persecutions of the Christians ceased, pilgrims from wherever the name of Christ was glorified began directing their paths to that city, beginning with Empress Helen, who found Christ's Cross and built several magnificent churches on sites associated with Christ's earthly sojourn.

These places likewise filled up with monasteries, where ascetics sought for themselves, and indicated to others, the path to salvation.

The subjugation of these countries by heterodox peoples of the east did not diminish the Christians' devotion to the Holy Land. Western peoples undertook crusades to liberate them, although they did not achieve their objective.

With the baptism of Rus', from the very inception of Christianity there, came new pilgrims. The Russian Church, from the first, forged strong links with the Holy Land. Everything that came or was brought from the Holy Land was sacred in the eyes of the Russian people. The ultimate goal of devout people was to visit the Holy Land. Individuals managed to do this even when such a journey entailed incredible difficulties. In the last century the flow of pilgrims was continuous.

To facilitate such pilgrimages, the Russian Ecclesiastical Mission in Jerusalem and the Palestine Society were founded. These acquired ownership of a number of plots of land in holy places, and on them monastic communities were established.

These monasteries allowed visiting Russians a place to stay while they were venerating the holy places, and even to the end of their lives for those who so desired. Thanks to the flood of donations from Russia, these communities could also develop widespread missionary activity among the local inhabitants and give essential support to the local Jerusalem patriarchate.

All this changed when sorrowful times came upon Russia.

With the onset of the First World War the stream of pilgrims and donations in support of the work of our holy communities came to a halt, and by the end of the war, with the Russian government shattered, their situation became still more difficult. The Second World War and the partition of Palestine between the Jordanian kingdom and the emerging state of Israel brought new adversities and dangers.

Those communities which turned out to be in Israel were deprived of part of their property and handed over to the jurisdiction of the Moscow Patriarchate. Communities in Jordan remained within the body of the Russian Church Abroad, despite the attempts of the Moscow Patriarchate to lay hold of them; these communities, and other Orthodox Russian establishments there, refused to submit to the Moscow Patriarchate on account of its ties with the Soviet government.

The Patriarchate is striving to subjugate and spread its influence to all nations. To this end, the Soviet government, an enemy of the Church and religion, realizing the significance of Orthodox Russia and its renown among Orthodox peoples, is positioning itself in the Near East as their protector, and is trying by all means to establish the influence of the Moscow Patriarch, who is under their control.

If there were no opposition to this activity, it could be very successful, and places dear to the entire Christian world might well become bases for anti-Christian influence.

However, the poor and truly holy communities and Russian Orthodox institutions in the Holy Land have proved to be an insurmountable obstacle to their intent and actions.

Aware of the submission of the Moscow church authority to the Soviet government, and knowing that the Moscow Patriarch is not a free servant of God and His Church but rather a puppet of the godless authorities, those holy communities and institutions refused to recognize his authority and have remained in submission to the authority of the free part of the Russian Church—to the Synod of Bishops of the Russian Orthodox Church abroad, although such recognition would have brought great advantage materially.

The Russian monastic communities in the Holy Land embody a pure Christian conscience in the Near East, and their presence and their confession prevent the Orthodox people there from opening their hearts to the influence of that church authority dependent on the enemy of God and the Church.

The courageous exploit of those communities in confessing the faith inspires a feeling of compunction, and we should bow down before them.

It is both natural and necessary that Russian people abroad recognize as their duty to support, morally and materially, the glorious exploit of those elderly monks and nuns who are enduring great need in all respects, although they remain strong in spirit.

To organize this effort, the Synod of Bishops has established the Palestine Committee under my leadership.

In undertaking the establishment of representatives of the Committee throughout the Diaspora, I appeal to all Orthodox to give them their cooperation, and to consider as their sacred duty to assist the monasteries and Orthodox institutions in the Holy Land, a duty before the Church and Holy Russia, which has had such sincere and devoted veneration for Jerusalem.

If I forget thee, O Jerusalem, let my right hand be forgotten.

Ukase addressed to clergy
and church singers

It is always necessary to remember and be aware that church singing is prayer, and prayers must be chanted with reverence in order to stimulate the faithful who stand in church to pray. Chants and hymns which only delight the ear but by content or manner of performance do not dispose one to prayer are unacceptable. The same applies to those chants and hymns which are incompatible with the given church service, commemoration, or church rubrics. In addition, the behavior of the singers must be reverent and compatible with the high calling of church singers, who unite their voices with the voices of the angels. It is the responsibility of the choir director and the celebrating priest to oversee this, and the priest's directives must be fulfilled without question.

Ukase concerning order
in church services

To avoid confusion and misunderstanding when several clergy are serving together, the order of seniority according to consecration is to be observed: archimandrites stand according to seniority in their elevation, archpriests according to seniority when they were made archpriests, other priests according to seniority of ordination. The same order is to be observed by deacons, subdeacons and readers, although it is not forbidden to voluntarily yield the honor to one's brother for some reason. Clergy who arrive late for the beginning of the service are to stand at the end of the row of clergy so as not to cause confusion during the service, for the grace of God rests upon them equally wherever they stand before the Lord God.

Ukase concerning the proper abbreviation for the name of the cathedral

In view of the abbreviated name of the Cathedral, "Holy Sorrowing" (Свято-Скорбященский) which has come into use, it is to be made clear that the cathedral dedicated to the Most Holy Mother of God has as its patronal icon not an image of the Sorrowing Mother of God but the image, "Joy of All Who Sorrow," representing the joy of all those whom she nourishes and comforts. Because it personifies joy and not sorrow, this icon and the cathedral bearing its name should be called "Joy of the Sorrowing" or "Joy to the Sorrowing," whenever its name is abbreviated.

Ukase regarding collections

This confirms the decree that church wardens and other persons who conduct collections for the church and other benefits during services should not enter the altar and distract clergy from prayer; rather, they should stand with collection plates at the front of the church, facing the Royal Doors, before the hierarch or priest gives the general blessing, when at the same time he blesses those making the collections.

Ukase concerning the transfer of feasts

Clergy and faithful are reminded that feast days were established in Old Testament times by the command of God—*which God appointed and sanctified*—as also were days of fasting and lamentation.

The Lord Jesus Christ, teaching the true understanding of the significance of a feast, did not abolish these but confirmed the observance of feast days, and from the beginning the New Testament Church of Christ observed holy days.

In establishing the yearly cycle of services, the Church designated feast days, giving special distinction to those which manifest Divine providence and which pour forth God's grace to this day. Along with these, the Church enjoins us to honor days commemorating significant events in the life of the Saviour and the Mother of God, signs of God's mercy, and the memory of God-pleasers. The Church precisely established the significance and the order of their celebration, as also the days when these are held and, in special cases, their transfer to another day. When possible, the commemoration of the saints and sacred events are celebrated at the same time, so that Orthodox Christians may be united in the same thought and the same feeling, raising with one soul their prayers and praise. This does not, however, exclude the special local celebration of an event or saint known or specially revered in a particular locale.

In addition to major feast days, each parish has a patronal feast, i.e., a day when the sacred event or saint to whom the church is dedicated is celebrated. According to the Church typicon, patronal feasts hold equal rank with the Great Feasts of the Lord and the Mother of God, and they are marked with a corresponding service appointed for that particular day, which is a solemn and grace-filled occasion for those praying in the church and for its parish community.

For this reason, it is inadmissible to willfully transfer a parish feast for the sake of convenience. Both the clergy and laity should be aware that transferring the celebration to another day does not make that day the parish feast; likewise, if a parish feast is not celebrated this does not lessen its spiritual significance, which is preserved regardless of how it is treated by either the clergy or the parishioners. Clergy and laity should try in every possible way to worthily observe their patronal feast, to gather in church and take part in the Divine services of that day. Those unable to make it to church even briefly on that day should transport themselves in mind and heart, and at least in this way receive in themselves the emanating rays of grace.

Ukase concerning the inadmissibility of venerating icons when wearing lipstick

It is the responsibility of the clergy and, in particular, of parish rectors to insure that those who wear lipstick do not venerate icons, the Cross, or anything holy, leaving lipstick marks on them. A notice to this effect should be posted near the entrance of the church, and, in sermons, it should repeatedly be explained that it is a great sin to defile something holy by such contact. Women should refrain from wearing lipstick to church or not venerate anything. In any case, they should not commune Christ's Holy Gifts without having thoroughly washed their lips.

241

Appendix

TROPARION

to the Holy Hierarch and wonderworker
JOHN of Shanghai and San Francisco

Tone 5

*Lo, thy care for thy flock in its sojourn / hath prefigured
the supplications / which thou dost ever offer up for the
whole world. / Thus do we believe, having come to know
thy love, / O holy hierarch and wonderworker John! /
Wholly sanctified by God through the ministry of the
all-pure Mysteries, / and thyself ever strengthened
thereby, / thou didst hasten unto the suffering,
O most gladsome healer. // Hasten now also to
the aid of us who honor thee
with all our heart.*

Report to the Synod of Bishops by the Commission which examined the remains of the Hierarch John of Shanghai and San Francisco

ON SEPTEMBER 28/October 11, in connection with the approaching glorification of Archbishop John of Shanghai and San Francisco (which is to take place June 19/July 2, 1994), with the blessing of His Eminence Archbishop Anthony of Western America and San Francisco, Vladika John's tomb was opened in his sepulchre beneath the Diocesan Cathedral of the Most Holy Theotokos "Joy of All Who Sorrow" in the city of San Francisco.

Before the opening and examination of the honorable remains of the venerable Vladika John, preparation both practical and spiritual was required. From the practical aspect it was necessary to determine how complicated it would be to open the sarcophagus which held Vladika's coffin, in what condition was the coffin, and was there free access to it. This work was carried out on September 17/30, on the day of commemoration of the Holy Martyrs Faith, Hope, Charity, and their mother, Sophia. That evening, Archbishop Anthony, Priest George Kurtow, Protodeacon Nicholai Porshnikoff, Reader Vladimir Krassovsky, and Boris M. Troyan descended into the sepulchre and, after Vladika Anthony had served a litia, they set to work. In the course of two hours they managed to remove the lid on the sarcophagus and placed it on the floor. The lid weighed approximately 400 pounds. Having removed the lid, the first thing they noticed was Vladika John's mantia, shining like new. Underneath the mantia was his coffin. There was no odor of any kind. On the lid of the coffin there were several rust spots. After inspecting the coffin, the sarcophagus was closed in anticipation of the examination of the very remains of Vladika John.

His Eminence, Archbishop Laurus of Syracuse and Holy Trinity, a member of the Committee which was established by the Synod of Bishops of the Russian Orthodox Church Abroad for the preparations of the up-coming glorification, arrived for the examination of the relics, which took place on the day of the commemoration of Saint Chariton the Confessor. Another member of the Committee, Archbishop Alypy, was unable to come because of two parish feast days in his diocese. His Eminence, Bishop Kyrill of Seattle, as Vicar of the Western American Diocese, was also a member of the Committee. Several of the clergy from the Diocesan Council, as well as clergy of the cathedral, were likewise assigned to participate in the examination. In all, three bishops, seven priests, three deacons, one reader and one layman participated in the examination. All of the participants of this sacred work observed a strict fast that day. Several prepared through the Mystery of Confession, others by serving the Divine Liturgy and receiving Christ's Holy Mysteries.

After Vespers and Matins in the cathedral, those taking part in the examination of the relics gradually descended to the sepulchre. The participants were Archbishop Anthony, Archbishop Laurus, Bishop Kyrill, Archpriest Stefan Pavlenko, Archpriest Peter Perekrestov, Priest George Kurtow, Priest Sergei Kotar, Priest Alexander Krassovsky, Hieromonk Peter (Lukianov), Priest Paul Iwaszewicz, Protodeacon Nicholai Porshnikoff, Deacon Alexei Kotar, Hierodeacon Andronik (Taratuchin), Reader Vladimir Krassovsky, and the custodian of the sepulchre, Boris Troyan. All of the archpastors and priests in turn read the Gospel over the tomb. At precisely 9:00 P.M. a panikhida for Vladika

John was served by Their Eminences. After the panikhida, Archbishop Anthony gave a brief sermon calling all of the participants of this sacred work to be at peace and then, having bowed to the ground, asked forgiveness of everyone.

With reverence, vested in epitrachelia, with the singing of the troparion, "Have mercy on us, O Lord, have mercy on us," they began to open the sarcophagus. A wooden coffin, which had been brought to the sepulchre, had been constructed in advance by Priest George Kurtow. Thanks to the preparatory work on September 17/30, the lid of the sarcophagus was removed without any difficulty. After wrapping straps around the bottom of the coffin, the clergy lifted the coffin and placed it on a board, laid over the top of the sarcophagus. It turned out that the coffin had rusted through in many places, including the base. Hieromonk Peter produced the key to Vladika John's coffin, which he had kept for the past twenty-seven years, but because of the rust, he was unable to open the coffin. An attempt was made to unscrew the hinges on the side of the coffin opposite the lock, but the screws had also rusted. Not wishing to apply crude force in such a sacred task, the clergy tried to slowly pry off the lid. Vladika Anthony, seeing that there was difficulty, sang "We have no other Help . . . , " and almost immediately the lock was opened. Everyone stepped back, giving Archbishop Anthony way to the loosened lid of the coffin.

At 10:10 P.M. Vladika Anthony, with trembling and fear of God, opened the coffin with the honorable remains of the Ever-memorable Archbishop John. With the exception of Bishop Kyrill, who had participated in the uncovering of the relics of the New Martyrs Grand Duchess Elizabeth and Nun Barbara in Jerusalem, not one of those present had ever been a witness to the uncovering of relics, and this intensified the awe with which everyone surrounded the coffin. The face of Vladika John was covered, and everyone immediately turned their attention to his white, incorrupt hands.* The white vestments and miter had

---

* This whiteness turned out to be a mildew. Later, when the relics were washed with a mixture of rose water and white wine, they proved to be a dark bronze color.

turned green. Having blessed himself and reading Psalm 50, Vladika Anthony removed the aër from Vladika John's face and everyone saw the incorrupt face of the Ever-memorable Hierarch. The skin on his face was white. His beard had been completely preserved. In the place of the eyes were small openings, but this was barely noticeable since the miter on Vladika John's head was set very low. Vladika's under-vestment was almost completely decayed and his legs were visible. They were dark. (It is well known that Vladika John had poor legs, and during his life they were dark from wounds.) A spot was noticed on Vladika's leg in the place where there had been an open wound. There was neither a fragrant nor unpleasant odor. However, a slight smell of dampness was detected, that of earth or rust. After the uncovering of the face, there was an extraordinary silence. Then everyone attentively began to examine the sacred relics and quietly remark on the condition of the remains, the vestments, the cross, etc. In turn everyone venerated the incorrupt relics.

It was decided to place the relics in the new wooden coffin. The clergy did not know how fragile the body was, and so they laid a sheet underneath it and only then did they transfer the relics to the new coffin, while singing the irmoi of the Great Canon of St. Andrew [from the Service of the Burial of a Priest], "He is my Helper and Protector, and has become my salvation .... Establish Thy Church upon the rock of Thy commandments, O Christ." With the remains of Vladika John now in the new coffin, the clergy began to clean them of the decayed lining (and pillow) from the old coffin. The body of Vladika John, when it was lifted up high, turned out to be relatively light in weight and stiff, not flexible or fragile as would have been expected. It is worth noting what was experienced by the participants of the examination: after the uncovering of Vladika John's face an extraordinary spiritual peace and reverent silence were felt. No one was amazed, no one spoke. All sensed a feeling of well being and how grace-filling it was to stand by the relics. There was no hurrying or fussing. No one wanted to leave the relics; there was a desire simply to stand by them, pray, and touch them.

Having cleaned the relics from the decayed lining and also from earth which had been sprinkled over them during the funeral, the clergy again laid the relics into the wooden coffin. During the reading of the kontakion of the Great Canon, "My soul, my soul, arise . . . , " Archbishop Anthony covered the face of the Ever-memorable Archbishop John with a new aër and his body was covered with a shroud. Then, Vladika Anthony informed everyone that the two-year-old son of one of the diocesan clergy, Priest Yaroslav Belikow, was very ill, and father and son were waiting not far away to venerate the relics. They sent for Father Yaroslav, and shortly thereafter he came down into the sepulchre, carrying his son Vsevolod, and touched the child to Vladika John's incorrupt hands. The wooden coffin was then lifted into the sarcophagus, which had been cleaned of rust. The coffin was closed and sealed and then covered with the mantia. The lid of the sarcophagus was brought in and put back in place. After the clergy sang the general troparion to a hierarch: "Teacher of the Orthodox Faith and good instructor of piety . . . ," a litia for the dead was served. Everyone venerated the tomb of Vladika John and was anointed with oil from the vigil lamp on top of the tomb. At 11:15 everyone began to disperse, thanking the Lord God for His great mercy to us, revealed in the incorrupt remains of the Ever-memorable Archbishop John, of which all of the undersigned were witnesses.

Archbishop Anthony
Archbishop Laurus
Bishop Kyrill

(and signatures of the other
members of the Commission)

28 September/11 October, 1993

250

Holy Virgin Cathedral, "Joy of All Who Sorrow," San Francisco, California.

GLOSSARY

analogion: a stand for icons or sacred books.

antidoron: bread distributed to the faithful at the end of Liturgy; literally "in place of the Gifts."

aposticha: verses chanted in memory of a saint or feast.

archimandrite: an abbot in priestly rank.

batiushka: a term of endearment for a priest.

canon: a series of hymns and verses in nine parts.

cliros: place where the choir or chanter stands in church, usually located at the front of the nave.

Horologion: Book of Hours; a service book containing the unchanging parts of the daily services.

irmos (pl. *irmosi*): initial hymn for each part of a canon.

kathisma: one of twenty sections into which the Psalter is divided.

klobuk: stiff, cylindrical monastic head covering.

kontakion: hymn that particularly honors and describes a feast or saint.

lavra: a large, cenobitic monastery.

litia: a shortened service for the dead; also, entreaty.

mantia: bishop's mantle; floor length, pleated and sleeveless monastic outer garment.

menologia: calendar of saints.

moleben: service of intercession for the living.

Octoechos: Book of the Eight Tones; contains all the hymns in the form of stichera, troparia, kontakia, canons, etc., which are divided into eight groups of melodies, or "tones."

O.S.: Old Style or Julian calendar, which is still followed by the Church, is now thirteen days behind the Gregorian or civil calendar, instituted by Pope Gregory in 1582.

panikhida: memorial service for the dead.

Pascha: the Resurrection of the Lord; the New Testament Passover.

podvig: spiritual or ascetic feat.

Polyeleos: in Matins, verses chanted from Psalms 134 and 135, glorifying the mercy of God.

prosphoron: a small, round, leavened bread used in preparation of the Holy Eucharist at the Divine Liturgy.

Quadragesima: Great Lent; a period of forty days preceding Passion Week.

starets: a spiritual elder.

stichera: verses.

trapeza: refectory; the communal meal served in the refectory.

troparion: see *kontakion.*

ACKNOWLEDGEMENTS

The publishers are grateful to the following persons for their valuable assistance in the translation and editing of this English-language edition:

Archpriest Peter Perekrestov
Archpriest Alexey Young
Hieromonk German Ciuba
Sister Anastasia
Elizabeth Avdienko
Barnabas Brown
Irina Krishpinovich
Daniel Olson
Alexei Ulanov

And the editors of *Orthodox Life* for permission to use several sermons which were previously printed in their publication.

254

The End and
Glory be to God